Srimad Devi Bhagavatam, also known as the Devi Purana, is one of the Puranas dedicated to the Shakta stream of Hinduism that primarily focuses on the worship of the Mother Goddess. This is an important part of the archive of ancient Indian scriptures. But, regrettably, modern urban Indians may not be as aware of this Text as they should be for various reasons. For one, there are not enough good English translations of it. Further, at 18,000 verses, the scripture is an intense read. And that is precisely where this book helps. Dinesh Bhatia has done a wonderful job of translating and simplifying the sacred scripture. He writes in eloquent, lucid English and has summarised the stories in the Purana very well. This is a wonderful introduction to the holy Devi Purana. Read it, and discover the magic of the Goddess. My compliments to Dinesh ji for this stellar contribution to our Texts.

Shri Amish Tripathi

DEVI PURANA

DEVI PURANA

A Rendition of Srimad Devi Bhagavatam

DINESH BHATIA

BLOOMSBURY

NEW DELHI • LONDON • OXFORD • NEW YORK • SYDNEY

BLOOMSBURY INDIA
Bloomsbury Publishing India Pvt. Ltd
Second Floor, LSC Building No. 4, DDA Complex, Pocket C – 6 & 7,
Vasant Kunj, New Delhi, 110070

BLOOMSBURY, BLOOMSBURY INDIA and the Diana logo
are trademarks of Bloomsbury Publishing Plc

First published in India 2023
This edition published 2023

ISBN: PB: 978-93-54359-85-9; eBook: 978-93-54359-73-6

2 4 6 8 10 9 7 5 3 1

Typeset in Adobe Caslon Pro by Manipal Technologies Limited
Printed and bound in India by Replika Press Pvt. Ltd.

सर्वं खल्विदमेवाहं नान्यदस्ति सनातनम्

Srimad Devi Bhagavatam, Book 1, Chapter 15, Shloka 52

It is I who is the entire creation. There is nothing eternal in this creation other than I

CONTENTS

Preface

All the Puranas are essentially collections of stories narrated by Suta who was the disciple of Maharishi Veda Vyasa, the composer of all the Vedas and Puranas.

The stories, in their original form, are woven like a web and not easy to comprehend as there is no defined order, be it chronological or otherwise. The spiritual concepts and philosophies are either intertwined in these stories or emerge out of the narration.

This rendition attempts to segregate and simplify the stories and their philosophies as well as present them in a simple comprehensible modern English language. This book also reorganises their flow and order and presents them as a direct narration by Vyasa to King Janamejaya, the grandson of Abhimanyu, while retaining the essence of the original work.

I have based this work on the original Sanskrit text of Srimad Devi Bhagavatam available in the public domain, its English translation by Swami Vijnanananda and also the abridged Hindi version published by Gita Press, Gorakhpur. Numerous other open sources on the internet were referred to while working on this publication.

The objective of this rendition is to introduce and generate interest in Devi Purana, in particular, and Puranas as well as other Indian scriptures, in general. As it is simply not possible to cover all the aspects of the original work in an abridged version like the present one, the original scripture, or its authentic translations, is recommended for a deeper understanding.

I wish to thank my wife, Seema, and my children, Barhayita and Deevyanshu, for their encouragement while writing the manuscript. I also take this opportunity to thank Bloomsbury and their editor for their support in enabling me to refine and publish this book.

Last but not least, I feel it was the handiwork of destiny that impelled me to accomplish this rendition and this would not have been possible without the Devi's blessings.

Prologue

The great war of Mahabharata had just ended. The eighteen-day war resulted in a pyrrhic victory of the five Pandava brothers over their cousins. The war had extirpated the entire future generations of the Kaurava family. Duryodhana was the last of the hundred Kaurava brothers to be killed.

This victory could not be celebrated. The battlefield of Kurukshetra laid thickly strewn with corpses of warriors from both sides, the victorious and the defeated. Nothing but deafening silence and dense smoke arising out of burning pyres remained in Hastinapur, the capital of the Chandravanshi[1] Kuru clan.

The year was 3139 BCE.

The new King, Yudhishthira, the eldest Pandava brother, who should have been the rightful king earlier but for the fateful turn of events deciding it otherwise, had the huge responsibility of building the kingdom again. He was also faced with the challenge of instilling confidence and hope among his subjects. Yudhishthira ruled for the next thirty-six years.

In another predestined development, all the descendants of the Yadava clan were killed in internecine fighting at Prabhas[2] because of Gandhari's (mother of the hundred Kaurava brothers) curse. Arjuna cremated all of them along with the mortal coil of Lord Krishna and went back to Hastinapur with a heavy heart.

When Yudhishthira came to know about the killings in Prabhas and the passing away of Narayana incarnate, Krishna, he decided to leave the kingdom and go to the Himalayas. His four brothers – Bheema, Arjuna, Nakul and Sahadeva – and Draupadi, their common wife, joined Yudhishthira in his final voyage.

Yudhishthira anointed Parikshit, son of Uttara and the great warrior Abhimanyu who was killed in the Mahabharata war, on the throne of Hastinapur. Parikshit, who was in Uttara's womb at the time of the war, became the king of Hastinapur at the age of thirty-six in 3102 BCE. It is the year when Dvapara Yuga gave way to Kali Yuga.[3]

Parikshit, the grandson of Arjuna, ruled Hastinapur for sixty years.

The Death of King Parikshit

One day, King Parikshit went on a hunting expedition to a dense forest. He shot a deer. In the chase that followed while searching for the animal, he eventually reached a hermitage, the abode of a sage.

After a long pursuit of the deer, Parikshit was thirsty, hungry and tired. He asked the sage, who was engrossed in meditation, 'Where can I have water?'

The sage, deep in meditation and under the vow of silence, did not respond. This irritated the thirsty king – influenced no doubt by Kali, the lord of Kali Yuga. Unable to control his anger, he lifted a dead serpent with the curved end of his bow and coiled it around the sage's neck.

Unperturbed, the sage remained in his state of samadhi.[4] Getting no response from the sage, a frustrated Parikshit left the hermitage, joined his contingent and returned home.

The sage had a son named Shringi, who was himself a great ascetic born from a cow's womb. Shringi was playing in the nearby forest when he heard of this sacrilege. He could not control his anger. As customary, he took water in his hand[5] and cursed, 'He who has coiled a dead serpent around my father's neck, let him be bitten by the serpent Takshaka within one week from this day.'

The news of Shringi's curse spread across the kingdom and Parikshit too learnt of it. He was aware that the curse was from a devotee of Goddess Mahashakti[6] and, therefore, infallible. He convened an assembly of his ministers and advisers.

Accepting that his act was equivalent to a sin, Parikshit asked the assembly, 'I understand that death in my case is inevitable. However, the Shastras prescribe that one ought to fight it. Sages also advise one to take actions through the powers of mani,[7] mantras[8] and aushadhhi.[9] I have heard of a sage giving half his life to his wife who died of a snakebite and brought her alive again. Therefore, wise and industrious people do not believe that whatever is inevitable must come to pass. That means one must make one's best efforts in the present to shape the future and not depend solely on destiny.'

Parikshit's assembly was surprised to hear the reference to the sage who had brought his wife back to life. They requested him, 'O King! Do tell us which sage did it and how.'

The king began, 'O ministers! You all have heard of Maharishi Bhrigu. He had a gorgeous wife, Puloma. Their son Muni[10] Chyavana married Sukanya. They were blessed with a handsome son, whom they named Pramati. Pramati and his beautiful wife Pratapi had a child, Ruru, who became a great ascetic.

Around the same time, the apsara[11] Menaka from heaven fell in love with Visvavasu Gandharva[12] and conceived. Close to the time of the delivery of their child, Menaka arrived at the hermitage of the well-known sage Sthulakesha. She gave birth to a beautiful daughter and abandoned her at the hermitage. Sthulakesha adopted the girl and named her Pramadvara. Over time, Pramadvara grew up to be a charming beauty. While passing by the hermitage one day, Sage Ruru was smitten by her beauty and could not get her out of his mind. Pramati noticed his son's restlessness and asked him the reason for it.

Ruru told his father of his desire to make Pramadvara his wife. Pramati immediately went to the Sthulakesha's hermitage and requested his daughter's hand in marriage for his son. The proposal was accepted. Thus began the preparations for the marriage to be solemnised on an auspicious day.

Meanwhile, one fateful day Pramadvara unknowingly stepped on a serpent in the courtyard and was bitten by it. She died immediately. Ruru, hearing the news, reached the hermitage and cried aloud, blaming fate.

So grief-stricken was Ruru that he began to consider ending his life too. But the thought that suicide would amount to an irrevocable sin dissuaded him. He felt that his suicide would delight his enemies. Further, neither would it bring any gain to his dead beloved nor was there any surety that she would be his in the next birth.

Ruru bathed, performed aachaman[13] and took water in his hand. He said, "If in my entire life I have worshipped gods, did japam[14] and tapasya,[15] obeyed my teachers and elders, studied the Vedas and recited the Gayatri Mantra, then let my beloved Pramadvara be alive again. If she does not, I will relinquish my life."

Saying this, Ruru prayed to the gods and threw the water in his hands on the ground. Hearing his resolve, the devas were shaken. They sent a messenger to him. He argued with Ruru that Pramadvara could not get her life back as she had exhausted her prescribed life span. The messenger suggested he get married to another girl.

Ruru could not be persuaded by the messenger's urgings and insisted on giving up his life. The messenger was impressed and said, "The only way to make her alive again is by your giving up half your life."

The words of the messenger brought Visvavasu Gandharva, Pramadvara's father, down from heaven. Visvavasu, joined by the messenger, proceeded to meet Yama, the Dharmaraaj. They narrated the whole story to him and pleaded with him to give back Pramadvara's life in return for Sage Ruru sacrificing half his life for her.

Yamaraj, son of Surya, agreed, "If the girl becomes alive again, Ruru's life will be reduced by an equal amount of time." The words of Yamaraj took effect and the girl became alive. Thus, Ruru and Pramadvara got married on the auspicious day, as planned.'

Parikshit completed his story and asked, 'O ministers! Don't you all agree that one should use all the means available to save one's life?'

After discussing with his assembly of ministers and advisers, the king got a tall building of seven floors erected. He surrounded the building with his best guards and highly accomplished people having knowledge of the powers of mani, mantras and aushadhhi. He placed himself on the top storey.

Not willing to take any chances, Parikshit also sent a sage named Gaurmukha to talk to Muni Shringi, but it was of no avail.

The king, while awaiting the D-day to arrive, continued with his daily routine and ruled his kingdom from the seventh floor, well-protected by armed men, elephants and wise people. The building was so secure that it was claimed that not even air could enter it.

A brahmin named Kashyapa also came to know of this curse on the king. Kashyapa, who was highly skilled in mantras, believed that he had the remedy for Takshaka's poison. He contemplated that if he managed to save the king, he would be handsomely rewarded. Hoping to win the largesse, Kashyapa embarked on his voyage towards Parikshit's palace.

Meanwhile, Takshaka became aware of Shringi's curse and his obligation to fulfil it. He also learnt about Kashyapa's mission. Assuming the disguise of an old brahmin, he met Kashyapa on his way to the king's palace and engaged with him. 'O Brahmin! Where are you going in such a hurry?'

Unaware that the brahmin was Takshaka in disguise, Kashyapa said, 'I know the mantra that can nullify the poison of the serpent Takshaka. If the king is destined to live further, then I can help him to live on.'

At this, Takshaka revealed his identity and said, 'Dear Brahmin, your mission is futile as you will not be able to help the king if I bite him.'

Kashyapa said, 'O Naagdeva, the head serpent! I am confident in the ability of my mantras to give life to the king even after you bite him.'

Takshaka nudged the brahmin. 'I am going to bite this nyagrodha tree. Why don't you show me your strength by making it alive again?'

As Takshaka bit the tree, it burst into flames and turned into ashes. Kashyapa collected the ashes and took some water in his palm. Infusing the water with the power of his mantras, he sprinkled it on the remains of the tree. And before Takshaka's incredulous eyes, the nyagrodha tree became lush green again.

Takshaka could not hide his amazement. He asked Kashyapa, 'Why do you want to apply this mantra on the king? What would you gain from it? Tell me. Perhaps I can fulfil your desires.'

Kashyapa told Takshaka that he hoped the grateful king would make him rich beyond his wildest dreams.

Takshaka asked the brahmin slyly, 'If I give you a fortune matching your desire, will you abandon your mission and go back?'

The wise Kashyapa mulled over the offer. One option was to take the riches from Takshaka and return home. But this would mean that he would miss out on the potential fame after reviving the king from the snakebite. The other was to bring the king back to life, which would give him immense wealth and fame while earning punya, good karma.

While Kashyapa was carefully weighing the two options, of earning only wealth or of earning wealth with fame, he slipped into meditation. In his deep meditation, the power of his mantras revealed to him that the king's lifespan was coming to an end. So he realised that he was left with no other option but to accept Takshaka's offer.

Kashyapa took the amount of wealth he desired from Takshaka and returned home satisfied.

Takshaka continued to Hastinapur to fulfil Shringi's curse. He reached the city on the seventh and the last day of the curse.

There he learnt that Parikshit had shifted to the well-guarded seven-storeyed tower. He wondered how he could enter the palace to accomplish his mission.

At the same time, he was surprised at the foolishness of the king in trying to prevent his death in spite of knowing fully well that nothing could thwart it.

He also felt that when death was knocking on the door, the king should have been making charities and doing good karma as only such acts could help him prolong his life. Instead, here he was, depending on security and the powers of mani, mantras and aushadhhi. Only through good acts in accordance with dharma can one reach heaven and avoid hell. He wondered if no one could make the king realise this.

Takshaka came up with a plan. He turned the other serpents accompanying him into brahmins. The group of snakes masquerading as brahmins carried roots and fruits to be taken to the king. Assuming the form of an insect, Takshaka entered one of the fruits. They reached the tall tower where Parikshit was residing.

They were stopped by royal guards, who enquired, 'Who are you? Why are you here?'

One of the brahmins responded, 'We have come from our ashram[16] praying for the long life of our King Parikshit, the son of the great warrior Abhimanyu and grandson of Arjuna. We have been chanting mantras from the Atharva Veda. We have come to greet and bless the king with the prasadam[17] of fruits.'

The sentries, knowing well that the king was trying to elude a brahmin's curse, replied, 'O men of knowledge! Your meeting with the king is not possible as brahmins are not allowed inside this fortified palace due to another brahmin's curse.'

But the serpents had a job to accomplish. They insisted, 'Then we request you to carry this prasadam to the king and convey our blessings to him.'

The guards, not in a position to take a chance, went to the king and informed him about the brahmins wishing to bless him. The king ordered that the prasadam be brought inside.

The king received the large tray of roots and fruits. He took only one ripe fruit for himself and offered the rest to his ministers. No sooner had he cut the fruit, he saw in it a copper-coloured insect with black eyes. The king and his ministers were equally shocked. But the king said, 'The sun is about to set and then I have no fear of being poisoned. Let this insect bite me.'

Uttering these words, the king placed the insect on his neck. It was the time of sunset and Takshaka lost no time in shedding his guise and returning to his original form. The dreadful serpent coiled himself around the king and with one bite killed King Parikshit with the severest venom that he had. The king dropped dead instantly.

All hell broke loose. The ministers, courtiers and guards began wailing. Many, struck with horror at the sight of Takshaka, fled from the building.

Takshaka rose to the sky after taking the life of the king and executing the curse of Shringi.

Sarpa Yagna

King Parikshit's ministers performed the funeral of his already ashened body but without reciting any of the mantras as he had an unnatural death from snakebite. They placed an effigy of the king made of kusha grass on the pyre of sandalwood and undertook the last rites and recited Vedic mantras. To secure the king a place in heaven, gold, clothing, food, etc., were distributed to brahmins in charity.

Although the son of Parikshit, Prince Janamejaya, was too young, he was crowned as the successor at an auspicious time. The people of Hastinapur were happy to accept him as their new king. As Janamejaya grew up, he showed all the qualities of an intelligent person.

Janamejaya was initiated into his formal studies at the age of eleven, with the invocation of the Gayatri Mantra. Guru Kripacharya undertook his teaching in archery as was taught by his brother-in-law, the celebrated Guru Dronacharya to Arjuna.

As time passed by, the young king became well-versed in the Vedas, Dharmashastras[18] and Arthashastras.[19] The knowledge of these scriptures was essential to be a powerful, effective and invincible king. Dignified, truthful, balanced and religious, Janamejaya governed his kingdom in a just manner like his great-grandfather Yudhishthira.

In time, Janamejaya married Vapushtama, the beautiful daughter of the king of Kashi.[20] It was a sense of déjà vu as Janamejaya's great-great-grandfather Vichitravirya had also married the daughter of the then king of Kashi. The king was delighted with his new wife and spent time with her while delegating the routine governance of the kingdom to his able ministers.

Around the same time, a sage called Uttanka came to Hastinapur to meet the king. Sage Uttanka had had an acrimonious relationship with the serpent Takshaka and wanted to use King Janamejaya to take revenge.

Uttanka met Janamejaya and prodded him, 'O King! It seems that you are not doing what you ought to do. You are rather doing what ought not to be done. You should have been angry with your enemy. Instead, you are behaving like a child, and as if everything is normal.'

Janamejaya was surprised to hear this and asked, 'O Brahmin! Who is my enemy? I have no idea. Kindly enlighten me by telling me what wrong was committed. I shall take corrective action once I know the truth.'

Uttanka said, 'O King! Takshaka, the serpent, killed your father, King Parikshit. You should enquire about the death of your father from your ministers.'

The ministers then narrated the episode to Janamejaya. He was explained all aspects of the incident, starting from the humiliation of the sage in the forest by his father to the killing of the king by the serpent. After grasping all the nuances, Janamejaya said to Uttanka, 'My father died of Muni Shringi's curse,' and asked him, 'what is Takshaka's fault in this?'

Uttanka, aware of the other part of the story, argued, 'O King! Takshaka not only killed your father by his venom but also dissuaded Kashyapa, by bribing him with lavish fortune, to reach your father. Had Kashyapa not gone back, he could have helped the king with his mantras. Therefore, it is not the brahmin's curse but Takshaka who killed your father. Hence, Takshaka is your enemy.'

Uttanka continued by recalling the same story that was narrated by King Parikshit to his ministers some years back, about Sage Ruru and his bride-to-be Pramadvara. He said, 'O Lord! It was Ruru's resolve that got the life of his beloved back. But after all that had happened, he pledged that whichever serpent he saw, he would kill it by striking with a club. And, thus, he began his mission by travelling around the world and killing serpents.

Once Ruru was travelling in a forest when he encountered an old dundubha, a non-venomous water snake. He angrily hit his club on the snake. The injured snake asked Ruru, "Why are you hitting me? I have not harmed you."

Ruru explained to dundubha, "My dear bride-to-be was killed by a snakebite. Though she became alive with a lot of effort and by the grace of the devas, I have vowed to kill all the snakes that I come across."

Dundubha replied, "O Muni! I am not one of those snakes who are poisonous although my form is similar to theirs. Therefore, your killing me would not fit into your resolve."

Ruru was intrigued by the snake talking to him in human language. He asked dundubha, "Who are you? How did you become a snake like this?"

The snake replied, "It was a long time ago that I was a brahmin. I had a friend called Khyaas who was known for all the right qualities that a brahmin ought to have. He was religious and without malice. Once he was performing agnihotra[21] when I teasingly but imprudently placed a fake snake made of leaves by me in front of him. Mistaking it for a real snake, he started shaking with fear. When he came to know of the truth, he cursed me that as I had petrified him with a snake having no poison, I would also become a similar snake. I have since turned into dundubha."

He continued, "After much persuasion and when he had calmed down, Khyaas told me that in the future Pramati's son Ruru would free me of this curse." He then asked the brahmin with the club, "Are you that Ruru?"

Ruru was dumbstruck, but he collected himself and responded, "Yes, I am."

The snake further added, "Now listen to these words carefully. The highest dharma for a brahmin is mercy and non-violence, that is, not killing someone. The only exception is when sacrificing a life during yagna[22] because the life sacrificed during such an act attains heaven. Therefore, the killing through a yagna does not account as an act of killing and no bad karma is earned by the one performing the sacrifice."'

Uttanka concluded the story, 'O King! The dundubha snake was freed of his curse and Ruru stopped further killing of serpents.'

The revengeful Uttanka did not stop at the conclusion of his story of Ruru and dundubha snake. He nudged King Janamejaya, 'O Head of Kuru clan! You have so far lived without seeking any revenge towards the culprit who killed your father. Your father died without getting the appropriate last rites and without performing charities as he had died an unnatural death. Your father cannot get out of hell unless you salvage him. You should perform the Sarpa Yagna to please the great Mother Goddess Amba and sacrifice all snakes.'

The words of Sage Uttanka moved the king to tears. The hitherto unknown truth troubled him. He thought to himself, 'What kind of a proud son am I if I cannot redeem the offence done to my father? I must perform the Sarpa Yagna and destroy all the serpents through sacrifice and deliver my father from hell.'

Having made his decision, King Janamejaya called his team of ministers and directed them, 'Let us have a holy site on the banks of River Ganga and make suitable arrangements for a splendid sacrifice in accordance with the advice of expert brahmins in the matter.' He added, 'Uttanka will be my sacrificial priest and Takshaka will be the prime sacrifice.'

As the great yagna began and the sacrifice of snakes was called for, a fearful Takshaka went to Lord Indra, the king of devas, and sought refuge. He prayed to Indra to save his life.

Indra gave his word to save the serpent, 'O Takshaka! Do not fear.'

When Sage Uttanka became aware of Lord Indra extending his word of protection to Takshaka, he called for both of them to the yagna fire.

Takshaka, in order to save the king of devas, ran away from Lord Indra's protection. He took the refuge of Aastik, a great sage and the son of Muni Jaratkaaru.

In response to the call for Takshaka to come to the sacrificial fire, Sage Aastik reached the yagna venue. As expected of a brahmin, he first sang praises of King Janamejaya.

The king, impressed with the young sage, asked him, 'What is the objective of your visiting me at this yagna? What can I do for you?'

As if Aastik was awaiting these words from the king, he responded immediately, 'O King of the Bharat clan! Do not proceed with this sacrificial yagna.'

Now that the king had already asked Sage Aastik for what he desired and was bound by his words, he dutifully stopped the yagna to honour the latter's wish.

The just king stopped the Sarpa Yagna, which, as Sage Uttanka had advised, would have delivered his father, King Parikshit, from hell. King Janamejaya turned unhappy and confused with this unexpected development.

Failing to see a way out of this situation, the king decided to talk to none else but the eldest surviving member of the family, Maharishi Veda Vyasa. It was the same Vyasa without whom the family tree of the Kuru clan could not have taken root.

Maharishi Vyasa, on learning that King Janamejaya needed him, reached the venue of the Sarpa Yagna immediately. The sage, in order to calm the king's mind, recited him the Mahabharata, the longest epic in the world. However, the recitation failed to provide the desired peace to the depressed king.

King Janamejaya begged Vyasa, 'O Son of Satyavati, O Maharishi! My mind is immersed in only one thought. My father, Abhimanyu's son and the great warrior Arjuna's grandson, Parikshit, died an unnatural death. What should I do to redeem him from hell and help him to go to heaven? My heart will find peace only after accomplishing this objective.'

Vyasa, in the assembly of ministers, courtiers and advisors of the king gathered to execute the yagna, said, 'O Son! You heard from me the Mahabharata. You venerated several munis and gave away alms in charity, yet your father did not attain heaven.

Janamejaya! I am now going to recite to you the highest Purana, Srimad Devi Bhagavatam, with all the secrets contained therein. It was first delivered by the Devi herself to Vishnu in the form of a half shloka – *Sarvam Khalvidam Evaham Nanya Dasti Sanatanam*[23] – and later expanded by Brahma into a billion shlokas.

I, in order to teach my son Shukadeva the Srimad Devi Bhagavatam, condensed them into eighteen thousand shlokas and twelve books although that voluminous compilation by Brahma is still available in the Devaloka. It is filled with many historical anecdotes elucidating the glory of the Devi. I have extracted these from Aagamas.

The hearing of Devi Purana will grant happiness and auspicious results to the listeners. It will bring in dharma,[24] artha,[25] kaam,[26] and moksha.[27]

You shall install and consecrate a temple dedicated to the Mother Goddess, Devi Bhagvati, who will fulfil all your desires. She will make your kingdom more prosperous and stable and will also bestow happiness on your family. You shall perform the Devimakha Yagna Yotistoma and please the Devi.

Those who worship the lotus feet of the Devi and listen to Devi Purana with utmost devoutness are able to move across the ocean of maya. Those who do not worship Devi Bhagvati, always remain afflicted with troubles in their lifetime. Those who worship her with deep devotion are fortunate and blessed; even Brahma and all the devas are always in her devotional service.

I have no doubt that its hearing will make your heart peaceful and, as a result, all your ancestors will attain heavenly life.'

Muni Aastik

King Janamejaya touched Vyasa's feet in reverence and got ready to listen to the rendition of Devi Purana from him. But unable to fathom who Aastik was and why he came to stop him from performing Sarpa Yagna, he decided to ask Veda Vyasa. Janamejaya said to Veda Vyasa, 'O Maharishi! Who is this Sage Aastik? Why did he want to stop me from sacrificing serpents? What was his motive in protecting the snakes? I request you to explain to me this in detail before you begin the recitation of the holy Purana.'

Vyasa understood Janamejaya's restlessness and spoke, 'In ancient times, there was a muni by the name of Jaratkaaru. Known for maintaining a calm composure and demeanour, he decided not to enter grihasthashram, the married householder's duties. It is the second part of one's life after brahmacharya that is devoted to learning and celibacy and is followed by vanaprastha[28] and sanyaas.[29]

Once Jaratkaaru was travelling, when he came across his pitris[30] in a cave in a forest. They all pleaded with him, "O Jaratkaaru! Do marry and beget a son. If your son will have good character, we will be freed from this condition and transcend to heaven."

A bachelor Jaratkaaru said to them, "I will marry only if I get a girl without asking for and also someone who is completely obedient to me." Jaratkaaru then continued on his journey.

At the same time, in some other place, the mother of all snakes called Kadru cursed her sons, "May you be burnt by fire."'

Vyasa paused and found that the king was deeply absorbed in the discourse. He said, 'Now you may be wondering who is Kadru. To understand this, I will have to narrate you another story.'

Veda Vyasa wanted the king to know the full details. He continued, 'Kashyapa Muni had two wives, Kadru and Vintaa. Once the two rival wives were watching the horse yoked in Surya's chariot. Kadru asked Vintaa, "O beautiful one! What do you think is the colour of the horse?"

Vintaa replied, "O auspicious one! To me, the horse is of white colour. What do you think? If you don't feel so, we can make a bet. Whoever will be defeated would become the slave of the other."

Kadru said, "I take your bet and I think the horse is black," and added smilingly, "be ready to be enslaved."

Kadru was hell-bent on winning the wager. She was the mother of all serpents. She asked all her sons to assemble and meet her.

She ordered them, "Go and use your bodies to cover the horse of Surya's chariot so that it looks black." Hearing her, some of the sons replied, "O Mother! This cannot and should not be done."

Their replies made Kadru angry and she cursed them, "Let you fall in the sacrificial fire of Janamejaya."

Fearing the wrath of their mother, the other snakes went immediately and coiled themselves around the back of the horse in such a way that it began to look black. Kadru and Vintaa both saw the horse again and it looked black because of Kadru's trickery. Vintaa was dejected as she had lost the bet and was going to be Kadru's slave.

Vintaa had two sons. One of them was the famed Garuda who was powerful and a known enemy of snakes. He loved to devour snakes. He saw his distraught mother and asked her, "O Mother! Why do you look so distressed? What has happened? Have you been shedding tears?"

He continued, "O Janani! You have two sons, Arun, the charioteer of Surya, and I. It is shameful for both of us if our mother has to suffer pain while we are alive. It is said that if the mother suffers while the son is capable and alive, then why did the mother give birth to such a son? The son will also go to hell due to this karma."

Garuda begged his mother, "Kindly tell me the reason for your anguish and I shall settle it immediately."

A sobbing Vintaa said, "O my dear son! Your words are like a balm to my wounds. But my days of misery are about to begin as I will now be the slave of my co-wife. She is now telling me to carry her on my back."

Garuda was perturbed, "Mother, I will carry her in your place and take her on my shoulders wherever she wants to go."'

Vyasa paused for a moment and resumed, 'At Kadru's command, Garuda, carried her with all her sons on his back across a sea. When they reached their destination, Garuda requested his stepmother to tell him how his mother could be freed from servitude.

Kadru smiled and said, "If you bring Amrita, the nectar, from Devaloka for my sons, your mother will be freed in return."

A determined Garuda, wanting to serve his mother, went to the abode of Indra and had an intense fight with the lord of the devas. He finally escaped with the jar of nectar and brought it to Kadru, thereby freeing his mother Vintaa from the slavery of her co-wife.

Meanwhile, all the snakes, Kadru's sons, went to take a ritualistic bath before partaking of the nectar. When they returned, they found the jar to be missing. Lord Indra, not losing any time, had stolen away the jar containing the nectar.

On not finding the jar of nectar where it was kept, the snakes became desperate and began to lick the kusha grass over which the jar of nectar had been kept. They faintly hoped that by doing so they would get a few droplets which might have spilled or seeped from the jar. Due to the sharp edges of kusha grass, the tongues of all the snakes got cleaved into two. Hence the snakes are also called dvijihva.[31]

Meanwhile, the snakes whom their mother Kadru had cursed to be dropped to King Janamejaya's sacrificial fire went to seek Brahma's refuge. Led by the serpent Vasuki, they told Brahma about their mother's curse. A compassionate Brahma advised them, "Get Vasuki's sister Jarat Kaaru, that is, Manasa, married to her namesake, the great Muni Jaratkaaru. She will deliver a son by the name of Aastik who will remedy your difficulties."

After getting Brahma's counsel, the snake brothers went to Jaratkaaru's ashram and requested him to accept their sister in marriage.'

'Do you recall what the sage had told his forefathers in the cave?' Vyasa asked Janamejaya in order to connect the two distant threads of the story. As he was not expecting an answer, Vyasa continued, 'He had said that he would marry only if he got a girl without asking for and also someone who was completely obedient to him.'

Vyasa could not control flashing a smile as if he admired the turn of fate. He continued, 'Jaratkaaru agreed to the marriage proposal by Vasuki and other snakes but on the condition that if their sister acted against his wishes, he would desert her immediately.

The bride's brothers agreed to this condition imposed by the sage and the wedding was solemnised in front of the pious fire. Vasuki with his brothers returned to their habitat.

Sage Jaratkaaru built a hut of leaves in the forest and started his married life happily with his namesake. One day, before retiring after a sumptuous lunch he instructed his wife not to wake him up under any circumstance. The lady Jarat Kaaru sat in the hut tending to her fast-asleep husband while the sun began to set.

The devout wife was well aware of the sage's routine. She realised that it was time for him to do his evening prayers or the sandhya. She was caught in a dilemma. She knew if she woke him up against his orders, the sage would abandon her. On the other hand, if she did not wake him up, he would miss an important part of his routine. She also knew that no amount of charities, sacrifices, fastings, austerities and worshipping all the devas would equal more than one-sixteenth part of serving one's husband.

Torn between the two options, she finally decided to wake him up as that was in accordance with her dharma. She reasoned that being forsaken by a husband or even death was a better choice than failure to comply with one's dharma.

Having so decided, she whispered in the sage's ears, "O great Muni! It is time to wake up and perform your sandhya."

The sage got up irritated and said,"You have disobeyed me by disturbing my sleep despite my directions."

The sage was so infuriated that he wanted to curse the crying lady Jarat Kaaru when Surya appeared before him. He said, "Seeing me at the verge of setting, your chaste wife, fearing that you would miss your dharma, woke you up. Now I have also come under your refuge. Kindly do not curse me."

On hearing these words from Surya, Jaratkaaru calmed down. But he was bound by his promise. He told his wife, "O my wife! I have no other option but to leave you as we had agreed upon before marriage."

The sage's words left Jarat Kaaru in tears. She somehow managed to compose herself and asked, "O high soul! My brothers married me to you with an objective. How will that be realised if you forsake me?"

The sage pointed to the slim belly of his beautiful wife and said with a calm mind and posture, "That has been achieved."

Both, the sage and his wife, were distressed by the unexpected and depressing turn of events. The sage went away to perform tapasya and his wife went to Mount Kailash to meditate upon Mahadeva.

After due time, a boy was born to her who later became famous as Muni Aastik. This child had already heard the highest knowledge from Mahadeva while he was in his mother's womb. Mahadeva had also taught the four Vedas to him.'

Vyasa looked at King Janamejaya and said, 'O King! It was Muni Aastik who came to dissuade you from performing Sarpa Yagna and sacrificing the snakes to save his mother's family, his maternal uncles. You have done a befitting deed by honouring his request.'

Devi's Darshana by the Trinity (The Parallel Worlds)

Janamejaya was curious. He had several questions for Vyasa on Devi Yagna.

Who was the Devi? What was this great yagna that was in the name of the Devi? Where and from whom the Devi was born? What were her qualities, her form and her nature?

With so many doubts in his mind, Janamejaya requested Vyasa, the curator of Devi Purana, to describe everything in detail he knew about the Devi and quench his thirst for knowledge.

Janamejaya asked, 'We all have heard that Brahma, Vishnu and Mahesh are the trinity of gods who create, preserve and destroy, respectively. Are they independent entities or do they also submit to another force? Are they also subject to the cycle of birth and death? Do their bodies consist of the seven dhaatus[32] and feel the senses like pain, pleasure, sleep and lethargy? How this whole universe came into being? Kindly enlighten me about the nature and dwellings of the trinity.'

Vyasa knew the answers to all of these questions as a result of a knowledge that he had been born with from the womb of a fisherman's daughter and the paternity of Maharishi Parashar along with the knowledge he had gained through his reflections and studies. Unfazed by this barrage of questions, Vyasa began responding to all the questions Janamejaya had asked.

He said, 'O intelligent King! Your questions are no ordinary ones, these are pertinent and immensely deep. In ancient times, I had also asked similar questions to Maharishi Narada, the son of Brahma. He gave me the replies that I will tell you now.'

Vyasa recalled his dialogue with Narada, 'Once I had met Maharishi Narada on the banks of the holy River Ganga. I touched his feet and took the seat on the sand offered by him.

I then asked him, "O Knower of all the Vedas! Who created this universe? From what, which, where and whom was it born? Is it eternal? As we have a result in the form of this universe, there has to be an effect or a cause. Is it one or many?"

Like you, I too had many doubts that needed to be clarified. I said that many knowledgeable people say that Mahadeva, the Rudra, is the lord of all and hence is the Supreme God. He is Aadi–Anadi, one with no beginning and no end. He is the one and only cause of creation, preservation and destruction. But many others say that it is Vishnu, the Aadipurusha or the first person in the universe, the Supreme God. He is the one who grants life, enjoyment and liberation to all living beings. He too has neither birth nor death.

Yet some others call Brahma, having four faces and, thus, looking in all directions, as the cause and the creator of this universe. There are many more who treat Surya Deva as god since, without him, there can be neither morning nor day. Again some others well-versed in the knowledge of this Brahmaanda worship Indra, the lord of the devas, as the god of this universe.

Many others opine that Varuna, the lord of the sky; Soma, Moon; Agni, fire; Yama, the god of death; Kubera, the god of wealth and prosperity; Pavana, the lord of air; and finally none other than Ganapathi, the first to be worshipped among all the gods, as the Supreme God.

Other learned people in the world say that the Supreme God is the Aadi Maya, the Shakti or the force behind all, who has the nature of with or without and attributes of the three gunas. She is worshipped in numerous forms and is at the root of this system of the universe. She is the mother of all the gods and beings – living and non-living. She has neither a beginning nor an end. One of her forms is Vidya, knowledge, without which there is no understanding and consequently no liberation.

Some intelligent people think God is an entity with infinite hands, infinite ears, infinite legs and infinite faces. Some others believe that this creation could not have been the handiwork of one God alone.'

Vyasa continued, 'In response to my questions, Narada, the lord of the munis, gave me the following reply.

He said that he too in the past had similar doubts. Narada said he wanted to know who was the supreme power in the Brahmaanda who ruled this universe and was fit to be worshipped. Thus, he approached his father, the creator of this universe, Brahma, and asked him the same questions.

He went on further, "O Father! Not knowing the ultimate truth, each person is under the effect of maya. No amount of meditation or visiting the pilgrimages can help in attaining the highest objective, that is, moksha, salvation, unless one knows what the highest truth is. Unless I know who the Supreme God is, who am I to worship?"

Brahma, the lord of creation, replied, "O my son! Your questions are so difficult that even Vishnu cannot answer. Those who are under the influence of maya, attached to this world, cannot find answers to these. However, those noble spirits who are unattached, free from envy and desires and are calm, know the secret of this universe."

He then told Narada, "In the early days of this world, an era difficult to measure and comprehend, there was only water everywhere. There was none and nothing – moving or non-moving. I was then born from the lotus navel of Vishnu.

Seeing nothing, I had questions like who created me, who is my protector and who will be my destroyer when this cycle ends? I could not see earth anywhere and wondered on what, then, this mass of water rested? Since a lotus is termed Pankaja because it springs from mud and dirt, there must exist earth underneath, or else this lotus cannot come out here.

In the quest to find the root of the lotus, I dived into the water but could not find earth anywhere in spite of a thousand years of search. Then a celestial voice told me, 'Practise tapasya.'

I began my meditation sitting on the lotus and continued for one thousand years. The same celestial voice again told me, 'Create.' I was dazed and did not know what and how to create.

While I was still deep in thought, I saw in the endless ocean of water, two terrible daityas, Madhu and Kaitabha, coming towards me. The two daityas asked me to fight with them. I was petrified. Having no other option, I held the stem of the lotus and went down into the water.

I saw towards the end of the stem someone sleeping on an infinite serpent, Ananta.[33] The person had magnificent deep blue skin like a rain cloud and was wearing yellow attire. He had four arms, which held conch shells, disc, club, lotus and other weapons.

Seeing him sleeping on a serpent bed, motionless and under the influence of Yoga Nidra, I contemplated how to awaken him. From my memory, I recollected the thought of auspicious Devi Yoga Nidra and began to meditate on her. The formless Devi, appeased with my prayer, left the body of Vishnu. Vishnu woke up and started fighting Madhu and Kaitabha. They fought for five thousand years and, eventually, Vishnu extended his thigh and slaughtered both of them on it.

At that moment, Rudra joined us and we three witnessed the beautiful Devi in celestial space. Dressed in red attire and adorned with divine ornaments, her body was of shining red colour and her limbs were marked with red sandal paste. While her forehead was decked with the crescent of the Chandra, she wore a crown of heavenly jewels on her head. We chanted hymns to her. She asked us to do our assigned task of creating, preserving and destroying the universe.

We three wondered and asked her how to do it as nothing existed. There was only a boundless ocean with no earth in sight. There were neither five elements nor the three gunas. Therefore, there was no base to work on.

The Devi smiled at our bewilderment and beckoned a beautiful aerial car. She asked us to get into the aerial car. The inside of it was beautifully decorated with gems, jewels and pearls. When she signalled, the car moved up. In a flicker of an eyelid, we landed.

We were dumbfounded to see there was no water where the car had landed. But there was earth with plants, grass and trees with green leaves and fruits; rivers, lakes and ponds; and men and women around. We saw a city in front of us with splendid buildings and palaces.

The aerial car, propelled by air, again took flight and arrived at the divine Nandana Garden. There we witnessed Kaamdhenu or Surabhi, the wish-fulfilling cow of plenty, under the shade of the parijaat[34] tree. We saw an elephant with four tusks. Menaka and other apsaras were busy with their gestures and postures; they were playing, dancing and singing. Among them, we saw Lord Indra with his extremely beautiful wife Sachi, the daughter of Puloma, and the other devas.

The aerial car, carrying three of us, again took flight and in no time, we reached Brahmaloka. What we saw there put us all in a quandary. We witnessed in the council hall a four-faced Brahma presiding over all the devas, who represented various elements of nature. We were speechless. Vishnu and Mahesh looked at me quizzingly but I had no explanation for it. I was equally puzzled and thought that if he were Brahma then who was I?

Then our car, moving as swiftly as mind, reached Mount Kailash. In the background of the enchanting sound of lutes and drums, we came across a five-faced, three-eyed Shiva. He was riding a bull and wore tiger skin and elephant skin. Ganesha and Kartikeya, his two unparalleled sons, were with him as were other ganas[35] chanting victories to him. This was again inexplicable to the three of us.

The aerial car once again took off and before we could fathom what was happening, we reached Vaikuntha. There at Vaikuntha, an outstanding city and abode of Lakshmi and Vishnu, we saw a four-armed Vishnu. The lord of preservation had the colour of the atasi[36] flower. He was wearing yellow garments and was bedecked with divine ornaments. Devi Lakshmi and Garuda were also present.

What we had experienced and witnessed was inexplicable and incomprehensible. We had seen another living Brahma, another Vishnu and another Shankar. With the swiftness of the wind, the aerial car then took us to Sudhaa Sagar, the ocean of nectar. It then crossed the ocean filled with marine life and charmingly sounding ripples. We landed at Mani Dvipa, the island of gems, in the middle of the Ocean."

Narada recalled Brahma closing his eyes as if he were soaking the ecstasy of being at the dvipa again and continuing, "O Narada! The dvipa is extraordinarily beautiful. It has mandar[37] and parijaat trees interspersed with kaleidoscopic trees of ashoka,[38] vakula,[39] ketaki,[40] champaka[41] and kuravaka.[42] The opulence of the island is compounded by the sweet cooing of the cuckoos and the humming sounds of the bees.

We saw on the island an exquisite shining cot with beautiful silken mats spread over it. It was decorated with various gems and jewels and inlaid with pearls. We saw a divine lady sitting on the cot. She was attired in red. The extraordinarily beautiful lady was more beautiful than millions of Lakshmis and was radiating like the sun. We were awestruck to witness the Devi sitting with a sweet smile on her lips as if she was waiting for her devotees to seek boons. She was all prepared to grant whatever her devotees could think of asking.

She was sitting in the middle of the Shatakona[43] Yantra, surrounded by celestial girls, attendants and maids. While we were gazing at her, the four-armed lady gradually became thousand-eyed, with thousand hands and thousand feet.

Vishnu, by his memory and intrinsic knowledge, recognised Bhagvati Bhuvneshvari and told us that she was Devi Bhagvati. He said that she was the eternal Mahavidya and non-eternal Maha Maya. She was also Prakriti, nature and the cause of us all. This Devi could only be seen by those who had yogic powers. These yogis could also see around her all the vibhutis.[44]

Vishnu said that, in times out of mind, when he was a baby and was sleeping on a cradle of immoveable fixed leaves of a banyan tree and tried to lick his toe, attempting to take it in his mouth and playing like an ordinary baby, she was the one who had rocked the cradle and sang lullabies like a mother. He suggested that we three take her blessings.

Mahesh and I gladly accepted Vishnu's words and chanted 'Aum'. We got out of the aerial car and started walking towards the Devi. And then, with a flash of her smile, she converted us into females. We were beautiful and youthful females wearing gorgeous garments and adorned with ornaments. Going closer to the Devi, we bent down to touch her lotus feet and saw the whole universe, moving and non-moving, including the three of us, in just one of her toenails.

This was enough for us to comprehend that she was the Mother of the universe, the Supreme Power. We also understood that she had brought us to Mani Dvipa to show her grandiose form and unlimited powers. No doubt, the dvipa was the ultimate place of happiness.

The realisation dawned upon us that if we could see our entire universe in her toenail, which included the three of us, then how many more universes with their respective trinity of Brahma, Vishnu, Mahesh and the devas existed. We three did our respective assigned tasks of creation, preservation and destruction with all the powers derived from her. If we three take birth and die as commanded by her, then similar must be the fate of Indra or other devas. It was only her that was eternal and manifested in various forms to craft the cycles of creation, obliteration and recreation of each of the existing universe.'"

Creation

Vyasa further explained to Janamejaya, 'Brahma had delivered the finality of Supreme God to Narada. But the trinity themselves, since they had a realisation about the enormity of the Cosmos and the possibility of several parallel worlds, needed to have answers to many more questions before they could leave the dvipa.

Brahma, thus, asked the Devi why there were cycles of creation and destruction.

The Devi, as if expecting the questions, was ready to quell all doubts from the minds of the three gods she had created.

She said that the need for creation, again and again, after each pralaya, that is destruction, was the result of the fructification of those karmas of the jivas, the souls, whose fruits had not been enjoyed before the pralayas. With the start of the creation, the balance karmas came into play. She told Brahma that it was he who was the custodian of these calculations and without him, maya would be impossible. Therefore, both Brahma and maya were interwoven.

Brahma asked again, "O Creatrix! People who have attained wisdom, who have knowledge of the Vedas, say that there is only one God and that is Brahman. Who is this Brahman, the one and second less? Is the One male or female? Also, whether the reality is dual or one?"

Devi Bhagvati spoke to the trinity in her incomparable sweet voice, "There is oneness between me and the Purusha. The Purusha is I and I am Purusha. It is I who manifests into Brahma at the time of creation. It is I who is the Shakti, the energy or force. Making Purusha the instrument, I perform all the actions.[45] I am the coolness in water, the heat in the fire, the lustre in the sun and the cooling rays in the Chandra. If I desert this universe, then it would become motionless.

As an illustration, if someone is weak, it is said that he is without shakti or energy. Nobody says that he is Shiva-less or Vishnu-less or Brahma-less. Anything living or non-living when combined with Shakti yields its properties, including gods and devas."

Devi Bhagvati continued, "Today, as we converse, there is no earth. That does not mean it does not exist. The earth exists in the form of atoms. All substances eternal, existing for a moment only, the void, and the substances of nature, both real and unreal, are due to a cause and ahamkara[46] is born first among them. O Brahma! Rajo Guna is your predominant quality."

Saying thus, the Devi presented Brahma with a part of her Shakti in the form of ever-smiling Devi Sarasvati as the Devi's vibhuti. She ordained Devi Sarasvati to be Brahma's companion and told him to perform his assigned role based on Prarabdha Karmas.[47] The Devi instructed Brahma to never disrespect Devi Sarasvati.

Devi Bhagvati also made it clear that Vishnu was superior to Brahma as his main quality was Sattva Guna. Therefore, Brahma should always respect and worship him. As and when Brahma experienced any difficulty, Vishnu would incarnate on earth and help Brahma tide over it. Saying this, she then presented the all-auspicious Maha Lakshmi to Vishnu.

With regard to the devas, she clarified that they would be appeased at the sound of another of her name "Svaha" at the end of all mantras during sacrificial oblations and ceremonies. And Shiva, who was the embodiment of Tamo Guna, would be revered and worshipped by all in every sacrifice. Shiva would also get Maha Kaali.

She then gave the three gods the nine-lettered mantra, "*Aum Hrim Shrim Chandikaayai Namah*", which is the best of all the mantras.

The Devi said, "But remember that you three are born of my gunas. Therefore you are one without any difference among you. There is nothing in this world that is devoid of the three gunas. Only the Supreme Self is without these gunas. However, at time I appear with gunas when I am causal[48]."

The Devi then explained that ahamkara, born out of reality, was embodied with the three gunas and, therefore, it was described as her effect. Ahamkara caused the effect called Mahattattva, Buddhi, and from it arose another ahamkara. This second ahamkara gave rise to the five subtle elements, the Tanmatraas.

From the Saattvika part of the five Tanmatraas, the five organs of perception came into being; from their Rajasika part, the five organs of action; and finally the five gross elements after a process called Panchikarana. The Saattvika portion of the five elements also gave birth to the mind. Thus, a total of sixteen things came into existence out of the three gunas. The Devi, thus, explained the creation at its beginning.

Brahma then told Narada that the three gods paid obeisance to the Devi and went to another place on the beautiful island where they turned into males again. Thereafter the three gods boarded the aerial car and when they looked back, they found no Mani Dvipa, no Devi and no ocean of nectar.'

Veda Vyasa opened his eyes from his deep meditational rendition and looked at Janamejaya. He said, 'This is what Narada Muni told me. But,' as if Vyasa knew the next volley of questions about to be thrown by the king, 'Narada Muni was in quest of more knowledge and he did not want to let go of this brilliant opportunity. I am sure, my son, you too have more doubts.'

The king nodded in agreement and waited for Vyasa to unfold the reality on his own.

On the subject of the utmost reality, Vyasa said, 'Narada had similar queries and, therefore, sought Brahma's help.

Brahma told Narada, "While the five gross elements, earth, ether, air, water and fire, are achieved through Panchikarana, their qualities also develop simultaneously. Ether has one quality only – sound; air has two – sound and touch; fire possesses three – sound, touch and form; water has four – sound, touch, form and taste; and the earth has five qualities – sound, touch, form, taste and smell. By the combination of these five gross elements, the grand Cosmos is produced."

Narada interrupted Brahma and asked his father to explain in detail the concept of Panchikarana.'

Vyasa said to Janamejaya, 'Brahma had no problem going into the depth of any of these subjects as he himself was the creator. Brahma replied, "Panchikarana is a simple process but yields results with complex properties as the end products are altogether different from its ingredients.

For instance, to create the gross element of water, divide the subtle element of water into two equal parts and divide the other four elements into two equal parts. Keep apart the first half of each of the five elements and divide the second half of each into four equal parts. Now mix the first half of water with the fourth part of each of the other four elements and you get one gross element of water.[49] When the five gross elements are, thus, produced, consciousness then enters into these elements as their presiding deities."

No sooner than Brahma finished, Narada put forth his observation on the concept of Nirguna.[50] He said, "I have observed severe austerities and performed meditation. I have also seen many siddha purusha,[51] high-souled sages, practise tapasya with completely controlling their passions and anger. However, none has been able to see the Nirguna form of the Supreme God."

Brahma replied, "As regards your observation of not being able to see the Nirguna form, it cannot be visible to anyone as anything that can be seen must have gunas. But it can be visualised only in the consciousness of sages through meditation and after achieving a heart free from ahamkara."

Narada intervened again, "I know that ahamkara is threefold: Saattvika, Rajasika and Tamasika. I wish to know in detail the difference between them. Having introduced the gunas, do explain their qualities and their configuration."

Brahma was pleased to get more queries from Narada and continued, "Hear Narada! The three types of ahamkara have different kinds of energy: Gyan Shakti, Kriya Shakti and Dravya or Artha Shakti, respectively. They, ad seriatim, are responsible for obtaining knowledge, producing action and generating material things or objects of the senses.

Sattva Guna, whose colour is white, is the source of pleasure and happiness. It is predominant in a man who has integrity, truthfulness, cleanliness, faith, forgiveness, fortitude, bashfulness, peace and contentment.

Rajo Guna, of the colour red, is the source of all troubles. It causes hatred, enmity, quarrelsome feelings, pride, want of faith, egoism, vanity and arrogance. Tamo Guna, of the colour black, gives rise to laziness, ignorance, sleep, poverty, fear, quarrels, miserliness, insincerity, anger, aberration of intellect and finding faults with others.

There is no one who has only one of these qualities. Every being has an intermingled combination of the three with one or the other as the inherent quality. It may sound paradoxical, but their co-existence is as if they are at war with each other to gain dominance over every being. The wise people, of course, always intend to enhance their sattva qualities, control the rajas qualities and destroy the tamas qualities."'

Vyasa concluded, 'O King! This is what Brahma told Narada and Narada explained it to me. Today I have passed on all that knowledge to you in this Kali Yuga when the universe needs this much more than any other time.

Now you know Supreme Goddess Devi Bhagvati, having many names and many manifestations, is the cause of this universe. Therefore, you should worship this Goddess and complete your yagna in her dedication to achieving the desired results.

In ancient times, the trinity of gods, the devas and the highest sages worshipped her on several occasions to achieve nirvana, liberation. Even if one takes her name with complete devotion, she, the merciful, grants the boon.

This is what happened to Satyavrata, an illiterate brahmin who had mistakenly uttered the word "*Aim*", the seed mantra of Sarasvati, the goddess of learning and, by her grace, turned into the best of poets.'

Satyavrata

Janamejaya became curious and asked Vyasa with childlike inquisitiveness, 'O Muni! Who was Satyavrata? What had happened to him? How did he turn into a great writer when he was illiterate?'

Vyasa replied, 'In one of my journeys to various pilgrimages, I went to the sacred forest of Naimisharanya. At that time, a congregation of several seers, sages and munis was being hosted. Many high-souled and liberated mind-born sons of Lord Brahma were present in the congregation. I had a great opportunity to enjoy the company of such sages.

I was given an appropriate place in the assembly and a discussion on deep religious and philosophical subjects started. In the congregation, Maharishi Jamadagni spoke of certain doubts that he had and sought others' opinions on them.'

Vyasa said to Janamejaya before proceeding further, 'His doubts were not very different from what you asked me,' and continued, 'Jamadagni asked, "In this gathering of some of the most knowledgeable souls in this universe, I wish to ask who is the best god and ought to be first worshipped. We have a trinity of gods: Brahma, Vishnu and Shiva. We also have many devas: Indra, Surya, Chandra, Varuna, Agni, Kubera, Vayu, Kartikeya, Ganesha and the two Ashvins. Who among them is easily satisfied and grants the desired boons?"

In response to his question, Maharishi Lomasha spoke with the objective to enlighten everyone in the assembly. He said, "I wish to submit to this august gathering that the highest god is the one who was omitted by Maharishi Jamadagni. It is the Devi, the goddess of shakti or energy. She is the one who created Brahma, Vishnu, Mahesh and all the devas. She is the Mother and the root of this Tree of universe. She is the most merciful. Anyone who worships her gets the desired boons and blessings. If I may, I would like to narrate a story to explain it to you all."

Maharishi Lomasha continued, "There once lived a brahmin by the name of Deva Datta in the country of Kosala,[52] located near River Sarayu. For a long time, his wife and he could not have a child. He decided to perform a sacrifice called 'Putreshti' to procreate.

An altar was constructed on the banks of River Tamsaa where Deva Datta invited other brahmins to perform the sacrifice. All the brahmins were well-versed in performing rites according to the Vedas. In the ceremony, Suhotra was appointed as the head priest and Govila as the Udgaataa, one of the four principal priests, who were to chant the hymns of the Saam Veda.

Govila began reciting the powerful hymns from the Saam Veda in the form of Svarita, which combined all the seven notes of music. While he was singing the Rathantar Mantra, he would draw his breath frequently. This resulted in several interruptions in the recitation, which irritated Deva Datta.

He scolded Govila and said despite being among the highest priests, Govila was reciting mantras like an illiterate man. Deva Datta went on to say that while he was performing an important sacrifice to procreate a son, Govila was acting stupid.

Govila felt humiliated and was enraged. Out of his uncontrolled fury, he cursed Deva Datta that his unborn son would be illiterate and foolish.

Despite being angry, Govila explained to Deva Datta the reasons for the interruption. He said, 'It was no fault of mine as respiration is integral to every living being. One cannot sing without breathing in between. I am shocked that even though you are an accomplished brahmin, you could not comprehend this.'

On hearing the curse of angry Govila, Deva Datta trembled with fear. He fell to Govila's feet and offered his sincerest apologies. Trying to reason out with the muni, he said, 'O High Priest! The wise people, the enlightened souls, are supposed to have won over their anger. Yet you cursed me out of rage so grievously for such a trivial fault of mine. You should have discerned that I was under severe mental stress being childless and now I am even more damned.'

Deva Datta lamented, 'They say that it is better to be sonless than to have a stupid son. How will an illiterate son of a brahmin perform his duties of learning and teaching the Vedas and worshipping on behalf of his patrons? He will get neither invited to any auspicious ceremonies nor any benefaction from the king. He will end up working as a farmer or a labourer.'

A weeping Deva Datta made his final appeal, 'As a brahmin, I would rather die than have an illiterate son. Therefore, O Muni! I bow down to you. Have some mercy on me and rethink your tormenting words,' and prostrated at Govila's feet."

Lomasha paused to gauge the reaction of those present in the assembly of wise sages and continued, "As the anger of sagacious persons is usually ephemeral, Govila had also calmed down by the time Deva Datta finished.

Govila thus compassionately spoke to a devastated Deva Datta, 'You know a curse once cast cannot be withdrawn. Its power, however, can be reduced. Now listen carefully. Your son will be illiterate in his early life but will turn into an intelligent and prudent person thereafter.'

Deva Datta breathed a sigh of relief on hearing Muni Govila's words. He went ahead with the completion of the Putreshti sacrifice and awarded all the priests with suitable dakshina, the offerings.

It was not too long before his wife, Rohini, became pregnant. Deva Datta performed the ceremonies at the time of conception followed by the Pumsavan[53] ceremony in the third month. The Simantonnayana ceremonies[54] in the fourth, sixth and eighth months of the pregnancy were also undertaken in accordance with the prescribed rituals.

His wife delivered a son on an auspicious day, coincidently under the Rohini Nakshatra, which bestows creativity. He diligently performed Jaat Karma[55] on his son's birth. He named his son Utathya during the Naamkaran[56] ceremony.

Deva Datta had not forgotten the curse but he went ahead with the following ceremonies, performing Nishkraman when Utathya was taken out in the open air for the first time at the tender age of four months, Annaprashan when the child was first fed with rice as solid food and Chudakarana[57] ceremony at the time of the first tonsure.

At the Upanayana[58] ceremony, the eight-year-old boy wore a sacred thread known as Janeyu. Following this, Utathya began his formal studies under the vow of being a chaste bachelor, a brahmachari.

The child was completely dumb and could not learn anything. In spite of having the best teachers, he could not utter a single word from the Vedas. He also could not develop any abilities to read or write.

Utathya spent twelve years in the school but could not learn a single lesson. It became widely known that the boy, because of the curse of Govila, had turned illiterate. The boy and his parents became a subject of ridicule in their society and beyond.

The contempt faced from his family, particularly his parents, turned poor Utathya into a recluse. One day, when he finally could not bear the reprimand of his father, he renounced his home and left for the forest.

He reached the banks of River Ganga. There he chose a serene location and built himself a hut. He began to live there surviving on the natural roots and fruits of the forest. Keeping his mind composed, he made a vow that he would never utter a lie."

Lomasha explained the plight of Utathya, "The young man had failed to acquire any knowledge during his time spent in the school. Hence, he was oblivious to any kind of worshipping, prayers, yoga, mantras, ceremonies or even the Gayatri Mantra.

He spent his day performing daily errands. He got up in the morning, took bath in the river and collected food and ate. He could not even discern whether a certain fruit was good for eating or not. Meanwhile, his quality of not speaking any untruth earned him the name of Satyavrata among the local people.

Utathya continued to pass his life without doing anything significant and just running the daily chores. He neither did any good nor bad to anyone around him. It seemed to him that his life was comparable to a cow not giving milk or a tree not bearing fruits. He was always immersed in the thought of eventually meeting his death, which would release him from his ignorant life. He felt that death was perhaps a better option than to live a life of a cursed illiterate brahmin."

Maharishi Lomasha paused to take a deep breath and found everyone was attentively listening to him. He continued, "Fourteen years passed since Utathya had taken abode in the forest. In all these years, he could not learn anything more than what he had known. But he knew that he had no knowledge. However, his fame as a truth speaker under the sobriquet Satyavrata spread.

Then one day, a boar accidentally visited Satyavrata's hermitage. The boar was petrified, bleeding and had sharp arrows pierced into his body. Looking at his pitiable condition, Satyavrata was filled with mercy. As a natural reaction, he pointed the boar to a safe direction exclaiming 'Ai, Ai', little realising that it was the seed mantra of Devi Sarasvati, the goddess of learning. The words came out of his mouth accidentally.

The boar, though badly injured, hid in the bushes around Satyavrata's hut.

Within moments, a seemingly trained hunter equipped with bows and arms followed the boar. It was obvious that he was chasing the boar to kill it. The hunter had a dreadful and cruel appearance.

The hunter saw Satyavrata sitting outside his hut silently. He greeted him and asked about the boar.

Satyavrata was in a difficult position. He knew that if he told the truth to the hunter about the boar's whereabouts, then the boar would die. If, on the other hand, Satyavrata said that he had not seen the boar, then it would be a lie.

He then reasoned that truth, if it causes injury or loss of lives, is no truth. The welfare of beings is more important than the truth. In this case, a lie will save a life and, hence, has a higher purpose.

After the internal debate, Satyavrata replied in the form of a verse, 'The eye that sees never speaks and the tongue that speaks never sees. O Hunter! Don't ask me the same question again to fulfil your vested interest.'

The hunter was rather disappointed with Satyavrata's answer but he was aware that Satyavrata always spoke the truth. So he returned without the boar.

Satyavrata, on the other hand, had no idea how he thought about various options and arrived at a righteous decision in spite of being illiterate and an acknowledged stupid."

Lomasha concluded, "Without the knowledge of Utathya, he had spoken the seed mantra of the goddess of learning which made the Devi fill with mercy and compassion towards him. Having been pleased, she gave him the knowledge at once, turning him into a seer and a poet like the ancient Muni Valmiki.

Satyavrata started composing and reciting poems in praise of Devi Sarasvati and his reputation reached far and wide. Gradually, his father Deva Datta heard about him and his fame. He brought him back to the family fold with respect and warmth.'"

Addressing the king, Vyasa said 'This is what I heard from Maharishi Lomasha in that congregation. O King! It is the Devi who is the prime energy and the cause of this universe. She is the one who should be worshipped first with great devotion and selfless love. She is the Kaamdaa, the giver of all desired boons.

Therefore, if you see knowledge, prosperity, health, progress, enjoyment, joy and posterity in a family, be rest assured that they are there because the Devi is worshipped by that family.'

Elated with Vyasa's narration of the story, Janamejaya asked, 'O Knower of the Vedas! As we are about to initiate the Devi Yagna, do tell us about the prescribed rites and rituals that ought to be observed in its performance. I am keen to know about the materials required, the mantras, the number of brahmins required and finally the dakshinas to be offered to them. I shall try to follow them with all my might and without any delay.'

Vyasa replied, 'The preparation for a yagna is dependent on what kind of yagna it is. They are of three varieties: Saattvika, Rajasika and Tamasika. All these three are usually performed by brahmins, kings and rakshasas,[59] respectively. There is, though, another kind that is devoid of these qualities and is undertaken by only the liberated ones.

When the place, time, mantras, devotion, brahmins to perform sacrifice and materials for yagna collected from legal and right means are all saattvika, it is called Saattvika

Yagna. If any of these conditions are not met, the yagna could give contrary results.'

He recalled, 'You remember that your forefathers, the Pandava brothers, had to undergo severe adversities within three months of their famed Rajasuya Yagna.[60] Their common wife, Draupadi, was publicly insulted. They lost their kingdom and were exiled to the forest, although the yagna was done in accordance with the prescribed rites. Moreover, Lord Krishna and many other enlightened souls were present there too.

One can argue that the hardships that the Pandava brothers met with were either that the rituals of the yagna were not followed properly or their fate was to be blamed. Fate cannot be the singular reason as it alone does not determine the course of life. Else what use is the significance of mantras, worshipping and rituals? It is also true that whatever is destined according to Prarabdha will surely happen.

The Vedas merely recommend a mechanism that should be observed for achieving positive outcomes but they cannot be treated as a recipe for sure results. It also does not mean that they are of no use. Therefore, both destiny and human efforts are important to achieve success.

Thus, the yagna by Pandavas must have lacked in some form. Possibly the material may not have been righteous or it was performed with egoism.

It is, thus, important that the Saattvika Yagna be performed only by the vanaprasthi munis and no animal is sacrificed.

When a yagna is performed with the objective of getting material benefits or victory in a battle, it is called Rajasuya Yagna.

The yagna dedicated to the sole object of killing someone, including enemies, and accompanied by arrogance, anger and evil thoughts is Tamasika Yagna.

There is another yagna, called Maanasika, performed by sages with no desire but to achieve liberation from this world.

Only a Maanasika Yagna can be perfectly done whereas the other three are prone to some or the other deficiencies, arising out of time, place, materials used or the state of mind.'

Sudarshana

VedaVyasa had innumerable stories to recount that depicted the kindness and infinite power of the Devi. He narrated another one to the king while everyone was preparing for the Devi Yagna.

He began, 'O Janamejaya! In ancient times, the Kosala country, with its capital at the pious city of Ayodhya, had a Suryavanshi[61] king called Dhruvsandhi. He earned his fame as a just king promoting dharma and righteousness.

He had two wives, both youthful, beautiful and intelligent. The first wife's name was Manorama and the second one was Lilavati. In time, Manorama was blessed with Dhruvsandhi's son. He was named Sudarshana and the beautiful son had all the indications of a royal child.

Within a month, Lilavati too delivered a handsome son who was named Shatrujit.

With great fanfare, the king performed all the prescribed ceremonies at the birth of both his sons. He gave alms and charities to the poor and gifted presents to brahmins and courtiers in his kingdom. When the children were fifteen months old, their Chudakarana ceremony or shaving off their heads was performed.

Both the boys were apples of the king's eyes. Dhruvsandhi treated them with equal affection. The boys were also charming and enamoured anyone who saw them.

As the boys grew up, Shatrujit, the son of Lilavati, developed a sweet tongue. He gradually became a favourite of not only the king but also of ministers and people at large.

Once the king went on his usual hunting expedition. He killed many animals in the forest and was stalking a deer when a huge lion came out of the bushes. Before the lion could attack him, the king shot several arrows and badly injured him.

In retaliation, the lion collected all his energy and jumped towards the king. The king pulled out his sword and attacked the lion.

The king's guards too showered multiple arrows on the lion. Before the dreadful lion succumbed to his injuries, he ripped open the king's chest. By the time the soldiers could take the king out from under the hefty lion, he died.

The guards rushed to the capital city and provided all the information to the court ministers. Supervised by Muni Vashishtha, the funeral was performed in the forest to ensure the king's safe journey to the next world.

Once the last rites were over, Muni Vashishtha began consulting other ministers and select citizens to decide the successor to the throne of Kosala. As a natural choice, the ministers proposed Sudarshana's name as he was the elder of the two brothers and was endowed with all the requisite characteristics of being the king. Muni Vashishtha accepted their proposal.

When the news about the selection of the successor spread, Lilavati's father, King Yudhajit of Ujjain, and Manorama's father, King Virasena of Kalinga, hurriedly arrived in Ayodhya accompanied by their respective armies. Both kings wanted to ensure that their respective grandsons got the throne.

The second round of tense consultation took place. While Virasena argued in favour of Sudarshana as he was the elder son, Yudhajit claimed that his grandson Shatrujit was more qualified and intelligent. In the end, Yudhajit gave an ultimatum to the ministers that as long as he was alive, he would not let Sudarshana become the king.

Soon the vassal kings of both also joined in, swelling the number of armed soldiers in the city. On hearing about the potential war, robbers from various places also moved into the city intending to plunder the riches.

An inevitable war eventually broke out between the armies of Virasena and Yudhajit.'

Vyasa paused for a moment before resuming, 'Human greed and unjust behaviour have no confines. Both the kings' hunger for the kingdom of Kosala for their respective grandsons led to a disastrous war. The war witnessed infantry, cavalry and elephant riders slaughtering their counterparts on the opposite side. What was left after the gruesome killings was a feast for vultures, crows and beasts from the forest. The nearby river had turned red with flowing blood and was clogged with piles of flesh and bones.

At the end of the decisive battle, Yudhajit slew Virasena with his sharp arrow.

As soon as this news reached Manorama, she knew that Yudhajit would not spare her minor son's life. She also realised that no one would be able to give shelter to her and Sudarshana in the entire kingdom because of Yudhajit's fear.

She decided to take a chance to save her son's life. She called in her confidant Minister Vidalla who had a reputation as an honest and sharp person. She cried, "O Vidalla! You know my father has been killed in the battle and Sudarshana, my son, is a minor. I have no reason to doubt that as soon as Yudhajit reaches this palace, Sudarshana and I will be his next target. What do you think I should do?"

The minister advised, "I think it would be best for you to leave the palace immediately. I will take you to Benares where my uncle Subaahu lives. He is very powerful and has his army. He will protect us." Vidalla further suggested, "You should get out of the city on the pretext of visiting Yudhajit. This seems to be the only way to escape from this imminent danger."

Manorama worked as per Vidalla's advice and informed her co-wife Lilavati. Accompanied by her son and a few attendants, she left in her chariot. She met Yudhajit and with his help, cremated her father Virasena. Soon after, she left in the dark of the night with her entourage. She travelled for two continuous days to reach the banks of River Ganga.

On seeing an affluent group on their way in the forest in the dark, some robbers plundered them of all their valuables. Left with nothing but her son and a few attendants including Vidalla, Manorama crossed the river and arrived at Chitrakuta mountain. She hastened to reach the hermitage of Maharishi Bharadwaja.

Maharishi Bharadwaja received her in his abode and asked, "O pretty one! Who are you? Where have you come from? From your attire, you seem like a royal. What happened to you?"

A despaired and grieving Manorama was unable to respond. Instead, Vidalla spoke on her behalf and narrated to Bharadwaja the complete episode. He begged Bharadwaja for protection from Yudhajit as such a deed was better than performing a sacrifice.

The maharishi accepted their request and permitted them to stay in his serene hermitage. He assured them that they did not need to worry about their enemies while living in his hermitage. He also blessed Sudarshana and told Manorama that her son would be a king.

Manorama, thus, began living in the hermitage peacefully and raised her son with the assistance of a maidservant and Vidalla.

Meanwhile, Yudhajit searched for Manorama and her son after his return to Kosala but could not find them there. He desperately wanted to kill Sudarshana.

He performed Shatrujit's coronation amidst chanting of auspicious hymns from the Atharva Veda by Maharishi Vashishtha. Thereafter, he returned to his kingdom. However, the citizens of Kosala continued to whisper about the injustice meted out to Sudarshana.

After reaching his kingdom, Yudhajit learnt that Manorama had taken shelter in Bharadwaja's hermitage. He once again marched with his army towards the hermitage.

At Manorama's request, the maharishi went out of his hermitage to talk to Yudhajit who was adamant to get the mother and son, by force, if required.

The maharishi challenged the king, "Don't even think about taking Manorama by force. If you dare, you will meet the same outcome as King Vishvamitra when he attempted to steal away the heavenly cow from the hermitage of Maharishi Vashishtha."'

Vyasa smiled at the reference to this interesting episode and did not attempt to hide it from an attentive Janamejaya.

An intrigued Janamejaya asked, 'What are you referring to Muni? It is difficult to believe that a maharishi stole something from another maharishi. Kindly tell me in detail.'

Vyasa nodded and said, 'As you insist Janamejaya. I will return to the story of Sudarshana in a bit,' and began the anecdote, 'In the days of yore, Vishvamitra was born as the son of King Gaadhi and succeeded his father as sovereign. While on leisurely travel, he accidentally arrived at the hermitage of Vashishtha.

The king paid his respects to Vashishtha. After spending some time discussing various subjects, Vashishtha invited Vishvamitra to dinner. The king pointed towards his large entourage and told the maharishi that it would be difficult to feed all of them.

The maharishi insisted and made several dishes from milk to feed the large entourage. Vishvamitra was pleasantly surprised. He soon realised that the maharishi had a cow called Nandini who had divine powers and was solely responsible for giving such a huge amount of milk.

The king requested Maharishi Vashishtha to give him Nandini and offered a thousand cows in lieu. Vashishtha, however, refused the offer. Vishvamitra increased the offer to tens of thousand of cows but Vashishtha did not agree.

The king was so enticed with the idea of owning Nandini that he threatened to take it away by force.

To this Vashishtha responded, "O King! I shall not be able to part with my cow. If you want to take her perforce, you may attempt."

The maharishi's words acted as a catalyst in hastening up the king's resolve to take away the cow. He ordered his guards to fasten a rope around her neck and pull her along.

The cow, Nandini, shuddered and cried to Vashishtha, "Save me! How can you leave me to be carried away like this?"

Vashishtha reassured Nandini, "I have no intention of parting away with you. You have always blessed me with your milk with which I have undertaken all my sacrifices. But what can I do against these royal guards using all their might."

On hearing this, the cow bellowed in anger and from her body came out terrible demons equipped with armour and weaponry. They destroyed Vishvamitra's entourage but spared his life. That moment of realisation changed him from a kshatriya to an ascetic. He left for penance and meditation and eventually attained sagehood.'

Veda Vyasa resumed his earlier narration that he had left midway, 'It is, therefore, advised not to pick a fight with ascetics as it might lead to great loss. And the same advice was also rendered by Yudhajit's ministers after he was warned by Maharishi Bharadwaja adding that since the boy had no power and no wealth, he did not pose any threat to his grandson's throne. The king heeded the advice and returned, very much against his wish of killing Manorama and Sudarshana.

One day, Sudarshana was playing with other children in the hermitage. He was five years old. The children saw Vidalla passing by and naughtily addressed him as "Klib, Klib".

Sudarshana too picked up this sound and began to resound the first part of it "Kli" repetitively in his mind. He was, of course, unaware that it was the root mantra of Kaamdeva[62], with the anusvara omitted. When he was eleven, he was initiated into formal studies after Maharishi Bharadwaja performed his Upanayana ceremony.

One night, Sudarshana had a dream of the Supreme Goddess attired in red and wearing red ornaments. Following his dream, he was bestowed a set of bows, arrows, a quiver and special armour by the Goddess.

Soon after, the king of Nishadas visited the hermitage and presented a chariot to Sudarshana. Drawn by four horses, it was befitting for a king. As Sudarshana had energised the seed mantra, his chariot under the influence of the mantra seemed to be surrounded by a large and powerful army of one Akshauhini[63].

Around the same time, King Subaahu's daughter Shashikala heard about Sudarshana from a clairvoyant. She started yearning for Sudarshana as her spouse. She received visions of the Devi and requested her to fulfil her desire of getting Sudarshana as her husband. The Devi blessed her.

Meanwhile, King Subaahu arranged for Shashikala's svayamvara[64] and invited all the kings and princes so that she could choose her husband from among them.

When the preparations for the ceremony were complete and the city of Kashi had received all the royal suitors for the princess, Shashikala told her mother about her desire to tie the knot with Sudarshana. She also told her mother about her visions of the Devi.

Shashikala's mother informed the king about their daughter's desire. But the king was least interested in marrying his daughter to an exiled and penniless prince. Instead, he suggested that Shashikala should marry Shatrujit, the reigning king of Kosala.

Shashikala, however, was adamant to marry Sudarshana. Through a wandering brahmin, she sent a message at the hermitage and conveyed to Sudarshana about the Devi giving her blessings to Shashikala's desire of getting married to Sudarshana. She also requested him to come immediately before her svayamvara or else she would commit suicide.

Considering this as Devi's desire, Sudarshana hurriedly left for Kashi in his grand chariot. Upon reaching Kashi, he was received with honour and made to stay at the royal guest house.

The city seemed like a festive ground with the presence of a plethora of kings and princes including Yudhajit and Shatrujit besides other important kings of Karusa, Madra, Sindhu, Mahismati, Panchala, Kamrupa, Chola and Vidharbha who had also come to take part in the svayamvara.

The news about Sudarshana's arrival led to a commotion among other kings. Yudhajit seized the opportunity and announced that he would kill Sudarshana in the svayamvara. But he was dissuaded by others as they highlighted that this was not the occasion to wage wars.

On the appointed day and time, the kings, attired in their best and bejewelled in their most expensive, gathered in the royal court. But Shashikala refused to come to the hall and insisted on getting married to Sudarshana only.'

Vyasa continued, 'On hearing his daughter's reiteration of having the blessings of the Devi, the king was forced to inform everyone that his daughter would not conduct the svayamvara. To avert the wrath of the annoyed kings, he offered huge quantities of wealth to each one of the kings present with the request to return to their kingdoms peacefully.

While all others kept the peace, Yudhajit was furious. He said angrily, "Why did you invite us in the first place? I will kill you and then Sudarshana if your daughter selects him. Let her choose any other king but Sudarshana."

The king returned to the palace to confer with his wife and daughter. Shashikala suggested, "Father! Get me married to Sudarshana and let the Devi protect us."

The king accepted his daughter's suggestion and requested the kings to return to the svayamvara hall the next day so that he could have the time to settle the matter with his daughter.

Having bought himself a day, the king married Shashikala and Sudarshana the same night with all the rites and ceremonies.

As the day broke and the sun was about to rise, the guest kings came to know about the wedding. They felt that they had been disgraced and cheated by Subaahu and decided to close all the exit routes of Kashi and kill Sudarshana. They waited for the newlywed couple to leave the city.

After six days of festivities and a post-wedding ceremony, Sudarshana sought the leave of the king and take his wife to the hermitage of Bharadwaja. He assured the king that the Goddess would take care of them.

As both were leaving the city, they were surrounded by the large armies-in-waiting of several kings. Sudarshana asked Shashikala to remain in the chariot and began reciting the seed mantra.

A dreadful battle ensued between Sudarshana and the armies in which Sudarshana was outnumbered. However, Devi Bhagvati appeared suddenly. She was smeared with red sandal paste and was mounted on her vehicle.

The most beautiful lady on the lion was also the most ferocious at the same time. Sudarshana bowed to her and announced to everyone on the battlefield, "O kings! Maha Devi Bhagvati Bhavani is here. Now I have no cause to worry about your large armies."

Yudhajit did not deter. He still wanted to kill Sudarshana and take away Shashikala. He urged the armies to attack and showered Sudarshana with his sharp arrows.

The Devi's lion then roared, which created shivers among the kings, soldiers, elephants and horses alike. The Devi herself joined the battle with her weapons and killed all including Yudhajit and Shatrujit.

Sudarshana, Shashikala, Manorama and Subaahu became ecstatic. They sang hymns in praise of Mother Goddess. She was pleased and told Subaahu to seek a boon.'

Janamejaya enjoyed listening to the narration as much as Vyasa telling it. Vyasa continued, 'Subaahu was speechless. But he gathered his wits to speak in front of the Devi, "O Mother! I am left with no desire after your vision. All I want is that my devotion to you continues unwavering and that you always remain in my city as Sri Durga Devi and bless it till it exists on this earth."

The Devi granted him his wish.

Sudarshana then, with folded hands, prostrated in front of the Devi and asked, "What shall I do, Mother?"

The Goddess blessed him and said, "O my great devotee! You go to Ayodhya, establish my image in your city of Ayodhya and rule the kingdom of your father. Also, continue to worship me unflinchingly as you have done, particularly on the fourth, eighth and ninth day of each lunar half month."

She added, "My great puja in spring and autumn for nine nights[65] should be done with the greatest devotion."

Equipped with the Devi's blessings and command, Sudarshana returned to Ayodhya with his wife and mother. He constructed the Devi's temple in the city and also in every village of his kingdom. He continued to rule in the footsteps of his most prominent ancestor Sri Rama.

Since then, the world has been celebrating Navratri in the Shukla Paksha[66] of months of Ashvin and Chaitra,' concluded Vyasa.

Navratri Puja

Janamejaya asked, 'O Creator of the Vedas! You just mentioned about the Navratras. Please explain to me in detail how men are supposed to observe Navratra. What results it may bring?'

Vyasa began to explain, 'The two seasons of spring and autumn are known as the teeth of Yama. Both seasons are known to inflict serious diseases that may cause loss of lives. Therefore, it is recommended that Devi Chandika be worshipped in the months of Chaitra and Ashvin.

Detailed prescribed preparations are required for the observance of Navaratras. It begins the day earlier, that is, on the day of amavasya, the new moon. One needs to collect all the materials required for the worship. One can eat only once on that day, that too a dish called habisyanna.[67] The place for the veneration should also be prepared beforehand by cleaning and creating a Vedi or a raised platform where the Devi has to be installed.

On the day of the first Navaratra, which is the Pratipada day of Shukla Paksha, one should take a bath and begin with the purification ceremony of the invited brahmins. They should be offered paadya[68], arghya[69] and madhuparka[70]. Then one should gift them as much as one is capable of, without being stingy. A sankalpa[71] can also be taken before initiating the ceremony.

The recitation of Chandi Paath and Bhagavatam has to be done by either nine, five, three or at least one brahmin. The objective of these recitations is to appease the Devi.

The Vedi may be decorated with a throne fitted with silken clothes. The image or statue of the Devi, decorated with beautiful clothing and ornaments, replete with four or eighteen arms should be installed on that throne.

If the image of the Devi or her statue is not available, then an earthen pot filled with water can be placed on the throne instead after purifying it according to Vedic mantras. The earthen pot represents the Devi. The pot should be decorated with five young shoots of plants, with the extremities of branches bearing new leaves immersed in water. A yantra signifying the nine-lettered mantra of Chandika should be also placed on the throne.

As far as possible, all the rules stipulated for the vow should be observed and the mantras recited accordingly.

The Devi has to be venerated by chandan,[72] aguru,[73] camphor, flowers, bel leaves and dhupa.[74] A lamp of ghee should be lighted. Fruits and specially cooked food, such as prasadam, should be offered accompanied by a heart full of devotion.

The meat-eaters can sacrifice animals in their worship. Goats and wild boar are considered the best options for this. Sacrifices made during these ceremonies are not considered as killing.

Worshipping has to be done all nine days accompanied by festivities comprising dancing, singing and music. If a person has taken the vow, he should sleep on the floor. During these nine days, Kumari puja, or worshipping the virgins (young girls from the age of two to the age of ten), is also prescribed. On the first day at least one girl should be worshipped and on the ninth day at least nine. The girls may be served with sweetmeats and gifts.'

Janamejaya interrupted Vyasa and asked, 'Are there any norms to be observed for this special puja of little girls?'

Vyasa elaborated, 'The girls have to be between the ages of two and ten. Those more than ten years cannot be part of these rites. Each age represents a particular form of the Devi and worshipping them respectively yields the following results. Those younger than two years of age also cannot be worshipped as they are considered to be oblivious to smell and taste.

The little girls for the worship ought to be chosen from those who are born from wedded mothers and have normal limbs and eyes as well as those who are not lepers or have sores and ulcers on their bodies.

The two-year-old girl is named the Kumari and her worship ends miseries and poverty. It also enhances wealth, longevity, power and victory over one's enemies. In her, the Kumari Devi is worshipped who had effortlessly created Brahma, the devas and the rest.

The worship of Trimurti, the Devi of three years, leads to the fulfilment of dharma, artha and kaam. It also bestows sons and grandsons. She personifies the Devi who is responsible for the three gunas: Sattva, Rajo and Tamo. She assumes multiple forms through the mixing of these gunas: from the inception to the end of this world.

Kalyani, the girl of four years, is the fructifier of all desires such as knowledge, success, kingdom and happiness. In her is embodied all auspicious Kumari Kalyani.

Worshipping Rohini, the girl of five years, cures all diseases. Devi Rohini is the keeper of all our karmas, past and present, in the seed form.

Worshipping of Kalika, the girl of six years, routs one's enemies. She signifies the Devi who in the form of Kaali had annihilated the whole universe at the end of the kalpa.

When we worship Chandika, the girl of seven years, we bring prosperity and wealth. She is the one whose worshipping destroys all evil. She is also the one who killed the two powerful demons Chanda and Munda.

Devi Shambhavi, represented in a girl of eight years, quells penury and wins over one's enemies. She signifies the Vedas and whose origin has not been caused by anything or anyone.

The devotion to Maa Durga, manifested in a girl of nine years, destroys enemies and brings happiness in subsequent life and beyond. She protects her devotees from all troubles and misfortunes.

Finally, worshipping a ten-year-old girl, that is Subhadra, leads to the accomplishment of all the wishes and for all the auspiciousness for her devotees.'

Vyasa paused so that the king could grasp all the information he had imparted. When Vyasa was convinced that Janamejaya had understood everything said till then, he continued, 'O King! It is possible that a devotee, in spite of his desire to do so, is not able to perform the ceremonies on all the days of Navaratras. In such a situation, one should do the special worship on the eighth day which is called Ashtami.

It was on this very day, Devi Bhadra Kaali arrived at the venue of Daksha's sacrifice with the objective of destroying it. It was the same Daksha who, though was the father-in-law of Shiva, had insulted him and did not invite Shiva to the sacrifice.

Devotees should offer payasam, a dish prepared with rice, milk and sugar, to the Devi. Those who eat meat can offer fresh fish.

Those who are unable to fast during all days of the Navaratras should fast on the last three days. If they do it on Saptami, Ashtami and Navami – the seventh, eighth and ninth day – they are endowed with the full blessings of the Devi.

O King! There are five heinous crimes. These are killing a brahmin, drinking alcohol, stealing gold, liaising with the guru's wife and being accomplices in any of these. When we worship the Devi during the Navaratras, we are absolved from these sins too.

Even Sri Rama, the incarnation of Vishnu, was blessed when he worshipped the Devi during Navaratras with utmost devotion.'

Hearing about Sri Rama and his link to Devi puja made Janamejaya more curious. He wondered how the incarnation of god could suffer so much and had to take the recourse to Devi puja. He asked, 'O Muni! Please explain to me in detail about Sri Rama performing this puja and getting rid of his sufferings.'

Vyasa understood Janamejaya's inquisitiveness and began explaining, 'Towards the end of the Treta Yuga, Vishnu was incarnated as Sri Rama and was born as the son of Ayodhya's King Dashratha. The ruling family of Ayodhya belonged to the Suryavanshi lineage and boasted of legendary ancestors like Ikshvaku and Raghu.

Dashratha was blessed with four sons – Rama, the eldest, born of Kaushalya, Bharat born of Kaikeyi and Lakshmana and Shatrughana born of Sumitra. All four sons had celebrated qualities and virtues.

Rama married Sita, the daughter of King Janak, after breaking the bow of Lord Shiva as the pre-condition during her svayamvara. Sita was part-incarnate of Devi Lakshmi.

King Janak married his younger daughter Urmila to Lakshmana. Bharat and Shatrughana married Mandavi and Shrutakirti, respectively, the daughters of King Kushadhvaja, the younger brother of Janak.

Dashratha announced his wish to coronate Rama as the king of Ayodhya. But destiny had some other plans in store.

Due to the two boons asked by Kaikeyi from Dashratha, Rama was exiled for fourteen years. Sita and Lakshmana accompanied him. Unable to come to terms with the grief of his son Rama leaving for the forest, Dashratha left his mortal body.

Kaikeyi's second boon of making Bharat the king of Ayodhya could not be fulfilled as he decided not to ascend the throne after witnessing his father die due to his mother seeking the undesirable boons.

Rama began living in the Panchavati forest with his wife and brother. One day, Surpanakha, the youngest sibling of Lanka King Ravana, saw Rama in the forest and was attracted to him. She wanted to express her love for Rama, but Lakshmana disfigured her by cutting off her nose and ears.

To avenge her insult and injury, her brothers Khara and Dushana came to kill Rama. Instead, they were slain by Rama.

On hearing of his sister's humiliation and killing of his cousins, the infuriated Ravana kidnapped Sita through trickery.

Both Rama and Lakshmana went out in search of Sita and found a moribund Jatayu, the king of birds. Jatayu told both the brothers that Ravana had taken away Sita slyly. When Jatayu had attempted to stop Ravana, he chopped off his wings.

While wandering in the forest in search of Sita, Rama and Lakshmana made friends with Sugriva, the king of monkeys. At Sugriva's request, Rama killed his cousin Bali and reinstated Sugriva to the kingship of Kishkindha.

Unable to find clues about Sita's whereabouts, Rama became anxious and was despaired. He spent four months of the rainy season with his brother in search of his wife. And at the end, grief-stricken Rama thinking that Janaki[75] was no more, wished to end his life as he could not live without his dear wife.'

Vyasa stopped for a moment to think and began again, 'While Lakshmana was consoling Rama, Maharishi Narada reached Kishkindha, playing his famous lute and singing hymns from the Saam Veda.

Rama was amazed to see Narada. He welcomed Narada and after washing his feet, offered him a respectable seat. After Rama finished worshipping the maharishi, Narada signalled him to take a seat close by.

In his characteristic soft and melodious voice, Narada asked Rama, "O Prince of Ayodhya! I have heard about Janaki being taken by the evil-minded Ravana, the descendant of Pulastya. But what is the point in lamenting like an ordinary mortal? Ravana does not know that you have been born to kill him and lessen the weight of evil from this earth. It is to fulfil this objective that he has stolen away Sita." Seeing Rama astonished, Narada added, "Let me explain it to you.

O Rama! Sita was born as the daughter of a muni in her previous birth. She was a great ascetic. One day, Ravana came to the muni's hermitage, the abode of Sita, and saw her. He liked her so much that he asked her to marry him. Being austere, she did not like the proposal and censured him. The wicked Ravana caught hold of her hair. Considering her body as being polluted by the touch of Ravana, she angrily decided to put an end to her life.

But before she parted with her life, she cursed Ravana, 'O one with evil eye! I am leaving this body but I will be born again, though not from any womb, and be the cause of your destruction.'

Sita, as part-incarnate of Devi Lakshmi and you, Rama, as the incarnation of Lord Vishnu, have been born in this yuga to fulfil that motive. You have to keep patience. Sita is in Ravana's captivity and meditating upon you. Indra, the king of the devas, is taking care of her. Daily he sends her milk from the heavenly cow on which she is surviving.

O Rama! In the days of yore, Brahma, Vishnu, Mahesh and the devas worshipped the Devi. Anyone desiring happiness and, in particular, those who are facing extreme difficulties must undertake this veneration of the Devi.

I recall that the same sacrifice was also done by Indra to decimate Vritrasura, by Shiva to kill Daitya Tripura and by Vishnu to slaughter Madhu and Kaitabha. Therefore, you should fast and worship the Devi for the first nine days of Shukla Paksha in the forthcoming month of Ashvin to bring an end to Ravana's life."

Narada then described to Rama, as I explained to you earlier, that the Goddess was eternal. She was the cause of everything in the universe, living or non-living. She was also the energy or shakti behind the trinity of gods and the devas. Without her, nothing could be created. She had neither origin nor culmination. She was supreme knowledge and had endless names and forms.

At Rama's request, Narada described how the Devi had to be worshipped during the Navaratras.

Following Narada's words, Rama fasted for nine days and offered the prescribed sacrifices.

It was on the night of the eighth day, when Rama had completed the vow, that Devi Bhagvati appeared to him. Mounted on the lion, she was pleased with Rama's worship. She said in her sweet motherly tone, "O Rama! You are the one who incarnated as a fish and then a tortoise to vertically hold the Mandar mountain to facilitate the churning of the ocean.

It is you who was born as a boar to hold the earth on your teeth. You assumed the form of Narasimha, the man-lion, and tore apart Hiranyakashipu with your sharp nails.

You then incarnated as Vamana, the dwarf, and taught a lesson to the daitya Bali. It was you again who was born as Parshurama, the son of brahmin Jamadagni, to extirpate the kshatriyas.

Now you are born in the lineage of Raghu as the son of Dashratha and Kaushalya to bring the end of Ravana. With you, the devas have also incarnated as these powerful monkeys. Your younger brother Lakshmana is the incarnate of Sheshanaag, your serpent.

You are born to kill Ravana. Rise, my son!

Go and complete your duty and then worship me in the vernal season. I bless you that you will rule for eleven thousand years on this earth and, thereafter, you will return to your heavenly abode."

The Devi's boons gave renewed confidence to Rama. With Lakshmana and the army of monkeys, he was able to create a bridge on the ocean. They fought valiantly against the demonic forces and killed the dreadful Kumbhakarna, Meghanada and Ravana.

Rama installed Vibhishana as the king of Lanka. He brought back Sita from Lanka and returned to Ayodhya. Rama reigned there as blessed by the Goddess,' told Vyasa to the king.

Vasudeva and Devaki

It was not that Janamejaya had not heard of some of these episodes earlier but a narration from Veda Vyasa had a whole different meaning. As Vyasa continued with his narration, the king came up with more and more queries.

Janamejaya said, 'O Vasaveya[76]! I wish to understand from you certain incomprehensible occurrences.

We all know that Sri Krishna was the incarnation of Vishnu. Yet he went through so many difficulties during his human life. So much so that his son Pradyumna was stolen away by asuras.

Why did Krishna take birth in a prison? Why did his pious parents Vasudeva and Devaki bear the hardships and sacrifice their seven children?

Who was that girl child born of Yashoda in Vrindavan who was killed by Kamsa and how did she assume the form of Ashtabhuja, the eight-armed Goddess?

Moreover, we always talk of Arjuna and Krishna as incarnations of Nara and Narayana. O Muni! Kindly enlighten me about who they were.

We know that the Yadava clan was destroyed due to Gandhari's curse. Why did it happen although Krishna was born in the same clan?

When several ancestors in my family had extraordinary powers, how was it that they could not understand dharma and were led to the path of eventual destruction of the family?

How was it that the righteous Pandava brothers went through such agonies in their life? Even their wife Draupadi was humiliated beyond imagination.

In the great war of Mahabharata, Sri Krishna used many forms of deceit to kill the stalwarts of Kauravas. Did these not count as acts earning negative karma?

Finally, my father, son of Abhimanyu and Uttara, died such an ignominious death after insulting a brahmin.

All these are unfathomable and, therefore, troubling my mind. I wonder if all these are because of the debt of karma of the past lives only. Kindly quell my doubts, O Muni.'

Vyasa dispassionately began quenching Janamejaya's thirst for knowledge. The knowledge that not many people in this world possess.

He said, 'Before I delve into each of your queries about several personalities that you have just mentioned, let me say that the arithmetic of karma in this universe is not easily intelligible. Even the gods and devas have difficulty comprehending it, let alone men.

As the universe began with the three gunas, everything tangible had its origin in karma. Karma acts as the seed for all the jivas[77]. The jivas continue to take births from one body to another till karma comes to an end. When that happens, the jiva is no more. It simply means the cessation of the cycle of birth and death.

Karma is of three types: Sanchita or the accumulated, Bhavishya or those awaiting in future and Prarabdha which have begun to fructify. The three kinds have three subcategories, namely, auspicious signifying Saattvika, inauspicious, that is, Tamasika and a mix of both kinds which is Rajasika Karma. They are present together in any body.

All the feelings of the body such as pleasure and pain, ageing, disease and death, joy and sorrow, lust, anger and greed and so on are due to the effect of the karmas. Karma manifests into what is commonly known as destiny.

So, my son! None is excluded from the influence of karma. Not even the gods.

Vishnu, the god of preservation, had to leave all his comforts of Vaikuntha, his consort Lakshmi and ambrosial nectar and take birth as a mortal. He had to go through the process of entering a womb and live unbearably with his face downwards for months.

Even after a jiva is born, life is difficult. For instance, a child cannot speak and depends on others for all its needs. After growing up, a person has to endure all the experiences, good and bad, pleasant and painful, beneficial and adversarial, opportunities and obstacles, auspicious and inauspicious. All of this is due to karma.

Everyone with a body, be it fine or gross, has to face the effect of karma, irrespective of being a deva, human or animal. Human beings have the ability to practise austerity, give alms and perform penance and sacrifices. It helps them to rise to the level of the devas. On the other hand, when the account of good karma finishes for the devas, they have to come down to take inferior births.

As I just told you, the devas had to incarnate themselves as monkeys with Sri Rama and, you will hear now, as cowherders with Sri Krishna.'

Having explained that everything is the effect of karma which spares no one, Vyasa moved on to other questions posed by the king, 'You also asked about Vasudeva, the father of Krishna. He was born of the part of Rishi Kashyapa.

His two wives Aditi and Sursa also incarnated with him as two sisters Devaki and Rohini. They were married to Vasudeva, the Aanakadundubhi.[78] Their reincarnations were on account of a curse by Varuna, the lord of water. Vasudeva was destined to tend cows as his occupation.'

Janamejaya was astonished and asked, 'A maharishi of the stature of Kashyapa? What crime had such an enlightened soul committed to be punished like this?'

Vyasa replied, 'In ancient times, Kashyapa had brought Kaamdhenu from Varuna for some sacrificial purposes. As you know, Kaamdhenu is the heavenly cow capable of yielding all desires. Thereafter, in spite of several requests that turned into pleadings by Varuna, Kashyapa did not return the cow to him.

Left with no option, Varuna went to Brahma. He narrated the entire account to Brahma. He also told Brahma, "O God of creation! Kashyapa seems to be obsessed with my cow and does not want to part with her despite my trying all possible means."

The lines of regret showed on Varuna's face as he added further, "I could no more hear bawling and baying of Kaamdhenu's calves. I, therefore, cursed Kashyapa that he would be born as a cowherd along with both his wives and suffer extreme difficulties and dangers. I did not stop at that and also cursed Aditi that she would be imprisoned and face severe problems.

O Father! I had to bring this to your notice."

On hearing this serious matter, Brahma summoned his grandson Kashyapa. He asked the muni, "A maharishi as accomplished as you knows very well that stealing is a sin. Yet you did not return Varuna's cow to him. Jealousy is something that does not befit the sages. In spite of knowing it, you acted under the influence of greed and committed an unlawful act."

Brahma, though he loved his grandson, cursed him in the name of upholding justice, "An amsha[79] of you will be born in Yadu clan where you will be joined by your wives," and reinforced Varuna's words, "and you will work as a cowherd."

Learning of this grievous curse on her husband, Diti, the other wife of Kashyapa, also cursed her sister and co-wife, Aditi. She cursed Aditi that seven of her newborn sons would be killed consecutively.'

Janamejaya could not stop but interrupted Vyasa, 'O Muni! Why did Diti curse her sister? It is a surprise to me. Kindly explain.'

Vyasa smiled because like earlier, he was required to delve into another story even before finishing the present one, owing to the queries of the king. He explained, 'Diti and Aditi were born to Daksha Prajapati, the son of Brahma, and were given in marriage to Kashyapa. Both sisters were favourites of their father. Aditi gave birth to the king of devas, Indra.

The beautiful Diti went to her husband and charmingly said, "I want a son too who is as strong and majestic as Indra."

Kashyapa advised her to practise a vow and assured her that after the prescribed period of the sacrifice, she would be blessed with a son like Indra.

Diti followed Kashyapa's advice and got impregnated. She followed the rites and regulations of the vow and lived only on milk and slept on the floor.

As Diti entered into full-blown pregnancy, she radiated with brilliance. Seeing her like this, an envious Aditi called Indra. She told him that if Diti was blessed with a son like him, he would lose prominence. She urged him to nip the enemy in the bud and, thus, destroy the baby in Diti's womb.

Indra, incited by his mother, thought about a plan and went to Diti with his evil intent. He sweetly spoke to her, "O Mother! You have turned weak practising your vow. I have come to help. Tell me what I should do for you."

He touched Diti's feet and started to softly massage them. A tired Diti fell asleep.

Indra, seeing her napping, took out his famous thunderbolt. Keeping it in his hand, he turned into a myopic form through yogic powers and entered the womb. He lost no time to tear apart the foetus into seven pieces.

The child in the womb, struck by the thunderbolt, screamed. Indra quietened the child and further cut these seven pieces into seven parts each.

Diti woke up with an ominous feeling and realised what Indra had done. She knew it must have been the handiwork of her sister and Indra's mother.

She angrily cursed that as Indra had deceitfully killed the foetus in her womb, his kingdom over the three worlds would be destroyed. And also, Aditi's sons too would die after their birth.

Kashyapa, in an attempt to assuage Diti's anger, blessed her, "O beautiful one! Your sons from this very foetus will also be very powerful and called Maruts. These forty-nine Maruts, instead of rivals or enemies to Indra, would be his companions.

Diti, your curse will fructify at the end of the twenty-eighth Dvapara Yuga in Vaivasvata Manvantara.[80] Aditi will pay for her jealousy when she would be born as a woman. Both the curses, yours and of Varuna, will make Aditi suffer concurrently."

Diti was thus placated by the words of Kashyapa and did not say any more unkind words. So, O King, Devaki was part-incarnate of Aditi,' informed Vyasa.

Nara and Narayana

Janamejaya became more puzzled once Vyasa completed his narration. He told Veda Vyasa, 'Your rendering of this history makes me even more confused and concerned. We consider these souls as enlightened. A high-souled sage like Kashyapa and his wives were greedy and prone to envy. The king of devas committed heinous crimes such as killing a foetus. Then how can the ordinary mortals under the influence of maya be free of such vices?

Even many of my forefathers including Bhishma and Yudhishthira and others like Drona, Kripa and Karna did such unjustifiable acts during the war of Mahabharata in spite of knowing the dharma well and having the wisdom to discern.

I have heard that seers of ancient times have declared that truth is the first pada[81] of dharma. The other three being cleanliness, compassion and charity. What dharma was being pursued by all of them?'

The king had raised deep-rooted questions. Vyasa wished these had simple answers. He, despite the questions being extremely difficult, did not shy away from answering them.

He began, 'As I explained to you earlier, maya created this world made of three gunas. Everything and every being has a component of each of these. There is nothing that is pure saattvika, the pure truth.

The sages and hermits were able to see the whole truth as they had neither attachments nor desires. The rest of the world, be it devas or ordinary mortals, is under the influence of a blend of these three gunas. Therefore, while truth exists, it may not be evident and is not completely comprehensible to different beings.

Even the scriptures including the Dharma Shastras, the Puranas and the Vedas give different interpretations as their interpreters and readers are under the effect of different gunas.

The body is an admixture of three qualities and will have an element of untruth. As soon as one takes birth and acquires a body, one is under the influence of maya.

Our indriyas, or the sense organs, push us towards the enjoyment of sensual things. These are primarily related to lust, anger and greed. When one does not get the desired sensual pleasures, one takes recourse to pretexts because one is unable to differentiate right from wrong. It ultimately leads to committing sins.

When a person acquires wealth and power, he develops ahamkara and harbours egoism and delusion. A person with ahamkara may perform sacrifices, give alms, visit places of pilgrimages, practise vows and undertake various religious rites and ceremonies. Many spend their ill-earned wealth on achieving these.

But these will not help the person afflicted with ahamkara as his objective of performing all these actions is personal interest and self-aggrandisement. To the extent that when materials acquired by any malefic intent or action are used for an auspicious rite, they yield contrary results at the time of fruition.

It is because of this reason that all materials are purified before the initiation of any auspicious ceremony. It is called Dravya Shuddhi.

Barring only a few exceptions, everyone in this world is afflicted by avarice, anger, covetousness and ahamkara. Even the devas who are the embodiment of Sattva Guna are not free of them.'

Vyasa sighed and continued, 'Even the Satya Yuga, the Golden Age and era of truth, was not devoid of envy and anger. Hence, it is futile and foolish to expect that the Kali Yuga or the Dark Age would be free of them.

Moreover, each yuga has or will see holy and unholy persons. For a holy person, even the Kali Yuga is holy and for an unholy person, even the Satya Yuga is unholy and dark.

To injure a person who is inflicting injury may be considered natural. But when this act is done without any cause and out of jealousy and enmity, it is certainly vicious and sinful.

The king of devas had been engaged in such acts since the Golden Age. Whenever a seer prayed and meditated to achieve progress, Indra would become insecure and create all possible deterrence to impede him.

He did the same to the legendary muni brothers Nara and Narayana.'

Janamejaya was again intrigued and asked, 'What did Indra do to the ascetics? What happened to them?'

Vyasa smiled as he recollected the connection between both the munis and the Kuru clan of which Janamejaya was the king, especially in relation to his great-grandfather, Arjuna. Without wasting time, he began his narration, 'Dharma was the son of Brahma. It is said that he was born of Brahma's heart. He was known for being truthful and a keen disciple of rites prescribed by the Vedas.

He married the ten daughters of Daksha Prajapati. From his wives, he was blessed with four sons. They were named Hari, Krishna, Nara and Narayana. Hari and Krishna took to the practice of yoga.

The twin brothers, Nara and Narayana, wished to pursue asceticism and left for the hermitage of Badrikashram[82] in the Himalayas.

Both of them, born of part of Vishnu, dedicated themselves to difficult tapasya on the banks of River Ganga. They continued to do penance for one thousand years.

The entire world became aware of their penance. And Indra, as his nature was, became concerned and anxious.

He thought that if these two munis continued their meditation, they would take over his seat in Devaloka. He, thus, thought to do something that would breach their tapasya.

He mounted his famous elephant, Airavata, obtained from the churning of the ocean, and reached the hills of Gandhamadan. He was dazed when he saw the two ascetics. The two shone like bright rising suns. It seemed like Vishnu himself was present in their bodily forms. Indra wondered what would happen when the brothers completed their tapasya.

Indra bowed down to the munis and said, "O sons of Dharma! I am pleased with your tapasya and wish to grant you boons. Tell me what you want. Even if you ask for something that is not worth giving, I shall give that to you."

The munis were deep in their meditation and had no inkling of their surroundings. Indra tried repeatedly to get through their state of trance but failed.

Unable to draw their attention to his presence even once, he decided to adopt other immoral means.

He created savage animals like wolves, lions and tigers through his mayic powers to disturb their meditation. Next, he produced tempests and terrible fires. But none of these could cause an iota of disturbance to the two meditating ascetics.

A desperate Indra returned to his abode in sheer despair. His tricks of saam[83], daam[84] and danda[85] had been unsuccessful in distracting the munis. He discerned the reason for his failure. The two ascetics were meditating upon the highest Shakti, Goddess Devi Bhuvneshvari, and as she was the supreme maya herself, the mayic powers of Indra did not work on them.

He then summoned Kaamdeva and Vasant[86]. He instructed them, "O Kaam! Take your wife Rati and apsaras including Tilottama and Rambha from the heaven to Badrikashram. Go and bewitch the two meditating rishis – Nara and Narayana – with your spells and bring them out of their tapasya.

Indra was sure that the whole entourage would be successful in breaching the trance of the two ascetics.

Before leaving, Kaamdeva cautioned Indra that had the two ascetics been meditating on Brahma, Vishnu or Shiva or any other deva, he would have had no difficulty in accomplishing the assigned task. But as the two ascetics were meditating on the Supreme Goddess, he did not think he would be able to seduce them.

Thus ordered, the whole constellation of enchanting experts and pretty damsels left for their destination where Nara and Narayana were engrossed in their meditation.

As soon as they arrived at the ashram, they made all the trees bloom with beautiful flowers, ripe fruits and green leaves. The entire area buzzed with the sweet singing of birds and the humming of bees.

The gentle breeze of that hermitage was filled with the fragrance and feelings of love. None remained untouched by it, be they animals or birds.

Then Kaamdeva entered with his wife Rati. The celestial beauties began their play and singing.

The two ascetics could not remain oblivious to this change any longer. Their sensual feelings were also aroused. They were forced to come out of their meditation. Both were amazed to see an untimely onset of the spring season.

Observing this extraordinary situation, Narayana spoke to his brother Nara, "Look at the trees and plants, birds and bees indicating the arrival of vasant. I can also hear the sweet singing of girls coming from someplace nearby. But I am pondering as to why it is happening. Someone is trying to obstruct our tapasya."

The enlightened souls had guessed who it was. Narayana spoke again, "It seems the handiwork of Indra to deviate us from our path. He is afraid of our meditation."

While Narayana was talking to Nara, they saw the entourage of Kaamdeva especially despatched by the lord of the devas. It included gorgeous apsaras of unparalleled fame like Menaka, Rambha, Tilottama, Puspagandha, Sukeshi, Mahashveta, Manorama, Pramadvara, Ghritachi, Charuhasini, Chandraprabha, Shobha, Vidyunmala, Ambujakshi, Kanchanamalini and several others, totalling sixteen thousand and fifty.

The deva girls, exquisitely dressed and ornamented, surrounded the ascetics. They paid their respects to them. To incite passion in their twin targets, the apsaras started their enchanting singing, dancing and music.

Delighted with their passionate performance, the brothers offered the apsaras to stay in the ashram.'

Vyasa said, 'You remember my son, none in this world is beyond ahamkara. The two munis, in spite of having performed severe penance for a thousand years, were not immune to it either. Their ego was already inflated when they came to realise that Indra had sent celestial beings to obstruct their tapasya.

Muni Narayana thought to himself that though the apsaras had not done anything against them, he needed to demonstrate to them the power of their meditation.

In the same vanity, he, by a simple clap of his hand against his thigh, created an apsara, a perfectly shaped curvaceous woman with intricate features and limbs. Her face was as pretty as the full moon and her deep eyes were mysterious.

This creation of the Narayana was given the name of Urvashi as she was born of uru part of the muni's body.

The muni also immediately created an equal number of women as the apsaras to attend to the latter. These newly created women were as beautiful and elegant, if not more, as the heavenly women sent by Indra.

The apsaras were dumbstruck at the muni's creations. They all prostrated in front of Narayana and said, "We are endowed with the qualities of enchanting anyone in this world. We are capable of igniting passion and lust in anyone. But we are no match for the steadfastness that you have achieved due to your long penance and meditation.

We don't doubt that you are part-incarnate of Vishnu himself. We were sent here by Indra to thwart your tapasya and not serve you."

Scared of the possibility of attracting the brothers' wrath, they begged for forgiveness.

The munis were not annoyed with the apsaras. They were instead pleased with their truthful behaviour and reassured them that they had nothing to worry about. They asked the apsaras to take the beautiful Urvashi to Indra and also offered to grant boons to them.

The apsaras were filled with devotion for the munis. They wished to serve the two brothers all their lives and said the new sixteen thousand fifty women created by the brothers could go to heaven in their place.

Narayana could not have any dearth of women if he wanted. In fact, he had created even more beautiful damsels. But here, there were sixteen thousand fifty celestial apsaras wanting to be in his service. He had to make a decision fast.

Narayana thus spoke, "O extraordinary beauties! We have been meditating for one thousand years. We have no intention of stopping our penance and enjoying the sensual pleasures of this world. We are rather relishing the highest bliss."

But the apsaras were in love with the muni. They were adamant to be with him and thus requested him, "O Muni! The sense of touch among the five senses[87] is the most pleasurable. We request you to bless us with your touch and then you can spend the rest of your life at this Gandhamadan mountain."

The exceptional request of the celestial beauties left Narayana speechless and led him to contemplate how to get out of this situation,' added Vyasa.

Vyasa continued, 'Narayana's mind was racing. He knew that involving himself in sensual pleasures at this juncture of his life would not only nullify his tapasya thus far but also make him a subject of mockery among his peers.

He realised that this situation had arisen from his ahamkara. He recalled what seers in the past had said, "If the creation was a tree, then ahamkara was at its root."

He thought that he should have kept quiet in accordance with the vow of silence when the women came. He realised that it was his ahamkara that made him talk and create other women to show his prowess.

He said to himself, "I, like a fool, did it at the expense of my dharma. Now, these apsaras are determined to destroy my tapasya. And I am caught in the consequences of my conduct like a spider in his own cobweb.

If I do not agree with their request, they may curse me out of their feeling of dejection. The silver lining though will be that I would be out of the present situation. I will also be free to perform further penance enabling me to deal with the curses."

Thinking along those lines, Narayana decided to show anger towards the apsaras and ask them to leave the ashram immediately.

No sooner than this thought crossed his mind, a counter-argument also hit him. He knew that after ahamkara, anger was the second biggest enemy of wisdom.

The muni was visibly shaken with only the bad and worse options available to him, and, that too, was of his own doing. Seeing him in that state of anxiety and dilemma, Nara told his brother, "O dear Brother! Anger does not suit a sage like you. You are intelligent to get rid of anger yourself.

Remember it was ahamkara and anger that destroyed our tapasya on an earlier occasion. We were forced to battle Prahlada, the king of asuras for one thousand years. Therefore, leave your anger and be peaceful. Let us go back to our tapasya once again."

Nara's words brought peace to Narayana immediately and turned him like a calm sea after the storm.'

Janamejaya was attentive and did not miss out on any of the threads in Vyasa's narration. Each time Vyasa explained an aspect, new questions and queries would arise in his mind.

The king asked, 'What happened to the request of the apsaras who wanted to be with Maharishi Narayana?'

Vyasa understood Janamejaya's anxiety and decided to put it to rest. He smilingly said, 'They did receive not only the touch of Narayana but also his company, though in a different birth.

Narayana addressed them thus, "O apsaras! I have vowed not to marry in this birth. But you will all be born again in the twenty-eighth Dvapara Yuga of the seventh Manvantara and will marry me."

Narayana's words came true when he part-reincarnated as Vishnu's incarnation – Sri Krishna.'

Prahlada

Janamejaya was very alert while listening to Vyasa and, as a result, he picked another finer point from Vyasa's account. He asked, 'O Muni! You mentioned about the twin brothers Nara and Narayana battling with the demon king Prahlada. How did it happen? The two excellent sages were known for their tapasya. They were not even from the warrior clan. What was the need for them to fight in the first place?

Moreover, Prahlada was an ardent devotee of Vishnu. He was known to be a knowledgeable and just king. Did he not know that the two brothers were part-incarnate of Vishnu himself?

I am a little confused, O Muni! Were Prahlada and the sages enemies from the past? Also who won the battle?'

A calm Vyasa readied himself to reply to the barrage of questions that Janamejaya had posed. He said, 'As I explained to you earlier, covetousness, anger and greed stem out of the core of ahamkara. No living being is immune from it, whether they are devas or gods. No amount of tapasya can win over ahamkara as you just heard in the anecdote about the great sages Nara and Narayana.

People try to get rid of ahamkara in all possible ways. They perform pilgrimages, study the Vedas and the Puranas, give alms, worship gods and undertake religious rites and ceremonies with the objective of being rid of ahamkara. But in spite of performing all these activities, anyone at any time can be overcome by the qualities of ahamkara.

Hostility is a corollary of ahamkara and usually arises out of claim and counter-claim over woman, wealth or territory. The twin brothers had none of these vices and thus no cause of hostility with Prahlada.'

Vyasa looked at Janamejaya who was waiting eagerly to hear the answers to his questions on this subject. Vyasa continued, 'O Kuru King! Narasimha, the incarnation of Vishnu had killed Prahlada's father, the demon king Hiranyakashipu, and anointed Prahlada as the successor king of the region of Patalaloka.[88]

During Prahlada's reign, peace and dharma existed on earth. Each person performed one's duties and undertook one's own trade under the able administration of Prahlada.

During this time, Muni Chyavana went to Vyarhtishwara, a place of pilgrimage along River Narmada.[89] He was the son of the famous Maharishi Bhrigu. He reached the river bank and as soon as he took a dip in the water, a huge snake encircled him and pulled him down to Patalaloka. Clueless, the only thing the muni could think of was to recite Lord Vishnu's name.

The moment he recited Lord Vishnu's name, the serpent turned poisonless and the muni calmly went down with it.

When both arrived at Patalaloka, the serpent realised Chyavana's prowess and fearing that he might be cursed, released him from his clench. Chyavana was then received by Naagkanyaas, the daughters of serpents.

Free to walk around, he took a stroll in the beautiful city of Patalaloka, which was inhabited by serpents and demons, and met King Prahlada.

The king was surprised to see a muni in his city as it was not a common sight. King Prahlada, however, offered him all due respect and began a conversation. He asked Chyavana, "O Muni! How come you are visiting this city in Patalaloka? I hope you have not been sent by Indra to spy on me and my people."

Sensing the asura king's discomfort, Chyavana smilingly answered, "What made you think so? O Prahlada! I have nothing to do with the lord of the devas.

I am Chyavana, son of Maharishi Bhrigu who needs no introduction. I am an accomplished brahmin with the knowledge of the Vedas. It was pure coincidence and my misfortune that a poisonous snake captured me in the holy waters of Narmada. I had gone there as a pilgrim but finally reached your city in Patalaloka.

When I took the name of the lord of preservation, Vishnu, the snake became poisonless and released me into this beautiful city. It is sheer serendipity that I met you. I know, King Prahlada, that you are a devotee of the same god –Vishnu – as I am."

On hearing the name of Vishnu – his master, guide and saviour – Prahlada immediately felt a connection with Chyavana. Prahlada also became curious about Chyavana's pilgrimage.

He said to Chyavana, "O Brahmin! I would like to hear from you about the places of pilgrimage on earth. Not only there, but also kindly tell me such places in Patalaloka and the heaven, which, if visited, turns a person holy and washes all his sins."

To this Chyavana said, "I think for someone whose mind, words and body are pure, every nook and corner is a place of pilgrimage. And for those with an impure mind, even sacred Ganga is unholy. The sacred places can instil holiness in only those who have a pure heart."

Chyavana continued, "For instance, a host of villages and towns exist along both the banks of River Ganga. The people in these places drink Ganga water daily as well as use the same water for bathing and other activities. But the holy water does not make them pure.

To attain purity, one must purify one's mind and thoughts and shed negative and sinful ideas. In fact, the sins accrued at a place of pilgrimage are everlasting and one ought to avoid bad company at these places of pilgrimage.

As you asked me about the places of pilgrimage that exist on earth, I will tell you about the best ones. The supreme place is Naimisharanya followed by Chakratirtha and Pushkar. There are, of course, several other innumerable sacred places in the world."

Hearing these words from Muni Chyavana, King Prahlada decided to visit Naimisharanya.'

Vyasa continued, 'With his entourage of demons and attendants, Prahlada left for the most sacred place of pilgrimage as was described by Chyavana. When he reached, he took a bath in the holy River Sarasvati and performed the prescribed ritual ceremonies on the river bank.

After finishing the rites, he went for a walk and saw a huge peepal tree that was giving shade to an exceptionally large area. He then saw a variety of magnificent arrows. The arrows had been well sharpened on stone and were adorned with feathers of vultures. He wondered who they belonged to, especially in this sacred hermitage.

While he was still contemplating the issue, he saw Nara and Narayana. The accomplished ascetics were deep in meditation, had long matted hair and wore black deerskin. He saw two shining bows kept in front of the meditating rishis.

The bows were called Sharangam and Ajagava as these had the markings of Vishnu and Shankar, respectively. They were accompanied by two inexhaustible quivers that would never be empty of arrows.

Prahlada was enraged to see two meditating rishis with bows and arrows. He growled at both, "O vain ascetics! Why are you showing off your hypocrisy? Meditation and holding of arms are contradictory to each other except for one person in all the yugas, that is Vishnu incarnated as Parshurama.

This inconsistency might be possible in Kali Yuga. But it does not befit you as rishis engaged in tapasya."

On hearing the piercing words of Prahlada, Nara said, "O king of asuras! It does behove you to speak about our tapasya. We are capable of accomplishing both simultaneously. Nevertheless, it is none of your concern. In any case, wise persons should not interfere in matters that are related to brahmins."

Both Prahlada and the munis refused to be cowed down.

As Prahlada wanted to stress his authority as a king, he roared, "I am the king of Patalaloka and all the kings on this earth are my vassals. I am the guardian of dharma in my territory. Therefore, I will not let you have your way in the sacred Naimisharanya.

O brahmins! If you also know how to fight with these bows and arrows, then fight me and show your abilities."

Nara replied calmly, "If you so wish, I shall fulfil your desire. But I assure you that after this you will not be able to battle anyone in the future."

The muni's words further acted as a catalyst in fomenting the anger of an already enraged daitya king.'

Veda Vyasa continued, 'Prahlada and Nara picked up their powerful weapons to fight. The stretching of the bowstrings of both caused an awful resonating sound in the three worlds. Both sides shot a flurry of arrows but were unable to hurt the other turning them frustrated and further aggravating the battle.

The terrible clamour of the battle forced the devas to come out of heaven to witness the duel.

At one point, Prahlada was successful in striking Nara and tore his bow. Next, Prahlada struck Nara's chest. As a counter-attack, Nara pierced Prahlada's arms. This infuriated Prahlada and he hurled a volley of arrows around the muni as if dark clouds had covered the earth.

Meanwhile, Narayana realised that his brother Nara was fatigued. Picking up his bow, Narayana took over Nara's side in the fray.

The indecisive battle favoured one challenger at one moment and the other the very following moment. The sky over the highest pilgrimage Naimisharanya was covered with the arrows of both the fighters. It seemed night had permanently enveloped the place as the cloud of arrows did not allow even a ray of sunlight to pierce through.

Seeing the duel, Narada commented that this frightful battle was even more appalling than the battles of devas with Tarakasura and Vritrasura.

As the arrows did not yield a final result in the battle, the two fighters took resort to other weapons and finally the use of shaktis or special powers. The battle was fought for full one thousand years.

And finally, Lord Vishnu came to Naimisharanya.

When King Prahlada saw his lord and benefactor, he left his weapons immediately and bowed down to him to seek Vishnu's blessings. He said, "O Jagannath! I am surprised that I have not been able to win this long battle against an ascetic. Kindly bless me so that I finish this soon."

The blue-skinned, four-armed Vishnu, with Sudarshana Chakra[90] in his hand, said, "O greatest of kings! These rishis Nara and Narayana are born of my amshas and, thus, are my part-incarnate. It is, therefore, not surprising that you have not been able to win the battle. Now, finish this duel right here and return to Patalaloka. There you continue to rule with your unflinching devotion to me."

The king of asuras, upon receiving the advice of his venerable god, returned to Patalaloka. The two sages also restarted their meditation and penance.'

Bhrigu's Curse on Vishnu

Janamejaya wondered loudly, 'It is difficult to comprehend why such high souls, Nara and Narayana, engaged in a battle. They were ascetics and completely devoted to their tapasya. Meditation is supposed to bring peace to a person within and outside. Moreover, both of them were part-incarnate of Vishnu himself. Then how did the brothers leave their path of asceticism and that too while being in the most important place of pilgrimage?

O Muni! You had earlier mentioned that women, wealth or territory are the sources of all fights. In this case, none of them existed. Did the rishis have any other kind of desire that they wanted to fulfil out of the battle? Didn't the fight nullify the accrued positivity of the two saattvika munis?'

Vyasa understood why Janamejaya was so confused and responded accordingly, 'O King! Let me reiterate that anyone born with bodily qualities in this world is impacted by ahamkara. The two munis were no exception.

Tapasya, worshipping, sacrifices and charities are all intended to enhance one's saattvika qualities. It means that sattva, in this case, asserts over rajas and tamas. However, the other two qualities too respond in their characteristic way.

Ahamkara is the cause of this universe and creates karma. Hence, the wheel of creation keeps on rolling because of action and reaction.

In the same way, Lord Vishnu took various incarnations on earth to honour Maharishi Bhrigu's curse on him.'

The king became wide-eyed. He could not control his curiosity and asked, 'What led Maharishi Bhrigu to curse god himself?'

Vyasa began a new narrative, 'After the killing of his father Hiranyakashipu by the Vishnu incarnation

Narasimha, Prahlada ruled the world. As you are aware, an incessant rivalry had always existed between the asuras and the devas. It continued during Prahlada's reign, and finally, he was defeated by the devas after a terrible battle that lasted over a hundred years.

Prahlada decided to quit the material world and dedicated himself to meditation. He left the royal affairs to his grandson Bali, who was born to his son Virochana, and anointed him as the king of Patalaloka. He left for Gandhamadan mountain to practice austerities.

But the conflict between the two warring sides continued. Bali too subsequently lost to the devas. After their defeat, the asuras went to their guru Shukracharya and sought his advice and protection. Shukracharya agreed and said, "You all can live with me without any fear. I will help you with my mantras and aushadhhi."

Indra came to know through his scouts about the asuras getting the protection of Shukracharya. He conferred with his council of devas. The council decided that before the asuras could get ready to fight again, the devas should mount an unanticipated strike and drive them back to Patalaloka.

When the asuras learnt about the devas' plan to attack and eliminate them, they pleaded with their guru again. Shukracharya intervened and as the devas were well aware of his power, they retreated.

Shukracharya explained to the asuras, "You are well aware that Bhagvan Hari Vishnu took incarnations earlier to slay the asuras. He might come again to extirpate you. If that happens, my mantras will not work against him and you will lose. I shall, therefore, worship Mahesh and seek more potent mantras from him."

Fearing the devas, the asuras requested Shukracharya not to leave them alone on earth. However, Shukracharya knew that it was the only way to take care of his disciples in the future.

He reassured the asuras, "Live in my ashram peacefully without engaging in any kind of hostilities with the devas. Appear submissive so that the devas get the message that you want peace. Wise people pick up their arms against their enemies only when they have the full strength and till such time, it is better to lie low. Therefore, wait for my return with the power of the mantras that I have taught you."

He then left to undertake penance to please Mahadeva.

After Shukracharya left for Mount Kailash, the asuras requested Prahlada to visit the devas as their emissary and seek conciliation. In reality, it was a ploy to buy time till Shukracharya returned.

Prahlada met the devas and convinced them that the daityas had given up their arms and were devoting themselves to penances. The devas considered Prahlada truthful and, thus, trusted his words.

In the meantime, Shukracharya reached Mount Kailash and paid his respects to Lord Mahesh. The lord asked him the purpose of his visit.

Joining his palms in reverence and praying to him, Shukracharya said, "I wish to possess the mantras that are not with Brihaspati, the guru of the devas. I would like to utilise them to help the auras win against the devas in their continual war."

Shukracharya's request put Lord Mahesh in a dilemma. He could not leave the devas in a disadvantageous position compared to the asuras as the revenge by the latter could destroy the immortal devas. Instead, he decided to divert Shukracharya by asking him to perform a near-impossible tapasya.

Mahadeva told Shukracharya, "Standing upside down, inhale the smoke of burnt husk. Do it for a thousand years. Then you may be considered for the mantra desired by you."

Shukracharya without blinking an eye began the penance as asked by Lord Mahesh.

The devas came to know about Shukracharya's penance and immediately understood the real reason. They quickly prepared themselves and marched to attack the asuras, who were ostensibly practising vows at the hermitage of Shukracharya.

The asuras tried to reason out with the devas and pleaded, "We have deserted our arms and the desire to fight. You have no fear from us. Why do you want to battle the weak and kill? You know that killing unarmed and debilitated will not be dharma."

The devas growled, "You have been deceiving us by pretending to be involved in asceticism while, at the same time, you sent your guru to receive mantras from Lord Mahesh. We will kill you. Pick up your arms and fight against us. Dharma says that you should finish your enemy when he is enfeebled."

The asuras fled in fear and took shelter at the hermitage of Shukracharya's mother. She accepted them under her refuge.

The devas, trailing the asuras, also reached the hermitage and began to slaughter them. Shukracharya's mother cautioned the devas not to kill the asuras but they did not pay any heed to her warning.

She then used her powers to order Nidra to put Indra and all the devas to sleep. Seeing the devas being crippled by sleep completely, Vishnu asked Indra to enter his body.

Shukracharya's mother was furious with Vishnu for entering the feud and siding with Indra. She threw another spell of her yogic powers on Vishnu and Indra and rendered them weak and ineffective.

Indra prayed to Vishnu to do something urgently before her powers overtook them. Vishnu, in the heat of the moment, used his Sudarshana Chakra, forgetting that it was forbidden to kill a woman. Shukracharya's mother was killed instantly as the invincible chakra chopped her head off.

While the devas rejoiced on becoming free of Shukracharya's mother's spell, her husband came to know about this gruesome and unethical murder. He was none other than Maharishi Bhrigu.

Maharishi Bhrigu, in a fit of rage, said to Vishnu, "O Madhusudana! You have committed a deplorable act of killing an innocent brahmin woman. It is a Tamasika act unbecoming of the lord of preservation.

I, thus, curse you Vishnu that you will have to take several births on earth and go through the agonies of being in wombs."

Maharishi Bhrigu took the severed head of his wife and planted it back on the corpse. Taking water in his hand, he said, "If I have practised dharma and austerities, duly learnt the Vedas and spoken truth always, then with my strength, my wife will be alive again."

He then threw the water in his hand on the body and the next moment, his wife became alive as if nothing had happened to her.'

Vyasa watched Janamejaya's face and it seemed that the king was spellbound.

Vyasa continued, 'On the other hand, Indra was still worried. He wondered what would happen when Shukracharya returned and that too with the mantras from Lord Mahesh.

He decided to adopt another strategy and summoned his daughter Jayanti.

He requested her, "Go to Muni Shukracharya who is doing severe penance and serve the muni in such a way that he would be pleased with you. Your objective would be to charm him and sooner or later, bring him under your control."

Jayanti travelled to the abode of Shukracharya. From the moment she arrived, she dedicated herself to assisting Shukracharya. She fanned him through the day when he was performing the penance of inhaling the smoke and shaded him from the sun with her clothes. She brought him water to drink and wash and fruits to eat. She laid his bed of soft leaves and performed all the duties as a true companion. She was, however, careful to not give any indication or gesture that would arouse his passion and disturb his meditation.

Eventually, thousand years passed like this and Shukracharya completed his vow.

On completion of his vow, Mahadeva granted Shukracharya the boon and said, "You will be blessed with whatever exists in the universe, whatever one can see and all that cannot be described in words. No mortal being will be able to kill you. You will be known as the best among brahmins."

Having received the fruits of his penance, Shukracharya's attention then diverted to Jayanti. He asked her, "O beautiful one! Who are you? Where did you come from?"

In the same breath, he also said, "I am extremely happy with your service. Ask me for boons."

Jayanti had waited for years to hear this. With shining eyes and a content face, she said, "O Muni! What can I say? You must have already read from my face what I desire."

Shukracharya said, "I would still like to hear it from you."

Jayanti responded, "I am Indra's daughter. My father gave me away to you. I would now like to live with you happily."

Shukracharya accepted her wish and said, "We will live together for ten years and, during this period, we will be invisible to all."

They both got married and started living together engrossed in each other, but invisible to others.'

A meaningful smile appeared on Vyasa's face indicating that he was thinking of the deceitful ways with which the devas hold on to their power. Without digressing, he continued, 'Meanwhile, news travelled to the asuras that their guru had completed the penance and received boons from Lord Mahesh. They went to meet him, but returned flustered and disheartened as they could not see him in his abode as he was invisible.

At the same time, Indra, waiting for this opportune moment, asked Guru Brihaspati to assume the guise of Shukracharya and go to the asuras.

As planned, Guru Brihaspati took the guise of Guru Shukracharya and started living amongst the asuras. The asuras were elated to see that their guru had returned.'

Janamejaya was not happy to learn about Brihaspati's impersonation of Shukracharya. He interrupted Vyasa and asked, 'How can a brahmin and that too the guru of the immortals commit such a fraud? He ought to be teaching and practising truth, one of the pillars of dharma.'

Vyasa answered, 'Let me return to the concept of ahamkara which is a must for all embodied beings. And that is the cause of lust, anger and greed. You recall, O King, that none is immune to it.

Many ascetics who wish to be free from the traits of ahamkara decide not to marry since a grihastha[91] can never be free of the bondage of worldly affairs. The only way to achieve freedom, while remaining in this embodied form, is to worship Devi Maheshani.

I will tell you about this a little more in a while but, for now, let us continue with the present narrative of Shukracharya.

After spending ten blissful years with Jayanti, Shukracharya returned to the asuras after bidding farewell to his consort.

But what he saw there, shocked him out of his wits. He saw Brihaspati masquerading as Shukracharya.

The asuras were comfortable in Brihaspati's company as they thought that the disguised Brihaspati was their guru.

Much to Shukracharya's chagrin, Brihaspati was teaching them Saattvika qualities like non-killing, no-envy, etc., which were contrary to the intrinsic nature of the asuras.

Shukracharya appeared in front of the asuras and told them that his look-alike was actually Brihaspati who was deceiving them. He asserted, "This man is Brihaspati, sent by the devas to cheat you all. He took advantage of my absence."

As soon as Shukracharya said this, Brihaspati also levelled similar charges on Shukracharya. The asuras were confused. Both Brihaspati and Shukracharya looked so similar that they could not identify who was the real one.

As the fake Shukracharya had been with them for ten years and they could not find any fault with him, the asuras posed their trust in Brihaspati masquerading as Shukracharya and turned the real Shukracharya away.

Before he left, the irritated Shukracharya cursed the asuras, "As you are so thick-headed as to believe in my look-alike, you will lose the war against devas."

Soon after, Brihaspati too left the company of asuras and returned to Devaloka. He told Indra about Shukracharya's curse on the asuras and suggested that the devas should attack the asuras immediately as they were not under their guru's protection and their situation had been compounded by the curse.

While the devas were preparing to wage war, the asuras were completely unprepared after the departure of their fake guru Brihaspati. It was then that the asuras realised the truth. They felt that they had been terribly deceived.

They gathered the courage to face their real guru and went to meet him. Shukracharya was still upset with them. Using unkind words for his visiting disciples, he drove them away.

Led by Prahlada, the asuras prayed for his forgiveness and said, "O Gurudeva! We were under the spell of Brihaspati and could not discern the real and the fake one. He took advantage of your absence. It all happened due to our ignorance. We seek your forgiveness and blessings again."

Shukracharya calmed down when he heard the emotional pleas of the asuras. He said, "You are my disciples. How can I abandon you?"

He added, "No one can divert the course of destiny. As I had uttered the words about your defeat, you will have to retreat to Patalaloka.

You will defeat the devas in Savarni Manvantara and reign over the three worlds again. Bali, Prahlada's grandson, will be the king. I am only reiterating what Lord Vishnu had said to Bali, the grandson of Prahlada, when he took away his kingdom. Lord Vishnu, incarnated as Vamana, had taken just three steps to dislodge Bali from the three worlds. Lord Vishnu had told Bali that he would become Indra in Savarni Manvantara.

Since then, Bali is hiding in the form of a donkey and is not visible to anyone.

In fact, once Indra, trying to trace him, had asked him, "Aren't you ashamed to take the form of a donkey."

Bali had replied, "If Vishnu can incarnate as a fish, a tortoise and a boar, what shame is there for me. It is all a matter of time. We must follow what is ordained by destiny."

Though the asuras received the blessings of their guru, they did not agree to return to Patalaloka. They did not want to accept their destiny. They prodded Prahlada to become their leader and wage war against the devas.

With Prahlada's experience and wisdom, the asuras won the hundred-year war. This outcome was unexpected and contrary to the predictions and the curse.

Brihaspati then advised Indra to invoke the Supreme Goddess. Without losing any time, Indra began singing praises to the Supreme Goddess. The Devi, appeased with Indra's worshipping, appeared before him. She came on an enormous yet awesome lion. Her four arms held conch shell, disc, mace and lotus. She blessed Indra and the other devas and told them not to fear.

Saying this, she went to the battlefield and faced the army of asuras. Her presence petrified them. They knew that Devi Chandika had come in support of the devas. In earlier times, she was the one who had killed Mahishasura and Chanda-Munda. The asuras began to tremble out of fear.

Prahlada then suggested, "We cannot fight the Goddess. It will be better if we immediately escape to Patalaloka."

But an intelligent asura by the name of Namuchi advised, "She can single-handedly kill us in an instant. There is no point in escaping. Let us worship her and take permission to leave."

Heeding Namuchi's advice, Prahlada initiated hymns in praise of the Devi and said, "O Maha Maya! The devas and we have originated from Rishi Kashyapa. It is only the difference in the composition of the three gunas that distinguishes us from them. They have their interests in mind and we have ours.

You are the creator of asuras, devas and the three qualities. The fight between us is your leela[92]. We both are your sons. Now you decide whether to kill us or save us. But as the mother, you ought not to discriminate between one and the other."

Appeased by the reasoning of Prahlada, the devotee of Vishnu, the Devi said, "Go back to Patalaloka and live there happily but do leave your anger against the devas here.

The time will come when you will get the fruits of your karma. Remember that those who are satisfied with what destiny brings them, live happy lives. But those who are greedy and covetous, the lordship of the three worlds also cannot bring them pleasure."

After counselling the asuras, the Devi disappeared. The asuras left for Patalaloka.'

Vyasa said, 'O King! It is of utmost importance for all beings to understand what the Devi told the asuras. One gets the fruits of one's karma only when the time comes. It is the key to live a happy and content life.'

Shukadeva

King Janamejaya interrupted again as he remembered an important remark that Veda Vyasa had made. Before the muni could move on, he wanted to understand the significance of it.

He asked, 'O Muni! You just talked about several ascetics not marrying, precisely because a grihastha can never be free of the bondage of worldly affairs. You said you would elaborate on this. Kindly explain what you meant.'

He also added, 'O Knower of the Vedas! I have another doubt in my mind. You had said that you delivered this Devi Purana to your son Shukadeva, but you were never married. How did you procreate a son? What happened to him?'

What Vyasa was asked was very personal, but he had no hesitation in sharing it with Janamejaya. He said smilingly, 'Long ago I was living in my hermitage on the banks of River Sarasvati when I saw a pair of chatak[93] birds in their nest trying to lovingly feed their newborns. The young birds had just come out of the eggs. Both the parent birds were bringing food and trying to put it into the beaks of their young ones. They seemed extremely happy.

I was amazed to see their affection, those who had not solemnised their marriage according to Vedic rites, for their children. I thought to myself that these young birds would fly away when they grew up. They would neither care for their parents in old age nor undertake their due funeral ceremonies. Yet, if this was the level of affection among birds, I wonder how much affection human parents would have for their children. How pleasurable would it be to bring up one's own sons?

I also recalled what is said in the Vedas and the Shastras that a sonless man never goes to heaven. With such thoughts in my mind, I was caught in the gloom. I decided to perform penance to beget a son. Without wasting any time, I left for Mount Meru.[94]

While I was still contemplating as to which god I should worship, Maharishi Narada arrived. I welcomed him and offered him due respect and a befitting seat.

Narada observed my restlessness and asked the reason. I candidly told him about my desire and sought his counsel.

Narada in his characteristic style said, "In the times of yore, my father Brahma had posed the same question to Lord Vishnu. Seeing the blue god, who wears the mark of Srivatsa on his breast, meditating, Brahma was surprised as Vishnu was for him the Supreme God, even superior to himself. He asked Vishnu who he was meditating to.

Vishnu recalled an incident when his head had been severed with the accidental cutting off of the bowstring. It was Brahma, who then had brought a horse's head and the great Vishvakarma had fixed that head on Vishnu's body. Since then Vishnu was also known as 'Hayagriva', that is, horse-faced. Vishnu said that if he had been all-powerful, then this would not have happened to him. Vishnu reiterated that all are commanded by a superior force, the prime energy, the shakti or the Devi. And it was she who Vishnu was meditating upon."

Thus, after learning from Narada, I started severe austerities at the mountain to appease the Devi. I spent nearly a hundred years meditating without eating anything. The heat of my penance reached Indra who, as his nature is, became insecure and wondered what I wanted. Indra went to Lord Shiva and enquired about the reason for my meditation.

Mahadeva told him the reason. He also said that since my hundred years of meditation were coming to an end, he would address me himself.

Mahadeva blessed me with his divine presence and granted me the boon, "O Son of Parashar! You will get a handsome son who would have all the Saattvika qualities. He would be wise, knowledgeable, mighty and famed."

After receiving the boon from Lord Shiva himself, I returned to my hermitage. I was tired and had not eaten for long. So I intended to kindle a fire by rubbing two arani[95] with each other.

I was simultaneously absorbed in my thoughts. I did not have a wife who could deliver a son to me. But if I got married, it would lead to permanent bondage, which was true even in the case of gods. While I was weighing on these transitory thoughts, I saw the most exquisite apsara Ghritachi and was immediately smitten by her.

I had two conflicting thoughts. First, if I took this apsara then my peers would laugh at me and my years of austerity would go astray. The other was that only a grihasthashram with a wife and son could receive liberation and heaven.

Thinking favourably of the second option, I suddenly recalled how Urvashi, the most beautiful apsara, had caused tremendous pain to King Pururava after taking control of him. I was, therefore, sceptical if this apsara Ghritachi was a suitable fit for me.

Ghritachi, seeing me pensive, thought that I might curse her. To escape my wrath, she took the form of a shuka[96] bird and flew away. She, of course, was unaware what was going on inside me.

Meanwhile, my mind was aroused by her exceptional beauty. In spite of all my power of penance, I could not take her out of my mind.

Then, as destiny must have ordained, my semen suddenly fell on the arani sticks. From the fire created by the friction of arani sticks arose the most handsome Shukadeva, my son. He had a glistening appearance, similar to the fire from which he was born.

Immediately after his birth, Shukadeva was showered with flowers and blessings from various sages and devas and I received felicitations on his birth. He grew up immediately, as I too had after my birth. He too had been born with immense knowledge of the Vedas and wisdom.

I decided to name him Shuka as this was the form of Ghritachi that I had seen at the time of my son's seeding.'

Hayagriva, Buddhadeva

Janamejaya appreciated the complexities of the narration as it had several layers of information. He wished to proceed with more on Shukadeva, but at the same time did not want to miss out on the two important references that Vyasa made earlier.

He stopped Vyasa, 'O Muni! Before you proceed further, I would like to ask you about "Hayagriva" and also what happened between apsara Urvashi and King Pururava. Is she the same Urvashi who was created by Muni Narayana?'

Vyasa was happy with the intelligent king as he knew that culling out the threads of interconnected information from his web of episodes was not easy. The king showed the right approach to attaining a deep understanding of it.

Vyasa began with the first query of the king. He said, 'Lord Vishnu fought several wars to uphold dharma and protect the sattva-embodied devas. In one such war, he fought for ten thousand years. Tired after the long war, Lord Vishnu went to Vaikuntha to take a little rest.

Lord Vishnu rested his bow erect on the ground and seated himself in front of it in Padmasana[97]. In no time, he fell into a deep sleep under the effect of Devi Yoga Nidra while resting partially on the bow.

At the same time, all the devas accompanied by Brahma and Shankar reached Vaikuntha to invite Vishnu to a sacrificial yagna that they had planned. They found Vishnu in a state of deep sleep.

Everyone was hesitant to wake up Vishnu in spite of the urgency of the yagna. Brahma thought of an idea. He created an insect called Vamri[98] and asked it to eat up one side of the bow resting on the ground so that the other end rose. The movement of the bow would thus wake the sleeping Vishnu.

Vamri said, "O Brahma! Waking up someone from sleep is like brahmahatya or murdering a brahmin. The other similar acts are interrupting one while speaking, creating a division between a husband and wife and separating an infant child from his mother. Everyone commits a sin only for vested interest. What is my interest in incurring such a vicious act?"

Brahma offered Vamri a share in the planned yagna for the devas through the ghee that would fall outside the havan kunda[99].

Vamri agreed to Brahma's proposition and ate one end of the bow on the ground. As a result, the other side of the bow moved and broke the bowstring. This led to a terrifying sound similar to the rumbling of thousands of clouds. It caused severe earthquakes and tsunamis on earth, falling of meteors from the sky, petrifying the devas. The entire surrounding turned pitch dark.

As the darkness gradually disappeared, everyone noticed Vishnu's headless blue body and the beautiful head with the gem-studded crown not in sight.

Everyone was in a deep state of shock. Many started wailing loudly. Guru Brihaspati, aware that the situation needed immediate redressal, said to Indra, "Whatever had to happen, has happened. Fate has played its role and now it is for us to perform our karma to rectify it."

Accepting it as a decree by Daiva[100], Brahma summoned the Vedas, in their incarnate forms, to sing hymns to appease Devi Maha Maya. They worshipped the Devi and begged, "O Devi! You are the Shakti behind the trinity of gods. You are well aware that Vishnu's head has been chopped off accidentally.

Is it because Vishnu committed a heinous sin or did the daityas receive a boon from you? Or is it because you are upset with Vishnu for some reason?

Whatever it may be, O Mother, Devi Lakshmi, who is your part, will be without her husband now. Kindly have mercy on her and give back her husband."

The Devi was pleased with the hymns from the Saam Veda and addressed the devas present in Vaikuntha, "Everything in this universe has a cause. I ought to tell you the reason behind cutting off Vishnu's head.

Once Vishnu was enjoying solace with his dear wife Devi Lakshmi. He looked at her beautiful face and, out of the affection he felt for her, laughed lovingly.

Lakshmi assumed that her husband had probably seen something ugly on her face and that is why he had laughed. Else why should one laugh without a reason? And then she thought why did he see any ugliness on her face? Yet another thought crossed her mind that perhaps Vishnu was involved with another beautiful woman and wanted to have her as her co-wife.

With such a stream of negative thoughts, the Saattvika Maha Lakshmi was gripped by Tamo Guna and lost her temper. In a fit of rage, she cursed Vishnu that his head would fall off.

Strange are the ways of destiny and equally of a woman's nature. As a woman, she thought that a co-wife would be more painful than her widowhood and thus she cursed him."

The Devi had not completed. She looked at the apprehensive faces of the devas and said, "But listen, O devas! This is not the sole reason for the beheading of Vishnu. In fact, there is a blessing in disguise for you."

The Devi's words intrigued the devas, making them even more attentive. She said, "In earlier days, there was a demon by the name of Hayagriva. He undertook severe austerities on the bank of River Sarasvati. For one thousand years without eating anything, he chanted the one-syllabled mantra of Maya-Bija and worshipped my Tamasika shakti.

I appeared before him in my Tamasika form and offered to grant him his desired boons.

As every daitya had desired in the past and will do in future too, Hayagriva, being no exception, sought immortality besides invincibility from suras and asuras alike.

I had to thus explain to him that death was inevitable. Because of this, the cycle of birth and rebirth continued in this universe. Those who are born must die and those who die are reborn. Therefore, he should ask for a boon other than immortality.

He agreed and asked that he may be killed only by a Hayagriva, the one who is horse-faced.

It is unfortunate that after getting this boon from me the evil daitya Hayagriva turned reckless and ruthless. He started troubling ascetics and people at large. But there was none in this world who could kill him. Now the time has brought us an opportunity to kill that sinful demon.

O devas! Let the legendary designer and architect Vishvakarma fix a horse's head on Vishnu's body for the time being. This would enable Madhusudana to exterminate the vicious daitya."

The Devi's words created a ripple of joy among the devas. Vishvakarma cut off a horse's head and planted it on the decapitated body of Vishnu.

As the Devi had ordained, Vishnu turned into Hayagriva and killed the daitya for the good of this world.'

Vyasa took a short breath and looked at Janamejaya's face. He then addressed Janamejaya's next query, 'O King! Pururava was born to Lord Buddha[101] and Ila. But before I talk about Pururava and quench your thirst to know about him, I will have to go back further to another episode of Chandra Deva stealing away Tara, the wife of

Guru Brihaspati. Pururava's father Buddha was born out of this liaison.'

Janamejaya was engrossed in the divine words that flowed out of Vyasa's lips. His eyes widened.

Vyasa said, 'It so happened that once Tara, the exceptionally gorgeous wife of Guru Brihaspati, visited the abode of Chandra Deva in relation to some sacrificial ceremony. Chandra was smitten by her beauty and fell under her spell the moment he saw her. The feelings were mutually reciprocated by the lady for the handsome Chandra Deva. Both fell in love and Tara stayed with Chandra Deva.

Brihaspati awaited his wife's return, which did not happen. He finally sent one of his disciples to Chandra's place. Tara, in complete awe of Chandra, rejected Brihaspati's request to return to her husband's house.

Several messages from Brihaspati did not yield any favourable result. Finally, a desperate Brihaspati decided to visit Chandra Deva himself. Upon reaching there, he encountered a sneering Chandra.

He begged Chandra, "Why are you committing this act of adultery? And that too with your guru's wife? You know that cheating with guru's wife is one of the five sins beyond redemption. The othes are killing a brahmin, stealing gold, consumption of alcohol and keeping company of any of those involved in these. You are, therefore, a mahapataki[102]. You don't deserve to be called a deva.

I implore you to release my beautiful Tara now and let her come back to me. Else I will have to curse you."

Chandra was ready with his side of the argument, "What kind of brahmin are you who is so consumed by anger? You are not merited to be worshipped. Be aware that Tara is here of her own volition and can leave whenever she wants to.

Remember that a brahmin, after committing sins, is purified again by performing good karmas. Similarly, a woman too is purified again after going through her menstrual period.

Brihaspati returned empty-handed with mixed feelings of embarrassment, disgrace, anger and frustration. After a few days, he decided to visit Chandra again. But this time, he was stopped right at the entrance of Chandra's house by the gatekeepers.

This left the guru fuming. He yelled at Chandra from outside and threatened him.

Chandra responded from inside, "Your curse will not have any effect on me as you are angry and acting under your personal interest. I am not going to return your wife. You can do whatever you wish."

Brihaspati left for the palace of Indra. Indra received him with honours prescribed for the guru and welcomed him with paadya, arghya and aachaman and enquired, "O Gurudeva! You are looking so grievous and worn out. Such a sorry state does not behove the lord of knowledge from whom we, the immortals, draw inspiration and skills. You are the chief priest of Devaloka. What is the cause of your concern? Let me know so that I immediately attend to it."

Brihaspati explained to him the entire situation and pleaded with him for assistance to ensure the return of his wife.

Indra chose a sharp emissary and sent him to Chandra. The emissary went and tried to counsel Chandra on behalf of Indra, "You are an intelligent and honourable Deva. You are the son of Maharishi Atri.

You have twenty-eight wives, all prettier than the other. Why do you want to take away someone else's wife and that too, of your guru? Such an incriminating act does not befit you.

Your guru is only trying to protect his wife as his duty is. Do not quarrel with him, even if his wife is exceptionally beautiful."

Chandra's reply was terse, justifying his action: "Go and tell the lord of the devas that the woman is with me willingly and happily. The Shastras framed by the guru himself says that I ought to safeguard her. In this situation, I will not be able to give her away."

Upon receiving Chandra's answer, Indra ordered forces to be ready to attack Chandra.

Such news and gossips travel like a forest fire.

Shukracharya heard of it and, out of his natural hostility with Brihaspati, came to meet Chandra. He advised him not to return Tara under any circumstances and assured him of his support if a war broke out with the devas. He went to the extent of offering his mantra shakti in Chandra's favour.

The war began and continued for many years. Brahma was forced to come and mediate. He admonished Chandra and said that if he did not return Tara, he would be forced to destroy his side. He also spoke with Shukracharya, who changed his opinion and asked Chandra to do as Brahma had said.

Chandra was surprised by the change in Shukracharya's stance. He returned Tara to Brihaspati who did not realise that Tara was already pregnant.

After some weeks, Tara delivered an all-auspicious son under the highly favourable constellation of stars. The newborn had beautiful facial features and other physical qualities of Chandra Deva.

Brihaspati undertook to perform all ceremonies like a father. On the other hand, Chandra, hearing of the birth, sent for the newborn. He asserted that the child was born of his seed.

The dispute over the fatherhood of the child turned into another full-fledged war between Chandra, supported by Shukracharya and daityas, and Brihaspati, assisted by all the devas.

Brahma had to intervene again. In order to put a stop to the raging controversy about the father of the child, he rightly queried Tara, "O beautiful one! A mother knows who the father of her child is. Do speak up."

An abashed Tara quietly replied, "This is Chandra Deva's child."

Chandra was exceedingly happy to get Tara's corroboration and took the child with him. He named him Buddha.'

Pururava

Vyasa paused for a moment and saw how Janamejaya was completely immersed in the narration. He continued, 'O King! King Pururava, as I mentioned earlier, was the son of this Buddha, the son of Chandra, and born of his mother Ila.

In the days of yore, there was a king called Sudyumna who was just, truthful and self-restrained. Once he went on a hunting expedition and was accompanied by his courtiers and soldiers. He had a special bow called Aajgab and his quiver was full of arrows sharpened on stone. He killed several animals in the forest and kept moving deeper into the forest.

He reached an exotic spot in the forest, located at the foothills of Mount Meru. The place was exceptionally beautiful. It was adorned with divine trees of parijaat, ashoka and vakula and many other fruit trees like mango and pomegranate. Beautiful creepers like tarkul, satyu, tamal, champa and kunda made the place fragrant. Apart from the soft humming of the bees, the air had a sound that was palatable to the ears. The freshwater ponds in the place were full of beautiful swans and ducks.

The king was delighted and eagerly entered this part of the forest. As soon as the king stepped in, he turned into a female and his horse became a mare. The king was flabbergasted as he could not fathom the reason.

Not being able to comprehend the reason for being transformed into a woman, he became exasperated and anxious at the same time. He felt he was duped and wondered how he would be able to return to his kingdom and show his face to his family and people.'

Hearing this, Janamejaya too was not able to control his amazement. Interrupting Vyasa, he asked, 'This is unheard of. How can it happen? Was this king's own doing or was there some other reason for this?'

Vyasa smiled and said, 'Long ago, Shiva was once alone with his consort Uma in this very place. They were both in an intimate moment when Maharishi Sanaka, accompanied by some other rishis, arrived to pay Shiva a visit.

Devi Uma, being unclothed, rushed to dress. But she was extremely embarrassed that caused her body to tremble. The group of rishis immediately left the place as they realised that they had come at the most inappropriate time.

Sensing her discomfiture, Shiva asked Uma, "Why are you so embarrassed? It was none of your fault as the rishis arrived unannounced."

Saying so, he added, "From now on, any male that steps into the confines of this forest area will turn into a female."

It is for this reason that Sudyumna turned into a female.

The people living in the forest knew about this curse. But Sudyumna was ignorant about it. Unbeknownst to his people, Sudyumna started living in the forest as a woman and assumed the name of Ila.

Sometime later, Buddha, the son of Chandra, happened to pass by and saw Ila. He was swept off his feet by her beauty. Ila too liked Buddha and both became passionately attracted to each other. They got married and in due time, were blessed with a son called Pururava.

Ila, having lived as a woman for so long, recalled Maharishi Vashishtha, the guru of Sudyumna's clan, in her thoughts. Vashishtha sensed the thought and came to meet Ila in the forest. On seeing Sudyumna as a woman, he prayed to none other than Shiva as it was his curse on the forest that had turned Sudyumna into Ila.

Shiva was pleased with Vashishtha's worship and asked him to seek boons. Maharishi Vashishtha asked Shiva to transform Ila back into King Sudyumna.

Shiva, in a dilemma between his curse and his offer of a boon to Vashishtha, said, "Sudyumna will alternate between being a man and a woman every month," and then disappeared.

The king returned to his kingdom in the male form and once again started ruling it. When it was his turn to become a woman, he self-isolated in the palace. After completing a month, he would appear to his subjects again as a man and perform his royal duties.

In the meantime, Pururava grew up as a handsome prince and became eligible to succeed to the throne. At an auspicious time, Sudyumna handed over the reign of the kingdom to Pururava and went to the forest to pursue tapasya. There Narada gave him the nine-lettered mantra to worship the Devi, which he chanted continuously.

Over time, the Devi appeared before him when he was in the female form of Ila. Ila sang devotional hymns in praise of the Devi and said, "O Bhagvati! You had turned Brahma, Vishnu and Mahesh into women when they visited you in Mani Dvipa. And when they were leaving the Dvipa, they assumed their male forms again. You are all-powerful and merciful. You decide who is to be male and who is to be female.

O Mother! Please bring me back to my natural state."

The Devi, appeased with Ila's devotion, changed her back into Sudyumna.

Sudyumna asked for one more boon, "I have come to realise that you are neither a man nor a woman. You are neither a Nirguna nor a Saguna.[103] O Devi, whichever form and whatever qualities you may have, I bow down to you. I wish that I continue to worship you till my final breath in this birth."

The Devi, pleased with Sudyumna's penance and sweet words, granted him the final refuge under her grace and the king transcended into heaven permanently.

As a king, Pururava was known for his intelligence and fairness. He ruled in accordance with dharma and prescribed rules under the Shastras.

He was also known for his religious duties and made charities. Gradually his fame reached Devaloka and apsara Urvashi felt attracted towards him. She wanted to meet him and spend time together.

A brahmin had once cursed Urvashi and she was obliged to come to earth to suffer the consequences of it. She decided that she would be with Pururava during the period of the curse.

She, accompanied by two sheep, met the king and said, "O King! I will live with you but I have two conditions. First, I will eat only the ghee that is made out of the milk from these two sheep and nothing else. Therefore, I want these two young sheep to be with us and I would like you to protect them in any condition.

Second, except when we make love, I shall not see you naked. If there is a breach in either of the conditions, I will leave you immediately."

Although both the requests were strange, Pururava could not resist accepting them as he was smitten by Urvashi the very moment he had seen her.

They got married and the king was so captivated by Urvashi that he did not leave her alone even for a moment. Several years passed by.

In Devaloka, Indra felt the absence of Urvashi, the most beautiful apsara. He enquired about her from other apsaras and gandharvas.[104] They informed him that Urvashi was consorting with King Pururava on earth and fulfilling the curse as well.

Indra longed to see her and felt as if the beauty of his kingdom was not the same in her absence. He told the gandharvas to bring her back from earth.

Led by Vishvavasu, the gandharvas went to Pururava's kingdom. While the king and Urvashi were alone in the night, the gandharvas sneaked into the palace and stole the two sheep who bleated loudly as they were being carried away by the gandharvas to heaven.

Urvashi, on hearing the sheep bleating, became upset. She told Pururava, "I had asked you to keep my sheep safe. Thieves are stealing them away. What kind of king are you who cannot keep his words?"

She demanded to see both her sheep immediately. Seeing Urvashi crying in sorrow and anger, Pururava ran after the gandharvas. He did not realise that he was naked. As planned, the gandharvas illuminated the chamber, which made Urvashi see the naked king while out of bed.

The gandharvas were successful in their plan. They left the sheep in the palace and ran away. An exasperated and naked king brought the sheep back to his palace chamber and handed them to Urvashi. But she had left for Devaloka by then as her second condition had been breached.

The heartbroken king roamed around like a vagabond. He visited many places but could not find Urvashi. At last, when he arrived at Kurukshetra, he found her. He said to her, "O my love! Please come back with me. Whatever happened that night, I was still able to bring back your sheep. Now you come back for my sake. I cannot live without you."

Giving him a disdainful glance, Urvashi said, "O King! Where are your wisdom and knowledge? Everything in this world is transitory. We met, our relationship bloomed and came to an end in accordance with fate. You should go back and rule your kingdom in peace. You should stop thinking about me."

With a heavy heart, the king went back but could not forget the pain of Urvashi leaving him.

O King! This is the feeling I wanted to avoid when I saw apsara Ghritachi and kept wondering if I should approach her,' said Vyasa.

Videha

Janamejaya, as if enlightened suddenly, shook his head and said, 'Yes, I now understand what you wished to convey. I have my answers now.' He added, 'But, O Muni, I am still unclear about the concept of the bondage of a grihastha. Kindly elaborate on this.'

Vyasa's ever-meaningful smile continued while he spoke, 'For my extraordinarily brilliant son Shuka, I needed a teacher who excelled among all. I, thus, requested Brihaspati to take him in his fold. He kindly accepted my request and began teaching Shuka.

Shuka was as devoted to Brihaspati as was Sri Rama to Vashishtha and Arjuna to Dronacharya. He took the vow of brahmacharya and stayed in Brihaspati's house. He became an expert on the four Vedas and the Dharma Shastras.

When Shuka finished his studies, he offered guru dakshina and returned. I was very happy to see him back. I embraced him and held him close. We had a brief discussion on what all he had learnt from the guru of the devas. Thereafter, he started living with me at my hermitage.

One day, I asked him, "O my son! You were born without a womb but from my seed. I undertook severe penance for one hundred years to beget you. I am, therefore, your father."

Shuka replied, "I have no doubt about this, Father. I will do whatever is required to fulfil my dharma as your son."

I took the opportunity to convey my desire. I said, "You have acquired impeccable mastery of the Vedas. Therefore, you know that a sonless person cannot go to heaven. Now the time has come for you to take a wife and be a grihastha. That way you will also free me from my father's debt and make me happy.

Any king in this Bharat Varsha will be happy to have a chief priest in his kingdom as sharp, knowledgeable and wise as you. You will be able to get ample means to live your life comfortably and enjoy your youth as a householder."

Shuka, however, had something else in his mind and said, "There is nothing called absolute pleasure. All earthly pleasure is adulterated with some kind of pain. Every married man is dependent on his wife and becomes tied to the children too. How can a person achieve happiness if he is dependent on anybody or anything?

The human body is composed of urine and faeces. Why should I desire these in the form of a woman?

O Father! I have studied the Vedas which show us the path of Karmayoga. But that path too is full of violence towards others. When I went to study from Guru Brihaspati and sought wisdom from him, I found he too was deep into the householder's duties and attached to his family and material objects. All these signify nothing but maya. I have wondered how a guru, mired in the web of maya, could help show the path of liberation to others.

I am amazed to see people who have studied the Vedas and acquired expertise in the various Shastras continue to be attached to worldly affairs. What use is studying them as the purpose of these is to liberate a man from maya?"

Though I was surprised to hear his views, I was not shocked. I said to him, "The grihastha life is no bondage and is the most important part of life. The others, be brahmachari or vanaprasthi, have to worship a grihastha after mid-day. A householder has to perform several duties including taking care of the family, performing all the rites prescribed by the Shastras and earning money for the family by just means. In spite of performing all these duties, a householder can attain liberation if he remains unattached.

Thus, several sages and seers too take recourse to a grihastha's life after studying the Vedas and the Shastras. The grihastha stage of life helps in controlling the senses and urges that are rather strong during one's youth. The householder life was created as one of the four stages and one must transcend from brahmacharya to grihastha, before taking up vanaprastha.

I, therefore, urge you to take up the householder's life and follow the natural course of the four stages of life."

Shuka was, however, adamant and said, "A householder is always worried about earning money and making ends meet. If one has wealth and power, then he is busy enhancing or guarding them. The devas and gods too, though they have everything, fight with the asuras. In contrast, a penniless ascetic is satisfied with whatever he gets and is involved only in worshipping gods and observing austerities."

Shuka's words made my heart ache and I was tearful. Seeing me in that condition, Shuka said, "O dear Father! You are troubled because you are under the control of maya. There is none, not even Brahma, Vishnu, Mahesh or the devas, who are beyond her influence. She is the strongest entity.

O great Muni! You are the one who divided the Vedas into four and composed the Puranas and the Mahabharata. Do advise me on how to win over ahamkara and get out of the cycle of birth and rebirth by exhausting my karma."

I had an inkling that Shuka wished to enter the fourth stage of life straightaway and defy my advice and wishes. Shuka had a natural instinct and ingrained intelligence.

Seeing his resolve, I said to him, "O my brilliant son! As you have made up your mind, I advise you to study and grasp all the knowledge enshrined in Srimad Devi Bhagavatam.

This is one of the Upapuranas[105] I had composed, yet I named it Mahapurana. The study of this Purana will reveal to you that Devi Maha Maya is supreme. She spoke to Sri Hari when he was lying on a banyan leaf as an infant and delivered him the eternal truth in half a shloka[106].

She said, "It is I who is the entire creation. There is nothing eternal[107] in this creation other than I."

This half-shloka was the bijamantra for Vishnu. Brahma received it from Vishnu when he was in the lotus arising out of the latter's navel. Brahma in turn gave it to Narada and I got it from none other than Narada. This half-shloka epitomises the entire Devi Bhagavatam that I expanded into twelve skandhas[108]. Its study is considered equal to that of the Vedas. You will find eighteen thousand shlokas in this Purana.

Shuka stayed in my hermitage and studied the Puranas. He learnt the shlokas by heart and discerned their interpretations. But he was nowhere close to achieving the peace that usually accrued to my other students. He spent a lot of time alone and showed no interest in eating or fasting or doing other rites and ceremonies.

One day, I could not help but ask him, "O intelligent one! You resemble a poor man who is constantly thinking about repaying his outstanding debt. Tell me whatever worries and concerns you have."

To help him get out of the ambiguous state of mind that he had been in for so long, I suggested to Shuka, "If you are not able to find inner peace, go to Mithila and meet King Janak. He is a liberated soul, follows dharma and practises truth in all circumstances. Ask him all the doubts you have on dharma and about the four stages of life. I am confident that he will be able to satisfy you."

Shuka was astonished to hear about King Janak and said, "O Muni! I have also heard about him. He is living but disembodied and ruling but liberated. A living person using five senses and six tastes[109] cannot be jivanmukta, a liberated one. How can a ruler treat a thief and an ascetic equal? There is an inherent contradiction in these. However, since you are advising me to go to Mithila, I shall do so."

Thus saying, Shuka took my blessings and left. But before leaving I embraced him and told him to come back to my hermitage after he had completed his mission.

Shuka crossed regions, kingdoms, cities, villages, temples, fields and forests, and met several new people en route. He reached Mithila as fast as he could.

He found the kingdom of Mithila to be replete with prosperity and peace. A general discipline and happiness existed among the populace.

He encountered the guards while finding his way to the capital city of Mithila. One of the guards stopped him and asked, "Who are you? Where do you wish to go?"

Shuka remained quiet and instead moved back. He stood in one place smiling to himself.

After some time, when Shuka did not move from where he stood and kept looking at the main entrance of the city, the guard walked up to him and said, "O Brahmin! You didn't answer earlier. Strangers, whose lineage and disposition are not known, are barred to enter the city. You seem a knowledgeable brahmin. Therefore, if you wish to enter the city, you will have to introduce yourself and tell me your objective of the visit."

Shuka said, "It is neither yours nor the king's fault that I have been stopped. I appreciate that it is your duty to identify a thief or an enemy and forbid their entry."

He added, "I have come from a hermitage located in Mount Meru and travelled a long distance to Mithila. I have no desire to get any riches. My only wish is to meet King Janak. But it seems that I will not be able to enter the city and meet him. I think I was destined to travel all this way for nothing, as was envisaged in my Prarabdha Karma."

The guard was impressed with Shuka's little discourse. He asked him, "Tell me, what are happiness and pain? How do you distinguish between an enemy and a friend?"

The accomplished Shuka said, "Based on their intrinsic natures, men are divided into kinds: attached and unattached. Men who are involved in worldly affairs are 'attached.' They feel the pleasure by getting a wife, son, wealth, prestige and victory over others. They feel the pain if they are denied one or more of these. They adopt all measures to achieve pleasures and anyone who impedes the fulfilment of their desires becomes their enemy. On the other hand, the one who helps them to achieve these becomes their friend.

These 'attached' men are of two kinds. The cunning attached man is not bemused by these desires whereas a stupid attached falls into their trap and gets perplexed and confused.

The 'unattached' man reflects on 'self' solitarily. He finds pleasure and peace in the study of the Vedas and pain in dealing with material possessions. His real enemies are lust, anger and greed and the real friend is contentment."

The guard understood that Shuka was no ordinary man and took him immediately inside the city precincts.

Shuka then walked through the city towards the king's palace. He noticed there were three kinds of men on the streets: good, bad and those in-between. The people in the city seemed affluent. The shops sold expensive clothes, jewellery and other commodities of luxury and there was no dearth of shoppers.

A radiant Shuka reached the palace gate. Once again a guard stopped him. Shuka, in his characteristic style, stepped back to a secluded place near the entrance and started meditating. Shuka's presence was conspicuous as he was handsome and had a perceptible aura on his face. Seeing him standing still in the same place, the guards informed the authorities. A minister came and requested Shuka to join him in the royal guest house.

He was made comfortable in the royal surroundings with several palace maids attending to Shuka. These were no ordinary maids. They were well-trained in pleasing the guests through dance, music, talking, cooking and amorous dealing.

Shuka's knowledge, soft speech and fine mannerism enchanted everyone. The maids cooked a delicious dinner and made a soft bed for him. Shuka with a clean-heart and pure mind treated them all as his mothers.

He performed his evening sandhya[110] and meditated for one prahara.[111] He slept for two praharas before getting up in the wee hours to worship again. He took his bath at Brahma Muhurata[112] and got ready to meet King Janak.

King Janak received Shuka with due honours as he was his guru's son. The king asked about his guru's well-being and enquired about the purpose of his visit to Mithila.

Shuka replied, "O King! My father insists that I take a wife and enter the grihasthashram. I have avoided fulfilling his desire so far, as I did not want to be tied down by this bondage. We had long discussions on this issue and neither of us could convince the other. Then my father suggested that I should come here and learn from you as you are a liberated soul, a jivanmukta. And here I am to understand from you what ought to be done to achieve moksha."

Janak smiled. This was not a new question for him but, this time, the person seeking answers was himself a man with knowledge and wisdom. He replied, "The road to achieving moksha is well laid out. One should practise brahmacharya and study; marry and take care of his family as a grihastha; enter the life of an ascetic as vanaprasthi after being blessed with sons and grandsons as a householder; finally, practise penance as a sanyaasi. Each of these stages must be completed by following the duties laid out for each and then gradually controlling the senses.

The Vedas have prescribed forty-eight samskaras[113] and out of these, forty are meant for the householder. Only the last eight are for the sanyaasi."

"Is it necessary to enter grihastha even if a person is able to control his mind and becomes dispassionate earlier?" asked Shuka.

Janak replied, "While a young person may feel that he has achieved dispassion or detachment through penance and yoga, he could still fall prey to his desires or enticement of lust. It is important that a person satisfies his needs and then controls his mind through gradual penance to achieve detachment. For instance, an ant travels slowly but does not get tired as quickly as a bird that flies away in the sky rapidly.

Detachment is achieved through wisdom, intelligence and patience. It means having a stable nature that enables one to take success without getting excited and failure without becoming anxious; pleasure without becoming ecstatic and pain without getting disheartened. Look at me. I am not affected by the two extreme feelings.

The body of a person is a medium for the Atman, the pure consciousness or the soul. Freedom from bondage has to be achieved from the mind and not from the body."

Still filled with doubts, Shuka said, "O King! The title of Videha, the body-less or jivanmukta was awarded to your family lineage. But you are a ruler and you are enjoying the pleasures of the five senses and six tastes. You fight battles to protect your kingdom, thereby killing enemies. You administer justice in your court and distinguish between a thief and an innocent. You are also happy when you succeed and disappointed when you face failure. You also have the feeling of being the owner of wealth and materials in your kingdom. You do distinguish between a diamond and a piece of coal. How can you be a Videha?

As for me, I wish to live without any attachment to wife or family or material trappings. That would give me peace."

Janak was ready with a reply, "O young Brahmin! You intend to leave the company of your father and live in the forest all by yourself. But I wonder if you would not have any company there. You will have the company of forest animals. You cannot be free of the five senses as long as the body lives. You will be eating and, therefore, would not be free of the taste buds. If you establish your hermitage, you will have to take care of the requirements of your staff such as food, clothing or skin hides, huts and related materials and so on. How can then you be free and not have any bondage?

Similarly, I have concerns about my kingdom and my people. I am convinced that this world cannot bind me and, therefore, I am living in peace and happiness. If I had kept pondering that I was stuck in this material world, I would have been confused and unhappy.

The understanding that 'this body is not mine' leads to freedom as you do not invest your love and affection in your body. Likewise, I consider this kingdom as not mine since I am not invested in it."

These words enlightened Shuka. His visit to Mithila had been successful. He returned to my hermitage without any delay.

I was extremely pleased to see him back. Shuka then married Pivari, the lovely daughter of a muni. They were blessed with four sons and a daughter. We named them Krishna, Gauraprabha, Bhuri, Devashruta and Kirti.

Kirti was married to a seer called Anuha, the son of a renowned seer Vibhraja. This beautiful and auspicious couple begot a son who, in time, became a king by the name of Brahmadatta.'

An attentive Janamejaya was unable to control his curiosity and instead of waiting, asked Vyasa, 'What happened to Shukadeva?'

Vyasa turned gloomy for a while but quickly controlled it. He said, 'Shuka had always liked to be solitary. Finally, he left me and went to Mount Kailash to perform his tapasya. He was endowed with param siddhis.[114] He rose in the air on top of the mountain and his shining body became dissolved in the supreme power amalgamating in the Paramatman.[115]

I was sad again to be separated from him. I searched for him and reached the mountain where he had been practising austerities. Looking at my distressed condition, he said from the celestial space, "O Father! Where I am now, I do not see any difference between you and me. We are all one, the Atman."

His words could not console me and I continued to be in grief. Finally, Lord Shiva visited me and explained, "Your son has achieved the highest state of moksha, which is not at all common for even the highest sages. So you ought to be happy for him."

And then, Lord Shiva granted me a boon that I would be able to see Shuka's shadow by my side.'

Vyasa then closed his eyes so that he could see his son Shuka clearly in his thoughts, which he could not do with his eyes open.

Bhishma and Satyavati

Now Janamejaya wished to again discuss the point that Vyasa had elaborated on before answering the queries about grihastha dharma.

He asked, 'O Best of muni! You had earlier talked about Bhrigu's curse on Vishnu causing his incarnations. Kindly tell me more about his incarnations.'

Vyasa replied, 'O Descendant of Bharat! I will now tell you about why Jagannath, the lord of preservation, himself had to reincarnate because of the curse on him by Maharishi Bhrigu.

Vishnu's part-incarnations were Dharma's two sons, Nara and Narayana, in the Chakshush Manvantara. In the tenth Treta Yuga of the ongoing Vaivasvata Manvantara, his part was again born as Dattatreya, the son of Rishi Atri and his wife Anusuya. Anusuya wanted to have Brahma, Vishnu and Mahadeva as her sons and all three agreed to be born from her womb. They were known as Rishi Soma, Rishi Dattatreya and Rishi Durvasa, respectively.

Vishnu took the form of Narasimha, man and lion in one body, in the fourth Treta Yuga of the present Manvantara. His sole purpose was to exterminate Daitya Hiranyakashipu, the father of Prahlada, who we talked about earlier.

The seventh Treta Yuga of the present Manvantara witnessed Vishnu incarnating as Vamana, the dwarf. He was born to Rishi Kashyapa to unseat the asura king Bali from the lordship of the three worlds and send him to Patalaloka. In the nineteenth Chatur Yuga[116] of Vaivasvata Manvantara, he incarnated as Parashurama, son of Rishi Jamadagni. It was followed by his reincarnation as Rama, Dashratha's son, in the Treta Yuga of the current Chatur Yuga. Lastly, he took birth as Sri Krishna in the Dvapara Yuga.'

It is not possible to decipher the flow of nature causing destiny to fructify. But Janamejaya had the best possible chance to fathom a significant part of it through Vyasa.

He wanted to know as much as his mental capabilities could grasp. He asked again, 'O Muni! Kindly elaborate on why only Devaki and Vasudeva were chosen as parents by Vishnu for his incarnation.

Why did Krishna leave Mathura and go to Dwarka, even after killing powerful Kamsa? Why did he dread Jarasandha?

Why did Pandavas and Draupadi suffer so many difficulties? Even Krishna, as god's incarnation, was not spared.

Also, tell me more about Bhishma and your mother Satyavati.'

Vyasa did not hesitate to speak on any of these topics as he was aware that Janamejaya genuinely desired to learn more. He began, 'You heard from me how Rishi Kashyapa and his two wives Aditi and Sursa were reborn as Vasudeva, Devaki and Rohini, respectively. Now hear, the story of why Devavrata, Bhishma, was born.

Ayodhya, the capital of Kosala, was ruled by the descendants of Ikshvaku. One of his worthy successors was a king called Mahabhisha. The just and religious king performed one thousand Ashvamedha[117] Yagnas and one hundred Vajapeya[118] Yagnas, thereby pleasing Indra. The lord of Devaloka gave him a place in heaven.

While living in Devaloka, Mahabhisha once accompanied other devas to Brahmaloka, the abode of the four-faced lord of creation, the Prajapati. Coincidentally, the greatest river Ganga was also there in her gorgeous feminine form.

While sitting at the feet of Brahma, Ganga's attire was displaced due to the blowing of strong winds. All the devas looked away except Mahabhisha who kept looking at Ganga. The lady Ganga also felt it and realised that the king had fallen for her.

Brahma saw them both staring at each other unabashedly in the presence of elders and became livid. In his anger, he cursed the king to go back to earth and take rebirth as a human being. He also asked him to again accumulate good karma and only then could he return to heaven. Brahma also cursed Ganga that she would be born as a human and both would meet in human life.

To fulfil the curse, Mahabhisha considered all the possibilities and decided to be born to King Pratipa of the Puru dynasty.

At the very same time, the Ashta-Vasus[119] were out on a leisure trip with their respective wives and arrived at the hermitage of Rishi Vashishtha. Seeing there the divine cow Nandini, the wife of one of the Vasus, Dyau, enquired about her from her husband. Dyau said, "This is the heavenly cow of Rishi Vashishtha. Anyone who drinks her milk has youthful longevity of ten thousand years."

Hearing Nandini's special qualities, she insisted on taking her and the calf with them to serve a friend of hers. Though Dyau did not have ill intentions, he, at his wife's prodding, stole the cow and the calf.

When Vashishtha returned to his abode, he noticed Nandini's absence. He searched but could not find Nandini and her calf. Then he sat in the lotus position to meditate and immediately came to know that the Vasus had taken her away. He became angry at their outrageous act and cursed them, "Let all the eight Vasus be born as men."

The Vasus learnt of this and came back rushing and sought Vashishtha's forgiveness. By this time the rishi had calmed down and told them that they would be free of his curse as soon as they were born as humans except for Dyau who was responsible for the theft.

While the disheartened Vasus were returning from the hermitage, they met the accursed Ganga who was in a similar plight. They exchanged their respective miseries. Then Vasus requested Ganga, "O Mother! Since you would be born as a woman, allow us to be born from your womb. But as soon as we are born, please throw us in your holy waters and free us of Vashishtha's curse."

Ganga agreed to their request.

One day, King Pratipa was worshipping Surya when Ganga took the form of an exquisite beautiful female and sat on the right thigh of the king. She asked him to marry her. But the chaste king said, "Since you sat on my right thigh, which is the place for daughters and daughters-in-law, I will make you my son's wife when he will be born. I hope, with your blessings, I will have a worthy son."

Ganga blessed the king and disappeared.

Soon after, Mahabhisha was born to King Pratipa and was named Shantanu. When Shantanu grew up, Pratipa wanted to leave for the forest to spend the rest of his life in meditation. Before leaving, he recalled the incident that had happened several years ago and advised his son, "If you come across an extraordinarily beautiful woman in the forest, do accept her as your wife without asking her whereabouts."

Pratipa left to worship Devi Ambika and in due time left his mortal body in the forest. Shantanu, in his place, became a popular king. He ruled according to the prescribed dharma and took great care of the welfare of his subjects.

During one of his hunting expeditions near the banks of the holy River Ganga, Shantanu came across the most beautiful woman. Seeing her, he recalled his father's words. Moreover, as he was swept off his feet by the woman's beauty, there was no question of not following his father's advice. The woman too, who was none other than Ganga, knew that it was Mahabhisha reborn as Shantanu.

Shantanu, unbeknownst to Ganga's reality, approached her, "O one with beautiful eyes and sweetest smile! I don't know if you are a human or an apsara or a gandharvi or a naag. But whoever you are, be my wife."

The accursed Shantanu was also a means for Ganga to release the Vasus and herself from their respective curses. She said smilingly, "I know who you are, O King Shantanu. Which woman on this earth would refuse to be your wife?"

Saying so, she added, "I will be glad to marry you only on one condition. If you agree to it, I will be yours for life." Pausing for a moment, she added, "Whatever I do, be it good or bad, you will not stop me from doing it, irrespective of whether you like it or not. The day you do so, I shall leave you and go wherever I like."

Hearing this condition, the king became perplexed, but remembering his father's words, he nodded in affirmative.

They married and began to enjoy. They lived happily like Indra and Sachi. Shantanu was passionately in love with Ganga. Many years passed by before Ganga became pregnant.

As had been agreed upon between her and the Vasus, she gave birth to one of them. As soon as she gave birth, Ganga took her newborn son to her waters and threw him in it.

Shantanu followed his wife and witnessed the end of his son in the flowing waters of Ganga. But he did not say anything as he was bound by his commitment to his wife.

The same thing happened to six more successive newborn sons.

When Ganga was pregnant for the eighth time, the king was in a dilemma. He knew if he asked her, she would leave him and go. If he did not, she would, in all likelihood, take the same course of action as she had done in the past to her seven infant sons. Moreover, he wanted a son who would succeed him on the throne.

The day Ganga gave birth to the eighth son, this time Vasu Dyau, Shantanu could not hold himself and fell at her feet. He pleaded, "You have killed seven of our sons by throwing them in River Ganga. I did not say anything, but I beg you to give this one son to me. How will I transcend to heaven without a son? Instead of this one thing, I will give you whatever you may ask for."

Ganga was adamant to free the Vasus from the curse and when she was about to take the recent born to the river, the king became furious and said, "What kind of vicious mother are you? I will not let you take my son with you. He will remain with me."

Ganga told Shantanu, "You have broken your promise to me. Now I will not be able to live with you." She then told him the truth, "O King! Be aware that I am Ganga and I was here to fulfil god's work. I have been able to free seven Vasus from their curse. Now, this is the eighth one.

Today I am taking him with me to the same place where we had met. But I will return him to you when he grows up. Remember he is a Vasu. He will grow up to be very powerful and will be famous by the name of Gangeya."[120]

Shantanu was in deep pain at the separation from his wife and the only surviving son. As time passed by, Shantanu became more occupied with his royal duties. After some years, he was out hunting near the banks of River Ganga, the same place where he had met his wife. There he saw a young boy shooting sharp arrows with precision.

The king asked the boy as to whose son he was. The boy did not answer. While Shantanu was enquiring around from others, Ganga appeared. She told him, "He is your son, O King, the same eighth Vasu. I have brought him up well as your scion. He has been trained in the Vedas and archery at the hermitage of Rishi Vashishtha. Take him with you. He will do you proud."

The king brought the young boy with him to his capital Hastinapur and at an auspicious time, declared him as his crown prince.'

Taking a deep breath, Vyasa resumed, 'Shantanu later married my mother Satyavati. Now hear, how she came to be known as Satyavati.

Once there was a king by the name of Uparichara who ruled the kingdom of Chedi. He was a virtuous and truthful king. Pleased with his worshipping, Indra gave him a celestial aerial car, decorated with gems and jewellery. He travelled in that aerial car most of the time. Thus, he came to be known as "Uparichara Vasu" signifying flying in the air.

He had a beautiful wife called Girika who begot five powerful sons to the king. Uparichara allocated separate kingdoms for his five sons and continued to live with Girika in Chedi.

One day, when Girika had just entered her fertile period, she desired another son with the king. At the same time, the manes of his ancestors also desired him to kill a deer to perform certain rites. He decided to first satisfy his ancestors and left for the forest with Girika's thoughts in his mind.

The thought of his wife was so strong in his mind that he involuntarily ejaculated his seed. He wished the seed to bear fruit. He carefully folded it in a banyan leaf and energised the package with his mantras. Then he directed an eagle nearby to take it to his queen.

While this eagle was flying high in the air with the package tightly gripped in his beak, a hawk thought that it was a piece of meat and attacked. In the fight between the two, the leaf fell into River Yamuna.

Sometime before this day, there was an apsara called Adrika who had come to the river to take bath while a brahmin was performing his evening meditation on the banks of the river at the same time. The apsara mistakenly caught the feet of the brahmin who was deep in his Pranayaam.[121] The brahmin's meditation was disturbed and he cursed her to be a fish.

The beautiful Adrika, now a fish, caught the banyan leaf package dropped by the eagle. She ate it and turned pregnant with Uparichara's seed. She was trapped in a fisherman's net around the time when she was due to deliver. The fisherman tore open the dead fish and found two little human babies: a boy and a girl. The amazed fisherman ran to inform the king.

The king kept the boy with him who later came to be known as Matsyaraj[122]. He returned the girl to the fisherman to be brought up. She was known as Kaali or Matsyodari. As her body had the odour of a fish, she was also called Matsyagandha[123].'

No detail passed unnoticed from an alert Janamejaya. He interrupted the Muni, 'What happened to apsara Adrika?'

Vyasa smiled and continued, 'I am glad you asked Janamejaya. When she was cursed she apologised to the brahmin and sought forgiveness as it was not intentional. The brahmin also realised it. Therefore, he curtailed his curse by adding that she would be free of it once she, like a fish, gave birth to two human offspring.

O King! I always say that kaal, time and karma combine in an incomprehensible manner. Else who could have thought that a human child out of a fish was possible.

Who would also have imagined that a maharishi like Parashar could be attracted to a fisherman's girl whose body smelling of fish? It was this Matsyagandha who is my mother. She was wooed by the maharishi and I was born of them on an island on River Ganga. With my father's blessings, Matsyagandha's body started emanating sweet smells and she came to be known as Satyavati. Since I was born on a dvipa, I, as everyone knows, am also called Dvaipayana.'

The Birth of Krishna

Vyasa remembered all the questions the king had asked. He continued, 'O Janamejaya! Let me now tell you about Krishna's incarnation in the Dvapara Yuga.

As you are aware, Sri Hari Bhagvan Vishnu incarnated on this earth to eliminate evil forces whenever they got out of proportion. It was for the same reason that he incarnated at the request of Prithvi, Earth.

A time came when the inhabitants on earth were tormented by the increasing evil of several sinful kings. Prithvi took the form of a cow and went to Devaloka to seek help. Indra received her graciously and asked, "O Devi Vasundhara[124]! You seem distressed. What brings you here?"

Hearing the kind words of Indra, she started crying profusely. She described, "O King of devas! I am being burdened with wily and wicked kings. These include the king of Magadha, Jarasandha; of Chedi, Shishupala; of Kashi, Rukmi; of Mathura, Kamsa besides Narakasura, Shalva, Keshi, Dhenukasura and Bakasura. They are full of malicious intent and actions. They are all daityas incarnated as kings in this age.

In the past whenever I had troubles, Sri Hari helped me. He became a boar and helped me from drowning in the ocean. Now the twenty-eighth Kali Yuga is knocking on the door and if I am not saved, I will fall to Rasatala[125]"

Indra and the other devas accompanied Prithvi to meet Brahma. Brahma too joined them and they all went to Vishnu to seek a solution for the serious issue posed by Prithvi.

Vishnu welcomed them in Vaikuntha and enquired about their well-being and the reason for their visit.

Brahma took the initiative and said, "O Lord of Lakshmi! Prithvi is reeling under the burden of daityas and scared of the impending arrival of Kali Yuga. She seeks your help to relieve her burden.

You should incarnate at the end of Dvapara Yuga and help her out."

Vishnu smiled and said, "I am not the one who decides that. In fact, it is none of us. We all are under the control of Yoga Maya. If she wills it, it would happen.

She is the puppeteer and we all are her puppets. Let us meditate on her and find a beneficial and auspicious solution to this issue."

Following Vishnu's advice, all of them including Brahma and Vishnu chanted hymns in praise of Shakti, the Supreme Goddess. Devi Bhuvneshvari appeared in her chaturbhuja[126] form. She was holding a noose, hook and red java flower in her three hands. The palm of the fourth hand showed all five fingers pointing upwards in Abhaya[127] Mudra,[128] as if she was asking them to be fearless and seek blessings.

Brahma, Vishnu and the devas joined Prithvi in praying to the Devi, "O Maha Devi! You are most gracious, most merciful and the kindest. Your reminiscence removes all difficulties. Today we seek from you removal of the problems that Devi Prithvi is facing. We request you to kill the daityas on earth incarnated as kings and relieve her burden."

The Devi was pleased with the devas for extolling her. She said, "O devas! I have already decided that all these daityas will see their end before long."

She then addressed Vishnu, "And for that, you will have to take birth as a human incarnation on earth. With my blessings and shakti, you will help Prithvi in lightening her ill-load."

She then ascribed a role to each. "Maharishi Kashyapa, you will go first with your wives Aditi and Sursa and incarnate as Vasudeva, Devaki and Rohini, respectively. You will procreate a son who would be the incarnation of

Sri Hari Vishnu who has to fulfil the curse of Maharishi Bhrigu.

I will be born from the womb of Yashoda and help you to achieve the desired results. I will be responsible for taking Vishnu's incarnation out of the prison. I will also transfer Ananta from Devaki's womb to that of Rohini. The incarnation of Vishnu accompanied by that of Ananta will grow up and exterminate or will be a means to end the evil forces on earth.

Similarly, the five Pandava brothers will be born from other devas: Yudhishthira as part-incarnate of Dharma, Bheema of Vayu, Arjuna of Indra and the twin brothers Nakul and Sahadeva of the two Ashvin brothers. Devavrata, the incarnation of the Vasu Dyau, will be born as the son of Ganga.

Many of these daityas will be destroyed in the battleground of Kurukshetra. I will be present there to help you with my immense powers. At the end of Dvapara Yuga, the conceited Yadavas, who have suffered from malicious covetousness, lust and the desire to be always victorious, will also be extirpated.

Go now, O devas, and prepare to incarnate along with your wives in the regions of Mathura and Gokula. Be a tool in the hands of Sri Hari and help him achieve your collective goal."

The Goddess had, thus, pronounced the future, and mitigated the concerns of not only Earth but of the devas too.'

Vyasa smiled and added, 'That is how Prithvi was relieved of her burden at the end of Dvapara Yuga with the Devi restoring the order of dharma.'

Feeling the need to further explain, Vyasa spoke, 'You may think that Vishnu had incarnated because of two reasons: the curse of Bhrigu and the desire of Devi Yoga Maya. But if you think deeper, the curse of Bhrigu is also the mandate of Yoga Maya. Therefore, whether Sri Hari is resting in

Vaikuntha or fighting the daityas or incarnating on earth or performing austerities on his own, he is always under the influence of Yoga Maya.

Likewise, Brahma or Shiva or other devas including Indra, Surya, Chandra, Varuna, Agni, Yama and Kubera or the munis like Bhrigu, Kashyapa and Vashishtha are all under her influence. As I said earlier, everyone is a puppet in her hands.

O King! Let me also remind you that no one is immortal. People misunderstand the terms used for devas and gods. If someone has taken birth or appeared, he would die or disappear after his prescribed life period. For instance, mosquitos and water-borne insects have a short life of less than a day to a few days whereas human beings will have a life of several years. Similarly, devas also have a certain lifespan though they live much longer than humans.

For humans, a day consists of eight praharas, four each during the day and night. Thirty such days make a month and twelve months constitute a year. One day of the devas is equal to one year for humans. Therefore, three hundred and sixty human Chatur Yugas are equal to one Deva Yuga. Seventy-one Deva Yugas make one Manvantara, equalling the life of an Indra.

Fourteen Manvantaras constitute one day of Brahma's life, called kalpa. With this one day in his life, Brahma lives for one hundred and eight years. Vishnu's life is twice as much as Brahma's. Mahesh lives twice the life period of Vishnu.

Each one lives according to the specified longevity. But since they take bodily shapes, each of them is prone to happiness, sorrow, pain, pleasure, lust, envy and greed at different times as decided by fate. Yoga Maya, the Supreme Goddess, decides fate. She also wields the power of maya and deludes everyone.'

Vyasa was aware that it was not easy for ordinary mortals to fathom this knowledge. He stopped for a brief moment so that the king could digest it all. But he was still a long way from delivering the complete Devi Bhagavatam to the king.

He resumed, 'I shall now return to the reincarnation of Vishnu. He took birth as Krishna to seemingly serve the purpose of devas but, in fact, to follow the path preordained by the Devi. Let me describe it to you.

In the days of yore, there was a forest named Madhuban on the banks of River Yamuna. A notorious demon called Lavansura lived there. His father was called Madhu.

Lavansura was killed by Shatrughana, the brother of Rama and Lakshmana. Thereafter, Shatrughana founded a beautiful city in the same place and named it Mathura. He left his two sons to govern the city.

After ages, the rule of Suryavanshi kings declined and Mathura was controlled by the clan of Yadavas, the descendants of Yayati. Rishi Kashyapa took birth in this lineage of Yadavas, to Shurasena. Shurasena turned himself into an agriculturist.

At the same time when Vasudeva was born, Mathura was ruled by Ugrasena. His son was the evil Kamsa.

To fulfil the curse, Devaki, the part-incarnate of Aditi, was born to King Devaka. In time, Devaki wedded Vasudeva. As soon as the marriage was solemnised and the newly wedded couple prepared to leave, there was a celestial announcement. It said, "O Kamsa! You are happily attending the marriage of your sister-like Devaki, but it will be her eighth son who will kill you."

Kamsa became nervous on hearing this celestial prophecy. He immediately thought of killing Devaki so that no cause would remain for bringing his murderer into this world. The counterargument also crossed his mind resisting his first thought, saying, "Devaki is my cousin sister. There is no way that I can kill her."

But evil thoughts always weigh more than virtuous ones. He decided that, although Devaki was like a sister to him, she needed to be killed in light of the prophecy. He justified to himself that to save one's life, one must use all tools. He further thought that even if it was a sin to murder a woman, he could later perform penance to redeem it.

O King! You remember that even your father thought of the same logic after being cursed by the brahmin.

Not one of those to lose time, Kamsa took out his sword and was ready to kill Devaki in the wedding hall. Vasudeva, and others in his clan, sensed Kamsa's desperation and took out their arms to fight him.

A scuffle broke out. Soon it turned into a major fight. When the elders of the Yadava family saw several of their clan being felled for no fault of their own, they pleaded with Kamsa not to kill Devaki at the wedding festivities.

They argued that a young girl and that too at her wedding ceremony should not be killed as it would amount to an unpardonable sin. Moreover, they said that the voice instead of being celestial could have been one of the enemies of Vasudeva.

Appealing to Kamsa's vanity and prestige, they requested him to spare his sister. But Kamsa was convinced of the celestial warning and did not want to take any chances.

Then the intelligent Vasudeva spoke up, "O Kamsa! The basis of the three worlds is truth and if you believe in my truth, I will deliver to you all the sons born of Devaki soon after they come into this world. If I do not do this, let my forefathers descend into hell Kumbhipaka[129]."

Appreciating the reputation of Vasudeva as a wise and truthful person, the elders persuaded Kamsa to accept his condition and leave Devaki with her husband.

Vasudeva and Devaki began their married life under the dreadful thought that their sons would be killed by Kamsa. Time passed by and Devaki was pregnant with her first child. In time, she delivered a beautiful baby boy. Vasudeva reminded her of his commitment to Kamsa and asked her to hand over the infant to him.

Devaki lamented, "O dear Husband! If we take everything as preordained, then what is the use of observing penance, reciting mantras and acquiring knowledge of the Vedas, Ayurveda and science or such acts that are meant to change one's destiny? If we believe that fate is the only force that would decide everything, then why should one make effort?

It is said in the Shastras that if a lie is spoken to save a life, it does not amount to sin. I beg you to find some way of saving this baby's life who just entered this world."

Vasudeva tried to convince his wife, "All beings are subject to their fate. While one makes the effort, the results are given by fate. Prarabdha Karma is the fate that one is born with. All karmas of previous lives continue to accumulate in the Sanchita Karma and remain in the seed form in the soul. Based on this, one enjoys heaven or suffers in hell.

We undertake penance and eliminate those karmas that have not been added to the seed.

Upon completion of the part of the karma in heaven or hell, other births are taken by the soul during which Prarabdha Karma comes into play again for that particular birth. Prarabdha Karmas are those which have matured and are ready to deliver their fruits, good or bad, in that birth. There is no escape from this. These cannot be atoned by any penance or worshipping.

Those who do not speak the truth, their life is wasted. If this life is in vain, what can be hoped for afterlife? We must go through our karmas and honour the truth that I spoke to Kamsa to reap the positive effects. Therefore, let us hand over the baby to Kamsa."

Vasudeva took the newborn baby to Kamsa. He was surprised by Vasudeva's commitment to keeping his word. Kamsa thought and decided that he did not want to commit the sin of unnecessary killing of an infant. He said, "O Vasudeva, the celestial voice said it will be your eighth son who would be responsible for my death. You, thus, take away this son of yours and come back to me with the eighth one. I hope you will honour your words of truth."

Kamsa's courtiers and ministers heaved high praises for him on his decision. But soon after, Muni Narada arrived Mathura. Kamsa received him with due honours and worshipped him in accordance with the prescribed rites.

On Kamsa's query as to the reason for his unannounced visit, Narada in his unique melodious voice said, "I was at Mount Meru where I overheard that Brahma and the devas were plotting to kill you and it would be done by Vishnu taking birth as the eighth son of Devaki."

Kamsa said, "O Muni! I also know this through a celestial warning."

"Then why did you leave the newborn son of Devaki alive."

"I decided to kill the eighth son because of the celestial prophecy and, therefore, I spared the first one."

Narada smiled, "O King! Are you unaware of the conspiracies of these devas? Or you are a foolhardy failing to fathom the real danger? The warning said 'the eighth son' which could mean anyone up to the eighth one depending upon where you begin the count from. An intelligent king never underestimates even the weakest enemy and you let go of your potential killer by sparing Devaki's son?"

No sooner than Narada left, Kamsa called Vasudeva back with his just-born son and killed the infant by slamming him on a rock.'

Rishi Narada's behaviour confused Janamejaya. He knew it was uncharacteristic of the son of Brahma to instigate someone with the intention to kill. Unable to control his amazement, Janamejaya was forced to interject Vyasa.

He asked, 'O Muni! Why did a high-souled Narada act in such an evil manner to get the infant killed by Kamsa? Didn't he know that he was doing a wicked act? What was the background of that newborn who was killed even before he could see the world with his eyes?

Vyasa did not mind the interjection and appreciated the obvious questions asked by an objectively thinking person. He responded, 'Narada was known for bringing news and messages among devas and others. Sometimes he enjoyed the tiffs seeded by him. But being a maharishi, he never spoke an untruth. An objective existed behind all his acts and this time too, it was no different. He incited Kamsa to accomplish the purposes of the destiny.'

Janamejaya frowned partially in disbelief and the rest in attentiveness.

Vyasa continued, 'The six sons born to Devaki were killed immediately as they were the cursed sons of Maharishi Marichi, the son of Brahma, and his wife Uma.

In one instance, when Brahma became passionate for his daughter, a mistake that he realised himself, these six grandsons of Brahma sneered at him. Brahma, in his anger, cursed them, "You will be born among daityas."

The six brothers were subsequently born to Daitya Kaalnemi. When the time came for them to take the second such birth, they were well aware of their first birth and the consequences of Brahma's curse. They took birth as sons of dreadful Daitya Hiranyakashipu but retained their knowledge and wisdom in this incarnation.

As they were aware of who they were, they undertook penances even though they were born to Hiranyakashipu. They appeased Brahma and he granted them boons.

They asked for invincibility against the devas, humans, mahoraga[130], gandharvas and the lord of siddhass. Brahma instantly granted them their boons.

Hearing this, an affronted Hiranyakashipu became angry with his sons. He called them and said, "You have not only disrespected me but also disregarded my affection for you by attempting to please Brahma. I now disown you. You go to Patalaloka and sleep till you are born from the womb of Devaki. Then your father in the previous birth Kaalnemi, who will be reborn as Kamsa, will kill you all as soon as you take birth."

As they were ordered to stay in Patalaloka, they came to be known as Shadgarbha. But the second curse of Hiranyakashipu was a blessing in disguise for them as after this they would be relieved of the first curse by Brahma.'

'What happened to the seventh son, O Muni?' an engrossed and curious Janamejaya asked.

Vyasa said, 'The seventh pregnancy of Devaki was miscarried in the fifth month but Devi Yoga Maya transplanted that foetus in Rohini's womb. Rohini, Devaki's sister, gave birth to the incarnation of Ananta who was called Balarama.

When Kamsa was informed of the miscarriage, he took a sigh of relief as he did not have to kill another newborn. At an auspicious time, Devaki's eighth pregnancy began and Vishnu entered her womb.

Around the same time, Yashoda, the wife of Nanda in the village of Gokula Vrindavan, became pregnant with Devi Yoga Maya in her womb. Earlier, in the same village, Rohini had delivered Balarama.

Kamsa did not want to take any chances with the eighth son of Devaki. Learning of her pregnancy, he imprisoned her. Vasudeva did not wish to leave his beloved wife alone in the prison and joined her there. As the day of the delivery neared, Kamsa fortified the security.

On that very day, Devaki said to her husband, "My friend Yashoda had agreed to take care of my son. She had offered to give her son to be sacrificed by Kamsa. O dear Husband, do something to save the life of my about-to-be-born son. Take him away somehow."

Devaki and Yashoda both delivered on the same night. It was a dark night. A terrible storm occurred and rains flooded River Yamuna.

Devaki and Vasudeva were mesmerised to see that their just-born son had a blue lustrous body. As Vasudeva brooded on the non-existence of options to save his son's life, a heavenly voice spoke, "O Vasudeva! Take this child and rush to Gokula and exchange him with Nanda's just-born daughter. You have no cause to worry as I have put all the guards to sleep and opened all the eight gates of this prison."

Vasudeva picked up his son and hastened to his destination. The flooding river gave way to him and became fordable in the middle of the night.

In the quiet of the night, he arrived at Nanda's house to see an awaiting maidservant with Yashoda's newborn daughter to be handed over to him. It was none other than Devi Yoga Maya herself who assumed the guise of the maid. Vasudeva exchanged the babies and hurried back to the prison in Mathura.

No sooner than he returned and gave the baby girl in the embrace of Devaki, the child cried aloud, which woke up everyone. The guards, ignorant of what had happened as they were fast asleep under the influence of Devi Yoga Maya, rushed to Kamsa to give him the news of the birth of a baby.

Kamsa came running to the prison and cried aloud, "I am now going to kill the cause of my death, the eighth son of Devaki and Vishnu's incarnation. This will rid me of all the fears."

The moment he mercilessly took the child in his hands, he was shocked to see a girl. He pondered over the words of the prophecy and those of Narada but could not decipher how a girl child was born to Devaki.

Irrespective, he decided to kill the child and holding her by the legs, he raised her high to bang her against a rock. In a jiffy, the girl vanished in thin air and spoke from the sky, "O cruel Kamsa! The one who is going to kill you has already been born."

A distraught Kamsa returned to his palace and called all the daityas he could muster. He ordered them to find the eighth son of Devaki, his killer in the future and kill him wherever he was. Since it was not possible to identify the boy, he instructed them to kill all the newborn children in his kingdom.'

With Veda Vyasa, Janamejaya joined his hands and bowed to the mention of the birth of Sri Krishna. He said to Vyasa, 'You have talked about several incarnations to relieve the earth from her burdens, but there are many more. Kindly describe all the other contemporary incarnations of devas and asuras.'

Vyasa said, 'Several suras and asuras were born again. Among the prominent suras, there were Karna, son of Kunti as part-incarnate of Surya; Vidura, incarnate of Dharmaraaj; Dronacharya, part-incarnate of Brihaspati; his son Ashvatthama, part-incarnate of Mahadeva; Virata, the lord of Matsya; Kritavarman, part-incarnate of Maruts; Kripacharya, as incarnate of Arishta Nemi; Suvarchakhya Somapraru of Murvacha, the son of Chandra; Dhristadyumna as part-incarnate of Agni; Pradyumna as part-incarnate of Sanatkumara; Drupada as part-incarnate of Varuna; Draupadi as incarnate of Lakshmi; Draupadi's five sons of Vishvadevas; Kunti of Siddhi; Madri of Dhriti; and Gandhari of Mati.

Among the asuras, there were the reincarnation of Daitya Hamsa as Dhritrashtra; Kali Yuga as Duryodhana; Dvapara as Shakuni; Hiranyakashipu as Shishupala; Biprachitti as Jarasandha; Prahlada as Shalya; Kaalnemi as Kamsa; Hayashira as Keshi; son of Bali as Arista cow; Anuradha as Dhrishtaketu; Vashkala as Bhagadatta; Lamba as Pralamba; Khara as Dhenuka; Varaha and Kishora as Chanura and Mushtika; and Arista, the son of Diti as Kubalaya, Kamsa's elephant.'

Krishna

The knowledge in these tales being narrated by Vyasa was immense and for a rapt listener, each one was more riveting than the former.

Vyasa, a skilful storyteller, continued with his narration, 'Where was I when I was telling you about Sri Krishna? Oh yes, we deviated to the incarnations of suras and asuras. Before that, I was telling you about the disappearance of Devi Yoga Maya from Kamsa's hands. Allow me to continue.

At dawn the next day, when people woke up in Nanda's house, they had no inkling of what had happened in the night. They began to prepare for the celebration of the birth of a boy.

Kamsa learnt that a baby boy was born to Nanda. His spies also informed him that Vasudeva's other wife Rohini and her attendants had been staying at Nanda's house in Gokula.

Kamsa summoned his top daityas: Putanaa, Bakasura, Vatsasura, Keshi, Pralamba and Dhenuka. Each attempted to kill the young Krishna but were eliminated instead. Finally, when Kamsa heard of Sri Krishna raising the Goverdhana hill on his little finger, he was convinced that both, the celestial voice and Narada, were correct.

He made another plan to kill Krishna and arranged a Dhanur Yagna. He sent Akrura, an important Yadu born to Svaphalka and Gandini, to fetch Krishna and Balarama from their abode in Gokula.

Krishna arrived in Mathura with his characteristic elan. He foiled all the plans hatched by Kamsa and killed him. Thereafter, he freed his parents, Vasudeva and Devaki, from prison. He installed Ugrasena back to the seat of power in Mathura.

Krishna with his brother Balarama then left for the hermitage of Rishi Sandipani in Ujjain. By the age of twelve, Krishna became proficient in all the sixteen branches of learning, required to be a perfect human, at the hermitage and returned to Mathura.

Meanwhile, Jarasandha, Kamsa's father-in-law and the king of Magadha, wished to invade Mathura to avenge Kamsa's death. He invaded Mathura seventeen times. Each time, he was defeated by Sri Krishna.

Unable to win on his own, he told the lord of mlechchhas[131] called Kaalyavana to wage a war on Mathura.

Kaalyavana was dreadful and his force was ruthless. When Krishna learnt of this, he collected all the members of the Yadava clan and said, "If we continue to live in Mathura, we will be under constant fear of attacks from Jarasandha or the likes of him. A life without peace does not bear fruits. We should migrate to a place safe from potential attacks of enemies."

The elders in the clan asked, "Where do you think such a place exists?"

Krishna had all the plans in place. Under his guidance, the people of Mathura with their families and friends left for Dwarka, a new city at the seashore near Raivataka mountain. They carried with them their goods, clothes, valuables, chariots, carts, cattle and horses. Following the caravans of Yadavas, Krishna, with his family, also started the journey while remaining at the rear end of the entourage.

Traversing the land of Bharat, they took several weeks to arrive at Dwarka. Employing the best of architects, Krishna had the parts of the city renovated and brought them to glory.

After making the people comfortable in the city, Krishna and Balarama returned immediately to the empty city of Mathura. They did not have to wait too long for the arrival of Kaalyavana and his army.

When he learnt of the arrival of the enemy forces, Krishna dressed in yellow attire and walked past Kaalyavana.

Seeing a relaxed and smiling Krishna walking past, Kaalyavana chased after him on foot.

In this game of chase, Krishna led him to the place where King Muchukunda, wearing a yellow robe, was deep in his sleep. No sooner than they both arrived there, Krishna suddenly disappeared. Kaalyavana mistook the sleeping king for Krishna and kicked him hard. The king awoke in fury and with his angry red eyes burnt Kaalyavana to ashes.

As soon as the good deed was realised, Krishna appeared there again. The king, seeing the Vishnu incarnate, venerated him and took his blessings.

The news of Kaalyavana's death reached his army who were waiting for his return to invade Mathura. The disheartened army on the loss of their king lost the war without even an arrow being shot. They returned to their land and resolved to never come back to Mathura again.

With their mission in Mathura accomplished, both brothers went back to Dwarka and coronated Ugrasena as the king.

Krishna abducted Rukmini from under the nose of Shishupala, the groom-to-be, at her svayamvara ceremony. He married her according to Rakshasa Vidhi.[132] He thereafter married Jambavati, Satyabhama, Mitravinda, Kalindi, Lakshmana, Bhadra and auspicious Nagnajiti. These eight comprised the most gorgeous among all the wives of Sri Krishna.

When Rukmini's newborn son Pradyumna was taken away stealthily by the demon Shambarasura, Krishna was disenchanted. With a grievous heart, he worshipped the Supreme Goddess, Devi Yoga Maya.

Krishna cried, "I have worshipped and appeased you, Devi, in my previous births. In this birth, my son has been stolen and that too from the lying-in chamber in the central part of my hugely protected palace in Dwarka. Is it the doing of your maya for your pleasure or an enemy of mine has done it?

O Mother! You blessed us with the son and now you have separated our child from us. The birth of a child is the greatest delight and its death the deepest pain to any household.

O Devi! Please return my son to me."

Krishna's lamentations, who himself was the incarnation of Jagannath, saviour of the world and whose name removes all obstacles in life, brought the Devi to him in her physical form.

She said, "O Vasudevaya! It was because of a previous curse on you that Shambarasura stole away your son. But be calm and patient. When Pradyumna turns sixteen, he will kill that demon and return to you."

Saying this, the Devi disappeared and Krishna began to live his life in peace under her assurance.'

Unable to control himself once again, Janamejaya asked Vyasa in disbelief, 'A daitya took away the son of the incarnation of the lord of preservation and that too from the most protected lying-in chamber of the holy city of Dwarka! How could it happen? Did Sri Krishna not anticipate this? Could he not avert this?'

Vyasa smiled and said, 'It is all due to maya that deludes all bodily beings. She is called by the name of Shambhavi in this form. The moment gods, devas or asuras take birth as human beings, they are bound to act with human traits. These traits include appetite, thirst, sleep, frightfulness, lethargy, attachment, sorrow, distrust, pleasure, ego, ageing, disease, death, knowledge and ignorance, anger, envy, pride and greed. These are present in all humans in varying proportions.

Sri Rama, the Vishnu incarnate, went through several troubles in his life without any foreknowing. He was deprived of his kingdom and lived in forests. His wife

Sita was abducted by Ravana. He searched for her like an ordinary mortal.

Sita, as Devi's incarnate, suffered through the ignominy of proving her innocence and chastity after her stay in Lanka. Not only that, she had to leave her home again and live in the hermitage on the slight pretext that a commoner had vilified her.

Ravana, the king of daityas, could not stop himself from committing the sin of abducting Sita.

Krishna had to move his people from Mathura to Dwarka out of continued fear of wars with Jarasandha. He also took away Rukmini against the established norms of Santana Dharma.

Krishna went through the pain of separation from his son and then the pleasure of being reunited with him. At the insistence of his wife Satyabhama, Krishna went to heaven to bring the parijaat tree. It was for the same wife that Krishna was tied to a tree and donated to Rishi Narada. Satyabhama freed him after paying an equivalent amount of gold.

So you see, the incarnations in human form had to suffer and enjoy as humans do.'

Janamejaya nodded and asked, 'While narrating the episode of rishis Nara and Narayana, you mentioned that a large number of apsaras wished to become the wife of Narayana and their wish was fulfilled when Narayana reincarnated as Krishna. Kindly explain this to me.'

Vyasa replied, 'When Jambavati asked for sons as capable and as handsome as Rukmini's son Pradyumna, Krishna received spiritual guidance from Upamanyu in the form of Pashupata Mantra and practised penance. After six months of severe tapasya, Shiva appeared to him and asked him to seek boons.

Krishna chanted hymns in praise of Shiva and requested him, "O Lord of destruction! I am undergoing a difficult life as a householder. I am always bonded to my wives. I meditated upon you as my wife Jambavati seeks to have brilliant sons like that of Rukmini."

Shiva was pleased with him and said, "You will have sixteen thousand fifty wives with each begetting ten sons. All your sons will be powerful and gallant."

Parvati, who had accompanied Shiva, also blessed Krishna, "O perfect human! You will be known as an exemplary householder. But your clan will be extirpated after one hundred years, due to the curse of some of the saptarishis and that of Gandhari.

O Krishna! You should avoid grief as wise men do not lament over unavoidable matters. There is no remedy for destiny."

Thus receiving the boons and being foretold about the extinction of the Yadu clan, Krishna returned to Dwarka.'

Vyasa then summarised the description of maya, 'The Supreme Goddess thus creates each living being who is under the control of the karmic account. This account of credit and debit based on karmic merits and demerits is all under the effect of maya. She is free of any dependence on anyone else. Therefore, one must meditate on and worship the great Maha Maya, the Supreme Devi.

If one hears this narrative of Devi Bhagavatam, it frees oneself from the sins and accrues the virtues.'

Mahishasura

Janamejaya asked, 'O Author of the Vedas! You narrated the grandeur of Maha Maya. I now wish to know about the character of the Devi.'

Vyasa agreed to Janamejaya's request and explained, 'O intelligent King! I will have to take you back to the times beyond comprehension when a daitya by the name of Danu lived. He had two sons, Rambha and Karambha. Both brothers were well respected among the daityas. But neither of them had any offspring. They decided to undertake penance to beget a child and went to the banks of River Panchanada.

Karambha submerged himself in the river and began his asceticism holding his breath. Rambha began to worship fire under a peepal[133] tree.

As the two brothers continued with their severe austerities, Indra learnt about them. He arrived at their location and assumed the form of a crocodile in the river. The crocodile held the legs of Karambha and killed him. When Rambha came to know of his brother's death, he became furious.

In his rage, he decided to sacrifice his head. He held the braid on his head in his left hand and took a sharp scimitar in his right hand to severe his head. At that moment, Agni Deva, the fire god, arrived.

Agni Deva stopped Rambha from committing suicide, an unatonable sin and asked the daitya to seek boons. Rambha prayed at Agni's feet and said, "O Deva! If you are pleased with me, then grant me a powerful son who will be invincible in the battle against suras, asuras and humans. A son who will rule the three worlds. A son who will be able to assume forms at will."

Agni Deva blessed him, "You will beget such a son from whichever female you cohabit with," and disappeared.

Paying his obeisance to the fire god, Rambha left for his abode in Patalaloka. The place he lived in was prosperous and surrounded by the yakshas. The moment he arrived there, his eyes fell on an enticing she-buffalo who was more than willing to yield to him.

The she-buffalo became pregnant after Rambha made love to her. Rambha married her.

One day, a buffalo got attracted to Rambha's wife and chased her. Rambha, to save her, came in front of the buffalo. The excited animal attacked him and struck his sharp horns into Rambha's heart. Rambha fell instantly to the ground and died.

The terrified she-buffalo ran to a peepal tree and sought the protection of the yakshas. The yakshas had liked Rambha and were distressed to see his wife in such a pitiable condition.

The buffalo, irritably excited, continued to pursue the she-buffalo and also reached the peepal tree where she had taken refuge. The yakshas shot arrows at the uncontrollable buffalo and killed him.

The yakshas started preparing for Rambha's funeral and last rites. The she-buffalo wanted to go away with her dead husband but the yakshas desisted her. As soon as the funeral pyre was lit, the pregnant she-buffalo jumped into it.

Then, from the midst of the burning pyre, arose a daitya with a human body and a buffalo head. It was Mahisha. From the same fire, also emerged Rambha in a different form and was called Raktabija. Soon after, the daityas clan coronated Mahisha on the throne of Patalaloka.

Mahishasura went to Mount Meru and performed difficult penance for ten thousand years to appease Brahma. Pleased with Mahishasura's penance, Brahma appeared to grant him boons.

Like all the daityas before and after him having undertaken such penances, Mahisha asked Brahma, "O lotus born! I want to become immortal. Grant me this boon and I shall be free from the fear of death."

This was neither the first nor the last time that Brahma would receive such a request. He said, "Whatever is born is destined to die. Birth is followed by death and death by birth. No one can change this eternal law. Not only men and devas, but even the high mountains and deep oceans will also face the brunt of death when their time comes. Therefore, ask anything other than immortality and I shall grant that to you."

Mahisha gave it a thought and then said, "No male deva, daitya or human should be able to cause my death. I may be killed only by a woman," and added smilingly, "and there is no woman who can kill me."

Brahma smiled too but for a different reason. He knew that no boon could lead to immortality irrespective of the perfect plan hatched by the seeker. He blessed Mahisha with what he desired and left.'

'And there began the story of Mahishasura's conquest,' Vyasa added before proceeding further.

'Upon receiving the boon from Brahma, Mahishasura became invincible. In his arrogance, he brought the entire earth under his control besides the Patalaloka. Every king on earth became his vassal. Those who protested his reign were killed in deadly battles. So much so that even the brahmins on earth also became his servants. They started giving a part of yagna offerings to Mahishasura.

Famed daityas were part of his team. Chikshur served as commander-in-chief and Tamra was in charge of the royal treasury guarded by ten thousand soldiers. Others like Asiloma, Udarka, Vidala, Vashkala, Trinetra and Kaalbandhaka had their own corps of armies protecting Mahishasura's empire.

Mahishasura now wished to control Devaloka. Before invading heaven, he decided to give diplomacy a try. A messenger was sent to Indra. The messenger narrated Mahishasura's message, "O Indra! Take protection of Mahisha or fight with him. He knows your abilities as you were conquered by Mahisha's ancestors in ancient times."

Indra was furious to hear the message but he controlled himself. He said, "I know where your erroneous vanity is rooted in. I will finish off the root cause of it. Fortunately for you, it will be adharma[134] to kill a messenger. But, O Messenger! Go back and tell your master the following.

O son of buffalo and enemy of horses[135]! You have a hideous presence and you live on grass. You derive your strength from the horns. You only know how to strike with your horns. That is the only cause of your misplaced arrogance. You have no idea how to wage a war. I will cut off your horns and make a bow out of them."

The messenger returned with Indra's sharply insulting words and told Mahisha, "My job as a messenger is to speak pleasant words and convey the message. But the harsh words of Indra cannot be described truthfully in a sweet tongue. I, your servant, cannot utter those words either."

Mahisha got the hint and turned red with anger. He summoned all his chieftains and said, "Indra has refused to accept our sovereignty. He is adamant about fighting a war. You know that he will not be able to stand in front of me in battle.

He is vicious and a hypocrite as he always wins with maya shakti and treachery. He only knows how to use his apsaras against meditating ascetics.

He and the devas have always received the help ofVishnu who assumes forms to kill daityas. He is not to be trusted either.

The devas cannot fight against me let alone Vishnu and Mahadeva. In any case, no man can kill me.

Let us prepare for the war and conquer heaven. Thereafter, we will be able to partake in Soma,[136] drink milk from heavenly cows, get a larger share in the yagnas and enjoy the singing and dancing of gandharvas as well as apsaras from Devaloka."

In the same breath, Mahishasura ordered his courtiers, "Call Guru Shukracharya to work out an auspicious time for marching on Devaloka and begin the sacrificial ceremonies praying for our safety and eventual victory."

At the same time, Indra began to confer with the devas. He briefed them about his encounter with Mahisha's emissary and all that was exchanged between him and the messenger.

He appealed to them for their counsel, "O devas! While one should exert their best efforts, the result of a war, victory or defeat, is not in one's hands. They are well destined in Prarabdha Karma.

One can make peace by entering into a treaty with the enemy but in this case, a daitya cannot be trusted.

A wise man should not ignore the threat from a weak enemy and certainly not from a powerful and energetic one. Mahishasura falls in the latter category. But what we do not know is the extent of his strength and his army. Let us send our honest and dispassionate spies to ascertain the size of his forces, armaments and formations."

The scouts returned with detailed information. What they told was worrisome for the devas. A meeting was immediately called with all the suras present. Guru Brihaspati, the chief priest of devas, was specially invited to obtain advice on the strategy for the war. Indra explained the situation to Brihaspati and sought his advice.'

Vyasa paused for a brief moment and then resumed the narrative. He told Janamejaya, 'O King! What Brihaspati told Indra is an important part of our philosophy. Hear it carefully.

Brihaspati was the chief priest and guru of the devas as Shukracharya was for the daityas. He said, "O Lord of the devas! All living beings are under the effect of fate. Therefore, one should not feel dejected after failure or turn ecstatic after being successful. One needs to be always patient and not get carried away by such feelings.

If one is calm and patient, the effect of pain does not feel as much as impatience. Similarly, one should be patient and not be exuberant at the time of pleasure.

Sometimes, success comes even without efforts and at other times, it is not achieved despite one's best endeavours. But what matters is that one should continue to exert the best efforts within one's abilities.

One should also always strive to be free from the six malaises - hunger and thirst connected to life; pain and delusion arising out of the mind; and age and death related to the physical body. The attachment to these feelings is the cause of all miseries.

Victory and defeat are predestined. Whatever is destined shall come to pass. One's energies are also diverted in the direction of the fated results. Therefore, one ought to assess in advance if one's efforts will be successful or not."

Hearing the meaningful and wise words of his guru, Indra said, "No results are achieved without prowess and no kingdoms are made without efforts. I am ready to battle Mahisha and kill him with the support of my devas. Like always, I have the blessings and support of Hari and Hara. You, O Guru, perform the ceremonies with appropriate mantras for my success."

Brihaspati smiled and said, "I shall neither motivate you to wage the war nor desist you from it. What is ordained, shall happen."

Indra then went to Brahma and sought his help in this fight against the mighty Mahisha and his huge army of daityas. Brahma advised him, "First we should go to Mount Kailash and request Shiva to accompany us to meet Vishnu.

Then we will hold a meeting in Vaikunth Dham, where all the devas can decide the time and place to wage the war."

Indra, accompanied by devas and Brahma, proceeded to Mount Kailash. There they worshipped Shiva and requested him to join them. The entourage, now complete, arrived at Vishnu's abode.

Indra described the situation to Vishnu. The almighty Vishnu responded by saying, "Let us fight Mahishasura and kill him."

Emboldened by Vishnu's support, the devas mounted their respective vehicles and marched towards the battleground. But on their way, the deva army met with the daityas and the fight began there and then.

Both sides had a huge variety of arms. They had arrows, axes, prasas,[137] masalas,[138] parashus,[139] gadas,[140] shulas,[141] chakras[142] and even energised weaponry – the shaktis.

Chikshur attacked Indra with five arrows sharpened on stone. Indra cut off all of them and shot Ardhachandra[143] arrow that was directed at Chikshur's heart. When the arrow struck him, Chikshur fell unconscious on the back of his elephant. Indra chopped off the elephant's trunk by using his potent Vajra.[144] The injured elephant fled away trampling the daitya soldiers.

On hearing this episode, Mahisha became upset and angry. He directed Vidala to march into the battle. Vidala's elephant too met the same fate. But Vidala did not give up and instead mounted a chariot and returned to the battlefield.

On the other side, Indra's son, Jayanta, joined him. Jayanta was no less a warrior. He shot a sharp arrow into the chest of Vidala that made him unconscious. To save his life, the daitya forces quickly removed Vidala from the field.

The devas lost no time in resounding the victory drums. Gandharvas sang and apsaras danced to celebrate the victory.

An affronted Mahisha directed Tamra to go to the battlefield. Tamra too faced the volley of arrows from the devas and was also left unconscious in the battle. This was the third important daitya commander that the Indra forces had struck down.

A manic Mahisha, left with no choice, picked up his gada and joined his distressed force. His gada was smashed by Indra's vajra in the fight. Mahisha then deployed the shakti that had been invented by Shambarasura. With its effect, thousands and thousands of daityas resembling Mahisha appeared on the battlefield. This caused confusion and anxiety among the deva force.

Unable to find a remedy to this shakti, several devas including Varuna, Kubera, Yama, Agni, Surya and Chandra fled in terror. Indra was unable to counter this magic shakti and began chanting the names of Brahma, Vishnu and Mahesh. The trinity of gods soon joined Indra. Vishnu used his Sudarshana Chakra to nullify the shakti. In the meantime, Mahisha's chief asuras joined him in the battle.

Deadly fights ensued between Mahisha and Rudra, Vashkala and Indra, Trinetra and Yama, Maha Hanu and Kubera, Asiloma and Varuna and Andhaka and Vishnu. Vishnu used his Sudarshana Chakra but Andhaka neutralised the discus, leaving Vishnu flummoxed and devas terrified. In the next instant, Vishnu used his Kaumodaki Gada to hit the daitya and made him senseless.

Vishnu then struck Mahisha who swooned on the ground. But in no time he got up again and hit Vishnu with his Parigha.[145] Struck by the mace, Vishnu became unconscious. Garuda, Vishnu's trusted vehicle, immediately took him away from the battlefield.

On regaining consciousness, Vishnu saw Mahisha striking Shiva several times. Unable to keep himself away from the battle, Vishnu joined Shiva to fight Mahisha.

Mahisha kept changing his forms, to buffalo, to human, back to buffalo, to a lion and finally again to a buffalo. In the form of a buffalo, he pierced Vishnu's chest with his sharp horns. Vishnu was forced to leave the battlefield again. Seeing Vishnu's plight, Shiva too fled and reached Mount Kailash.

On seeing the two gods leave the battle, Brahma and the other devas were filled with terror and left the battlefield. Indra sensed that he too could not remain there for too long. He also retreated. As he exited the war scene, Varuna, Yama, Kubera, Agni, Chandra and Surya too quit thc battlefield.

The victorious daitya forces wasted no time in reaching heaven and occupying it. The reign of Mahisha now extended up to Devaloka.

The devas had no place to go. They wandered in jungles for hundreds of years before congregating at the abode of their grandfather Brahma. They pleaded, "O Grandsire! We lost the war against the daityas and now they occupy heaven, enjoying all its beauty and privileges. They are audacious enough to take our share of sacrifices in yagnas performed by the brahmins.

O Creator of the world! We are your sons. How can you forget us in these difficult times when we are being oppressed by the asuras?"

The matter was too serious to be resolved by Brahma alone. He again advised that they take Shiva with them and go to Vaikuntha to hold a meeting.

While Brahma and the devas were en route to Kailash, Shiva learnt of their visit and received them with warmth. Once all of them had settled, Brahma described the deteriorating situation of the devas and their oppression by Mahisha.

Shiva said sarcastically, "O Brahma! It is you who is responsible for this. You are the one who gave this boon to him. The result is that he has become haughty knowing fully well that no one can kill him. There is no lady amongst us who can fight and eliminate him. Our respective wives are not so adept in warfare. That is not what they were brought up for. I suggest that let us all consult Vishnu in this matter."

Sensing the auspicious signs indicating the ripening of time for the desired results, Brahma, Shiva, Indra and other devas went to Vaikuntha.

On reaching Vishnu's abode, the devas met Jaya and Vijaya, the two gatekeepers, at the entrance. They requested both to inform Vishnu of the arrival of Shiva, Brahma and the other devas.

As soon as Vishnu was informed of devas' arrival, he came out to receive them. Seeing the group of fatigued and disheartened devas, he comforted them and enquired about their well-being.

Indra and the other devas started worshipping Vishnu. They explained their situation and said, "O Hari! While Mahisha has become invincible due to the boon granted by Brahma, he has taken over the territories in the three worlds. Moreover, he has brazenly usurped our share in the yagnas performed by the brahmins.

O Sankatmochana[146]! You are the preserver of the world and well-versed in all the possible ways of the world. Do find out a solution to our problem. How do we get a female to kill the daitya?"

Vishnu said, "I remember the deadly battle with Mahishasura. He could not be killed by all of us. We, therefore, need to create a female deity with the collective energy, the shaktis, of each of the devas. If we could do so, that lady will be able to match the daitya in the war and destroy him."

Vishnu called upon all the devas, "I now ask you all, along with your respective wives, to contribute from within you a part of the fiery energy residing in you. This collective energy of all will be manifested in the form of the Devi. We will then dedicate our specialised weapons to equip her for the task of killing the demons."

No sooner than Vishnu spoke these ominous words, a fierce fiery energy emitted from Brahma's face. While it was scorching red, it was also simultaneously cool. It gradually took a gorgeous form having a halo behind it. Next came the energy from Shiva. Though silvery white in colour, the Tamo Guna incarnate was a sight difficult to see.

Then sprung out the blue energy from Vishnu's body and joined the fiery light of Brahma and the white light of Shiva. Soon the energies of various hues emanated from the bodies of Indra, Kubera, Yama, Agni, Varuna and other devas. While the devas were awestruck by this phenomenon, this huge mass of multi-coloured energies in the form of fire and light turned into a divine female form.'

Devi Maha Lakshmi

Vyasa paused again. He saw the king was as much awestruck listening to the narration as the devas had been while witnessing the unification of their energies in one.

Vyasa continued, 'O Janamejaya! This divine lady was none other than Maha Lakshmi. She had the traits of all the three gunas: Sattva, Tamas and Rajas. She was extraordinarily beautiful with the fairest complexion, red lips and kohl black eyes. The Goddess had eighteen arms in her manifested form and thousand in un-manifested form.'

Janamejaya curiously asked, 'Kindly describe in more detail the birth of Maha Lakshmi. I desire to know if the energies of the gods amalgamated or remained distinct.'

Vyasa said, 'O King! No words can describe her form and beauty. The Nirguna Goddess assumes various Saguna body forms to achieve the goals of devas, whenever such a situation arises. Different names have been given to her in different forms. She took physical traits from the trinity of gods and devas and combined them into one persona.

Her appearance from the ethereal fire and light brought instant happiness among the devas as they had achieved their objective. At that moment, Vishnu asked all the suras to offer their ornaments and weaponry to the Devi.

Kshir Sagar[147] presented her with a well-fitted crystal necklace, red-coloured heavenly attires eternal in nature, divine jewellery comprising earrings, bracelets for arms and anklets and a crown that emitted light equivalent to millions of suns together. Vishvakarma, the architect of the heavens, offered beautiful ornaments for her neck and gemmed rings for her fingers.

Varuna presented Vaijayanti, a garland of lotuses, with timeless freshness. Himalaya, the king of mountains, offered several gems and also a ferocious golden lion as her vehicle.

Thereafter, all others offered several weapons: Vishnu gave a chakra; Shiva gave a trident; Varuna gave conch, paash[148] and lotus; Agni Deva gave shatagni[149]; Marut, the god of wind, gave a deadly bow and a quiver with unlimited arrows; Indra gave thunderbolt and resounding bells of the elephant Airavata; Yama gave a lethal staff; Samay, the god of time, an axe and a shield; Brahma gave a kamandala[150] filled with holy waters of Ganga; Vishvakarma gave Parashu and Kaumodaki Gada; Kubera gave a golden drinking cup, filled with Soma; and Surya offered sunrays.

All the devas prostrated in front of the Devi and worshipped her. She was called by all the names of Devi Bhagvati, the Supreme Energy. The Devi was pleased with the praises offered to her. Although the Devi was omniscient, she asked the devas what was desired of her.

The devas narrated their situation and suffering from the excesses of Mahishasura. They requested her to kill the asura in battle and liberate them from their agonies.

The omnipotent Devi said in her deep voice, "It is amazing that Brahma, Vishnu, Shiva and all the devas are terrified of a daitya. It is, therefore, clear that time in the form of Prarabdha is the most powerful. It is time that has brought you all to this state. Time that unfolds the destiny, is thus the god."

The Devi then laughed thunderously, so loud that it reverberated in the three worlds. It was felt by the tallest of mountains and the deepest of oceans. The sound also reached Mahishasura's ears.

Mahisha felt a tinge of terror. He asked his courtiers, "Whose sound is this? Go and find out immediately. Whoever had the temerity to make such a loud noise full of vanity, bring him to me and I will kill him."

Mahisha's scouts went in all directions to find the source of the troubling sound. Finally, some of them reached the place where the Devi was. They saw an exquisitely beautiful woman sitting on a gigantic lion. She had eighteen hands, each carrying a different weapon. Her grandeur was beyond words. She was wearing divine jewels, each emitting its own shining rays. She was drinking Soma from the golden cup in one of her hands and all the devas were worshipping her.

The scouts were frightened of seeing the Devi and immediately returned to Mahishasura to give him the news.

Mahisha heard about the Devi's beauty, glory and powerful weapons. Instead of being petrified, he fancied the idea of possessing her. He directed his prime minister, "Go at once and get this beautiful lady here. Try whatever means advised under saam, daam and bheda[151]. If she does not agree to come anyhow, then use the last technique of danda. But do ensure that she is not harmed. I would like to make her my queen."

The prime minister left with his entourage. He met the Devi from a distance and began singing praises of his master. He asked, "O beautiful one! Who are you? Where have you come from? My master Mahishasura wishes to know more about you.

O doe-eyed! Mahishasura cannot be killed by devas or men. He is the ruler of the three lokas. After learning about your beauty and grace, he desires to see you and make you his queen."

The Devi heard him and laughed at his audacity. She spoke in a soft yet deep voice that resembled the thundering clouds. "As you wish to know more about me, let me tell you that I am Maha Lakshmi. I am the mother of the gods. Mahishasura has long been oppressing the devas. They have requested me to kill Mahishasura.

O Minister of daityas! You are wise enough to respectfully offer me sweet words. If you had not done so, I would have killed you. But go back and give my message to your master. If he desires to live more, he should leave Devaloka and go back to Patalaloka."

The prime minister did not wish to surrender to a lady and that too after exchanging only words. He said, "Your mannerism and words do not befit a woman. You are asking for a battle all by yourself but you are a soft and petite woman whereas Mahishasura is the emperor of Devaloka and all-powerful. Therefore, he will be able to defeat you in no time. But he would not like to do it as he has been captivated by you upon hearing about your extraordinary beauty.

As my master is fascinated by you, it is my duty not to speak harsh words. I assure you that he will be your obedient servant. All his wealth will be yours to enjoy. His companionship will provide you with extreme happiness."

The Devi retorted, "Nature brings together people of similar nature. If Mahishasura has a prime minister like you, how can he be intelligent himself? He thought that Brahma's boon would save him but did not realise that death at the hands of a woman would be humiliating for someone who considers himself a great hero.

You do not seem to have given a thought before commenting on my feminine form. Let me tell you that I am also the Highest Purusha but I have acquired this feminine form to achieve the death of Mahishasura.

It is established that as soon as a soul enters the bodily form, it will experience pleasure, pain and death. Even Brahma is not above this. His birth and death are ordained. How then can your master think that he would never die after getting a boon from Brahma?"

Unable to either win over or convince the Devi, the prime minister considered if he should fight her or return to his king. His intelligence counselled him that if he fought the lady and no matter if he won or lost, the king would still be upset with him. Hence, he decided to return and let the king decide how to deal with the Devi.

The prime minister gave a detailed account of his conversation with the Devi to Mahisha. An outraged Mahisha called a meeting of all his advisors who were experienced and well-versed in statecraft and war.

One of the aged advisors said, "While one should always speak truth in pleasant words, sometimes that is not possible. There is no dearth of sycophants in the world. However, at times, unpleasant words are required to convey the truth and achieve the desired results like a bitter medicine helps cure a disease."

Mahisha got the hint. He said, "Wise men are supposed to make decisions after listening to all opinions and weighing their pros and cons in accordance with one's own intellect. Let me hear all of you."

Before anyone could respond to the king, Virupaksha, a powerful asura, spoke, "O King! This woman seems to be exaggerating her prowess. If you, the lord of the three worlds, bow down to her, you will be treated as inferior to her. Allow me to go alone with my army and kill that arrogant woman or tie her in ropes of snakes and bring her to you."

Virupaksha was supported by Durdhasha, another daitya. He said rhetorically, 'O King! What that lady meant by killing you with her arrows, was to hunt you with her arrow-like eyesight. When she uttered laying you on the deathbed on the battlefield, she wanted to convey her desire to have relations with you. And by saying that she would take away your life, she meant taking your virility which also means life.

O King! She is actually in awe of you. Permit me to go and use the tactics of saam and daam. I am sure I will bring her to you by sweetly talking to her."

When times are bad the intellect also leaves you,' sighed Vyasa and continued, 'it was the same situation with Mahishasura and his advisors. But there were some sane voices too in his court.

Another powerful daitya Tamra, who was an expert in deciphering secrets and mysteries, spoke in disagreement. He said "Who has ever heard of a beautiful woman with eighteen arms and that too holding powerful weapons in each hand? By the description, this lady does not seem to be a deva or a human or a gandharvi or a danava. She is certainly a creation of maya of the wily devas. There is nothing to suggest that she has amorous feelings for you.

O King! I may submit that I have been getting ominous signs in my dreams indicating inauspicious happenings around the corner. I suggest we prepare to deal with her with force."

Mahishasura heard the contrary opinions and mulled over them. He then ordered Tamra to proceed with the option of fighting her and said, "Go and bring her to me after defeating her. If you cannot capture her, then kill her. At the same time, do find out who is the creator of this maya."

Tamra's advancement to the battlefield was full of inauspicious signs. He decided to give another chance to diplomacy. He bowed down to the Devi and pleaded in a soft tone that she should accept Mahishasura as her husband.

The Devi laughed at the reiteration of the proposal made by the earlier emissary. Her roar shivered mountains and earth and made daitya women miscarry.

The Devi said in a loud voice, "I will not even take Vishnu, Brahma, Mahesh or any other deva as my husband, how can I accept the proposal of a beast? My husband is the lord of all the worlds, living and non-living. He is beyond any gunas, omniscient and omnipresent.

Your stupid Mahishasura has been hit by cupid's arrows and has forgotten to differentiate between right and wrong. Let him come, fight me and be killed. If he wants to live, let him return immediately to Patalaloka."

Tamra returned empty-handed and terrified. A surprised Mahishasura called for another meeting to assess the latest reportage from Tamra.

Vidalaksha, one of his main ministers, said, "It would be prudent to find out who this woman is, where she came from and what her objective is. I have the feeling that the devas, knowing fully well that you can be killed only by a woman, have created her. Moreover, all devas, who are waiting in the wings, will help her when the time comes. That seems to be the reason why this lady, all by herself, is able to intrepidly challenge us to fight."

Then spoke Durmukha and Vashkala in favour of war. Each one was more jingoistic than the other.

No sooner had they finished, Durdhara spoke. He said, "O King! There are ministers in every court who fall under three broad categories. The Saattvika ones are righteous and follow the policies of their kings in letter and spirit. They never mean any harm to their master.

The Rajasika ministers always place their interests above that of their king and perform their duties at their own will. The Tamasika ones are the inimical lot who use royal interests to achieve their covetous ends. It is the third kind who is prone to bribes and go against their king. They are cowards and never advise their king to take the course of bravery against enemies. You should never trust this kind of ministers. Therefore, O King, I will go to the battle myself and defeat that vicious woman."

Mahishasura ordered Vashkala and Durmukha to lead the fight against the Devi. Filled with the pride of being top generals of the daitya king, both of them reached the battlefield and again argued with the Devi on similar lines as had been done by the earlier envoys. But the reply from the Goddess was the same.

The Devi's resolute stand further angered the daityas. They launched an attack. Vashkala began to shoot the Devi who responded with equally potent arrows. The fight moved on with scimitars and clubs replacing arrows. Eventually, Vashkala was struck by the Devi's trident that pierced his chest. He died instantly.

Durmukha wasted no time in replacing Vashkala in the battle so that the daitya army was not discouraged by the latter's killing. The fight became more dreadful and multiple weapons, from arrows to clubs to musalas and finally shaktis, were used.

The blood of the slain asuras flowed as water flows in a river. The corpses were feasted upon by animals and birds.

The Devi destroyed Durmukha's chariot with her sharpened arrows. He ran towards the Devi with a club and hit the ferocious lion. But the Devi was ready and seeing the asura within her reach, she chopped off his head with her axe. The lifeless daitya fell down and the devas began to chant hymns to the Devi.

Mahisha could not accept the news that two of his trusted generals had been eliminated. He summoned the rest and consulted them. Chikshur offered to lead this time. Mahishasura told Tamra to join Chikshur. Both marched with their respective armies resonating the skies with their war cries.

The Devi was ready to fight. The place resonated from the sound of her conch, bowstring and the great bell of Airavata offered by Indra. This sound was unbearable for the daityas and led to many of them losing their eardrums and several turning their backs.

The commanding general Chikshur gave a clarion call to his army and told them not to fear the Devi. He said, "I will kill this woman now." Addressing the Devi, he said, "O gorgeous one! A delicate beauty like you will be hurt even by the throw of flowers and you wish to fight us with arrows! You ought to have accepted Mahishasura's offer to become his wife and enjoy life's pleasures. It will be a dishonour to kill a woman, let alone a sin. But if that is my destiny, I shall accept it without hesitation."

The Devi repeated her warning to all the daityas to go back to Patalaloka and yet again, it fell on deaf ears.

Having received a clear answer from the Divine Mother, Chikshur spent no more time in dialogue. He attacked with his sharpened arrows. The Devi struck him with the club knocking him down from the chariot. Tamra, seeing Chikshur in a weak position, jumped in to help his fellow daitya.

While Tamra continued with the battle, Chikshur also regained his senses and both began to fight like a team. Meanwhile, Devi Maha Lakshmi slaughtered the daitya forces. Tamra hit his club on the lion's head infuriating the Devi who cut off his head using the sharp divine axe.

Chikshur witnessed the end of Tamra and attacked with even more vigour. But he was immediately counter-attacked by five arrows cutting his axe, then both hands and finally his head. He died then and there.

The news of Chikshur and Tamra being slayed unnerved Mahisha. He despatched Asiloma and Vidalaksha along with several more battalions of the army. As soon as they both reached the battleground, they witnessed the grand appearance of the Divine Mother with eighteen hands equipped with a multitude of extraordinary weapons and sitting majestically on her lion.

Asiloma, a daitya with a composed disposition, paid respects to the Devi. He again offered her a truce. He said, "You know the thumb rule of life is to shed suffering and gain happiness. Happiness is of two kinds: eternal and ephemeral. The pleasure achieved out of knowing atmagyan is eternal and that out of material gains is ephemeral. On the other hand, war enhances pain and suffering. Why then do you want a war? Why are you killing these sinless asuras?

What is their fault? You can take whatever wealth you want and leave. We will be happy to conclude a treaty with you to attain peace."

The Devi replied, "I have the role of a third person in this world as far as pleasure and pain are concerned. I take note of rights and wrongs. Consequently, I preserve the virtue and eliminate the evil but I do not harbour enmity with anyone. I am the Supreme Goddess. I incarnate again and again to achieve my objectives, as may be required to preserve this world.

The vicious Mahisha has troubled the devas for far too long. It is time for him to leave Devaloka and go back to Patalaloka where Prahlada is residing too. If he does not accept, let him fight me and be destroyed."

The Devi's words removed all doubts from Asiloma and Vidalaksha's minds about who she was. Asiloma asked his companion if they should proceed with the war.

An intelligent Vidalaksha said, "Truth and pleasant words seldom come together. If we go to our king and tell him the truth that he should leave his wealth here and proceed to Patalaloka to save his life, he would not spare us. He will not be able to distinguish between the beneficial and the pleasant words. Therefore, let us do our duty and fight, even if death is inevitable for us."

Thus both the daityas entered the battlefield. In no time, Vidalaksha was hit by the Devi's arrows and fell to the ground. He did not get up thereafter.

Asiloma, as if he had resigned to fate, entered the war. He too was pierced with sharp arrows and his body oozed blood from several injuries. In angry retaliation, he hit the lion's head with the iron club. The lion, in turn, tore into his arms with his claws. The wounded daitya picked up his club and struck the Devi. The Devi was unfazed and swung her axe to sever Asiloma's head from his body.

The devas, joined by rishis, siddhas, gandharvas, vidyadharas,[152] kinnaras[153] and all other celestial beings, showered praises on the Devi and cried in unison, "Jaya, Jaya[155]! Triumph to the Devi!" They beat the victory drums and danced in pleasure.

The daitya army, seeing their generals falling in the battle like ripened mangoes from a tree, fled away in horror in various directions. Several were devoured by the Devi's lion.

Those who managed to reach Mahishasura alive, narrated to him what had transpired in the battle. Mahisha was numbed with grief on hearing what had transpired on the battlefield and became deeply distressed,' said Vyasa.

Mahishasurmardini

Vyasa continued, 'The enraged king ordered his charioteer Daruka to prepare his special chariot. The chariot was well ornated, decked with jewels, equipped with arms and ammunition and drawn by a thousand best-breed horses. As he was getting ready to mount the chariot, Mahishasura thought that no woman liked an ugly person. He then changed into a handsome person so that he could charm the Devi.

Looking like a glittering deva, wearing the best of attire and ornaments, the king, arrogant of his awesome and powerful appearance, capable of enchanting any woman, led his army to the battleground.

The Devi saw him from a distance and blew a loud and strong sound from her conch. The sound, however, did not deter Mahishasura. He brought his chariot close to the Devi as if he still had hopes of wooing her. He said, "The objective of each life is to maximise happiness and that comes from relationships with other persons. The relations between parents and children are attributable to affection. These have no motives and are in the excellent category.

The relations between siblings, which have an element of mutual interest, are at the average level. The still lower level is of co-passengers in a boat. These are natural but offer much less happiness.

The relations between a man and a woman who share qualities are the most important as they bring extreme happiness to both. Therefore, O beautiful one! Marry me and enjoy the best of pleasures and wealth in the world. I shall remain your servant. Have no doubt that I am smitten by you.

Though I have defeated gods and devas in the battle, I set aside my weapons and take your refuge. Be mine!"

The Devi, who was above the three gunas, sniggered at Mahishasura's impudence. She said, "O stupid one! You still have not understood that I am married to the Supreme Being. We draw from each other. I am His Willpower. It is because of Him that I can create and I am termed as the Eternal Consciousness.

It is lowly people like you who desire sexual union. But you do not discern that men can be freed from all bondages but of that of the women.

Instead of taking my refuge, take refuge in peace. Go back to Patalaloka and leave the devas in amity in Devaloka. Be aware that I am stronger than you and capable of killing you. By virtue of having had a verbal exchange, we have developed a friendship. Therefore, I shall grant safe passage to you."

Mahishasura insisted, "I have won over Brahma, Vishnu and Shiva. There is no one in the three worlds capable of battling me. And now that you have mentioned friendship between us, how can I fight you and kill you? As killing a woman, a child and a brahmin have later consequences, I will not kill you. I will rather carry you to my kingdom."

To give another try to convince the Devi, Mahishasura changed his tune and said, "O beautiful one! As you are hell bent on not becoming my consort, I sincerely hope that you do not repent later not marrying me. I am not sure if you know about Mandodari who also rejected marrying a beautiful and auspicious king and later ended up marrying a fool."

The Devi asked curiously, "Who is this Mandodari? Who was the king she rejected?"

Mahishasura began narrating the story, "Once in the prosperous land of Simhala on earth, there ruled a virtuous king called Chandrasena. His beautiful wife birthed an enchanting daughter who they named Mandodari. By the time she turned ten, the king began to worry about her match.

The wandering brahmins brought the news of the handsome and gifted prince Kambugriva, the son of King Sudhanva of Madra country.

Hearing of the potential match, Chandrasena consulted his wife and she took the proposal to Mandodari. But the daughter said, 'I have decided to spend my life as a chaste virgin. I have no desire to marry. Marriage leads to bondage, dependence and miseries. In the case of husband marrying again, it also leads to jealousy. In the event of death of the husband, widowhood is insufferable. Thus, marriage brings no happiness.'

Hence, even after attaining the age of puberty, Mandodari continued to live in her father's kingdom without showing any inclination to get into family life.

Once, she was visiting the beautiful gardens outside the city when King Virasena, the powerful king of Kosala, happened to visit the same locale. When Mandodari's companions saw him, they were impressed with his personality. They began to discuss the king, throwing clear hints to the princess as to how lucky she would be if she chose this king as her husband.

Meanwhile, the king's eyes fell on the princess and her pristine beauty. Swept off his feet, he walked up to her and asked for her introduction. A smart maidservant in turn asked him to introduce himself first.

Virasena told her that he was the king of Kosala and had descended from the Kakutstha lineage. He was on a hunting expedition but had lost his way. Once the king finished introducing himself, one of the attendants of the princess gave her introduction.

The king told the attendant to convey to Mandodari, 'I have fallen for Princess Mandodari and, therefore, can perform Gandharva marriage with her right away. As she comes from a noble family, I will be happy if her father obliges and marries her off to me according to social norms. In any case, I think I am fit to be her husband.'

The attendant conveyed Virasena's message faithfully to Mandodari. She added, 'O large-eyed one! You have been busy with asceticism performing Hatha Dharma. But remember serving the husband is the highest virtue of a woman.'

However, Mandodari rejected the proposal. The attendant gave the message to the king who was disheartened and left for Kosala.

In some years, Mandodari's younger sister Indumati attained marriageable age. Their father called for a svayamvara ceremony. Indumati selected a husband for her amongst the handsome and powerful kings in the assembly. Due to a strange turn of fate, Mandodari also fell for a sly king by the name of Charudeshna. She failed to see the hypocrisy of the king due to his suave behaviour.

She informed her father about her choice. Though he was not convinced, he relented and married her to the king. After marriage, Mandodari and Charudeshna started enjoying their blissful days as a couple.

However, after some time, one of Mandodari's confidants found the king in an intimate position with a maidservant of the queen. She reported this to Queen Mandodari.

Mandodari was furious and reproached the king. But she maintained her cool as she was the one who had chosen Charudeshna.

Alas, this was neither the first nor the last time for such acts by the king. Soon another incident of the similar nature came to light. Finally, when Mandodari personally witnessed him engrossed in amusement with an ordinary-looking servant, she was crestfallen.

She realised her folly in marrying such an unabashed person. She weighed her options of returning to her father, which would lead to derision, or committing suicide, an act that could not be condoned. She finally decided to return to her life of austerities without any sensual pleasures."

Mahishasura paused and concluded, "O gorgeous one! Here I am, the king of the three worlds and you are refusing to marry me, as did Mandodari to Virasena."

The Devi heard Mahishasura patiently and said, "O foolish King! You refuse to pay heed to what I have consistently told you and your generals. I am the Supreme Energy, formless, birth less and death less. It would be in your best interest to leave immediately for Patalaloka or I shall slaughter you."

The daitya was forced to pick up his weaponry and a terrible war broke out between him and the Devi. Durdhara also joined in with his arrows to support his King. The Devi cut his arrows and shot him dead. He was replaced by another strong demon Trinetra. But he too could not survive long as he got hit by the Devi's energised trident. Another general called Andhaka joined in to assist Mahishasura. But he too was soon killed by the razor-sharp claws of the lion.

Mahisha was surprised by the quick defeat and deaths of his top commanders. He attacked the Devi with arrows. The Devi, cutting his arrows into smithereens, struck him on his chest with the club. Mahisha fell into a swoon but got up the next moment and hit the lion's head with his club. The lion retaliated in full force with his claws.

A frustrated Mahishasura changed his appearance from a man to a lion and again wounded the Devi's lion who also struck back. Mahishasura again changed his form to a male elephant and started hurling hillocks by his trunk. Meanwhile, the lion struck his claws on the elephant's head causing him to bleed profusely.

Mahishasura turned into a sharabha[155]. The Devi struck her axe on the sharabha's head. Having tried various appearances, Mahishasura assumed his original form of a buffalo and attacked with his most potent weapon, his horns.

The Devi paused to drink her sweet Soma and then pierced her trident into the chest of the buffalo demon. The daitya again got up but not for too long. The Devi finally beheaded him instantly with her disc that had a thousand spokes.

Having accomplished the mission, Devi Bhagvati left the battlefield. Joined by rishis, siddhas, gandharvas, kinnaras and other celestial beings, the devas chanted hymns in praise of her and followed her. The victory drums were played from all corners of the world.

The devas said in unison, "O Mother! You are our liberator, whether in happiness or distress. You are our protector. We are what we are due to the blessings of the dust of your feet."

After being venerated by the devas, the Devi was appeased and said, "O my sons! My blessings are with you. Go back to your abodes and start ruling the world according to dharma. If you come across more such difficulties, remember me and I shall destroy the evil."

While the devas continued their veneration, the Devi disappeared from there.'

Janamejaya asked, 'O Muni! How is it that the Mother Goddess Bhagvati, created by the combined energies of all the devas, disappear? Where did she disappear to? Where does she live now? Kindly explain and satisfy my quest.'

Vyasa smiled and said, 'You are a fortunate soul, O King! You must have done some excellent karmas in your past lives that you are able to hear this Devi Purana in this birth. Those who do not worship the Devi in their human birth land up with difficulties in their next births.

They may be reborn in poverty, misery, diseased, blind, deaf or dumb, leper or die childless. If you see someone wealthy, prosperous and enjoying the worldly pleasures in the present birth, he must have worshipped the lotus feet of the Devi in his past lives.

O King! Before I tell you where she went away, remember the Devi was thenceforth also called Mahishasurmardini, the slayer of Mahishasura.

Now, you may remember I had mentioned Mani Dvipa, the island in the ocean of nectar and Devi's abode. I had described its beauty and opulence. Devi Bhagvati assumed various forms whenever she was required to help the gods, devas or even mortals. After she finished her task, she returned to Mani Dvipa.

After the Devi vanished from amongst the devas, brahmins stopped sharing the proceeds of sacrifices with the daityas. Life on earth returned to usual where people lived according to the prescribed dharma. The rain came in normal cycles and the land gave abundant grains, fruits and vegetables. The cows began to milk auspiciously. The water from the rivers was again sweet and cool. The animals and birds lived in tandem with nature.

In sum, everyone began to live peacefully again under the blessings of Devi Chandika.'

Shumbha-Nishumbha

Janamejaya stopped the muni once again and asked, 'I have heard of daitya brothers Shumbha and Nishumbha who were also killed by the Devi. O Muni! Kindly enlighten me by describing in detail who they were and what happened to them.'

Vyasa went into a state of trance while thinking of the Devi. But that did not stop him from rendering the Purana to King Janamejaya. He was willing to pass on all the knowledge he had, to Janamejaya. Without wasting even a moment, he again began, 'I am glad that you remembered that episode. Let me tell you.

It was long, long ago when two asura brothers Shumbha and Nishumbha lived in their natural habitat, the Patalaloka. They both decided to come to earth and perform austerities. They went to the holy city of Pushkar and performed sacrifices. To begin with, they quit consuming rice grain and water.

Ten thousand years swung by while they kept themselves occupied with penance. Finally, the god of creation, the four-faced Brahma appeared before them in Pushkar. Sitting on his swan, he offered to grant boons to the two brothers.

The brothers stopped their meditation, prostrated before Brahma and circumambulated him. Then they sat in front of him and worshipped him with their debilitated bodies after a long meditation.

Brahma smiled as soon as they spoke, as if he knew what they were going to seek. They said, "O Prajapati! Remove the fear of death in us. Grant us immortality."

Brahma had heard this request umpteen times and he knew he could not grant it as he himself was subject to the cycle of life and death. He explained, "Immortality is against the law of nature. Each being assuming a body form is subject to a beginning and an end. Therefore, ask for anything else and I shall grant it to you."

The asura brothers were speechless for some time before they spoke up after giving due thought and consulting each other. They folded their hands and said, "O Brahma! Then grant us invulnerability from all species of males including devas, men, animals and birds. Grant us that we cannot be killed by a male."

Then thinking to themselves, they both laughed and added, "Which woman in the three worlds can fight us anyway?"

Brahma understood their intention and was filled with a sense of déjà vu. He recalled that Mahishasura too had asked for a similar boon from him. Brahma was aware that destiny and the wheel of time would prove to be a resolution for the boon granted by him.

The elated asuras returned to Patalaloka and appointed Maharishi Bhrigu as their chief priest. At an auspicious time selected by Bhrigu, he anointed Shumbha as the king.

The news of their boon travelled far and wide. The top daityas accepted their suzerainty. Famed Chanda and Munda brothers, the powerful Dhumralochana, the valiant warrior Raktabija and others joined the burgeoning army of Shumbha, along with their daityas, chariots, horses and elephants.

Raktabija, among all, was monstrously strong due to a special boon that he had received from Mahadeva. Every drop of his blood spilled over the ground created an innumerable number of similar daityas, resembling him in form and shape as well as in strength and ghastliness. He was, thus, an unconquerable foe on the battlefield.

The daitya army conquered the kings on earth and finally Nishumbha attacked Devaloka. Indra hit Nishumbha's chest with his potent thunderbolt, which made him fall unconscious. Shumbha came to his brother's rescue and after a terrible fight, drove away the devas' army from heaven. Shumbha became the lord of Devaloka and controlled all the heavenly assets.

The defeated devas left Nandana Garden and wandered around looking for a safe haven.

O Janamejaya! The turn of fate can make the strongest of kings, even devas, into beggars or refugees and vice versa.'

Vyasa gasped at the inevitability of fate and continued, 'While Shumbha ruled for good thousand years, the dejected wandering devas reached their guru, Brihaspati. They sought his counsel and said, "O Gurudeva! You the knower of all the mantras, kindly perform all the requisite yagnas and mantras to end the reign of the daityas."

The wise Brihaspati replied, "You, Indra, with Agni, Varuna, Kubera and the rest are presiding deities of the mantras and yagnas. Look at your own plight. It is therefore clear that mantras can do nothing on their own. They are subject to destiny. The wise neither depend on fate nor on remedies alone. The strategy is in propitiation of fate through remedies while continuing to exert the best of karmas."

He reminded the devas, "Remember when Devi Chandika had killed Mahishasura, she had said before departing that she would return to help you whenever you were in difficulty. The time has come to seek her blessings. Go to the Himalayas and worship her."

As advised by Brihaspati, the devas collectively eulogised the Devi and sang hymns to her.

The appeased Devi Bhagvati appeared to them in her most auspicious form. The Devi asked, "O Suras! Why are you all looking so depressed and miserable? Why have you been praising me for so long? What do you want?"

The devas prostrated before her and said, "O Devi! In ancient times, you had said that whenever an insurmountable difficulty arose, you would appear to resolve it as soon as we remembered you.

The time has come, O Mother!

Brahma gave a boon to Shumbha and Nishumbha, the two asura brothers, that they could not be killed by a male. Since then, they have rampaged and won over the three lokas. Indra and all of us have been ousted from the Nandana Garden for more than a thousand years already. We beg you to rid us of the reign of the daityas."

The Goddess created another form from her body. This equally beautiful, effulgent and graceful form was called Kaushiki.

No sooner than the second body came out, the original body turned black and was known as Kalika. Kalika also acquired the name of Kaalratri, which means the night of destruction.

Devi Kaushiki smiled at the devas and said, "So be it. If that removes the difficulties in your lives, I shall eliminate the two tormentors."

Devi Kaushiki mounted her lion and marched towards the abode of Shumbha. Devi Kalika joined too. Kaushiki went to a garden next to the city of Shumbha and began to sing in an enchanting melodious voice.

Coincidentally, the other two daitya brothers Chanda and Munda were also there. They noticed Devi Kaushiki's exquisite beauty and immediately went to King Shumbha and described to him the splendour of the woman visiting their gardens.

They added, "We have never witnessed such an alluring woman among the devas or apsaras or gandharvas or asuras or humans. We suggest that you take her as your consort. You are the master of best of gems in the three worlds and she will be best gem in the form of a lady that you would enjoy. However, let us first find out who she is and where she has come from."

Shumbha was excited to hear these words. As he did not wish to lose any time, he asked Sugriva to go to the lady as his messenger. He instructed him, "A woman is attracted only through two means: saam, soft and suave words, and daam, tasteful gifts.

The other two, bheda and danda, repulse a woman. Bheda is an inappropriate manifestation of love and danda has no feeling of love. Make use of your diplomacy and bring that woman to me."

Unbeknownst as to who she was, the arrogant messenger reached her and started singing paeans about his asura king. He added, "O delicate one! The lord of the three worlds has sent his kindest salutations full of affection for you. He has the rights over the offerings during the sacrifices made by the brahmins. He has all the wealth and lordship of the world. But after hearing about your bewitching beauty that ignited passion in him, he wants to become your servant."

Sugriva's gentle delivery of sweet words made the Devi smile. She said, "I have also heard a lot about your King Shumbha and his brother Nishumbha. They are acknowledged warriors and have all the qualities; they are handsome, charitable, strong, learned and, above all, the conqueror of devas. Go back and tell him that as a jewel studded in gold enhances its own lustre, I have come this far to seek a husband like him.

There is, however, a minor impediment. When I was a child, I had vowed to my companions that I would marry the one who could defeat me in battle. It was partly out of childishness and partly because of being proud of my own strength.

Therefore, O Messenger, tell your king that he can come himself or send his brother to fulfil my pledge by defeating me and then take me as his wife."

The messenger tried to convince the Devi that she was too delicate to fight the great Shumbha and that she should accept the daitya king as her husband, but it was all in vain.'

Vyasa added, 'This form of Devi was very different from that of Devi Bhagvati, the destructor of Mahisha. But every form of the Devi has varied behaviour and certainly one learns from each one of them.'

Vyasa continued, 'The messenger went back and conveyed Devi Kaushiki's message to Shumbha.

With hesitation, he added, "The lady is adamant for a fight with the prospective husband. She says even though she is a weaker sex, she is capable to fight. If the king is afraid then he can go to Patalaloka leaving the earth and heaven."

Shumbha consulted Nishumbha who was annoyed with the vanity of the Devi and said, "O King! To begin with, it would be inappropriate for you or even for me to go to the battleground. Let us send our general Dhumralochana and task him to defeat this arrogant lady. Once he brings her defeated, you can marry her."

Shumbha sent Dhumralochana with a daitya army of sixty thousand. He was instructed to kill anyone who helped her but ensure no harm to her.

Dhumralochana reached the battleground and humbly addressed the Devi, "It seems the messenger of King Shumbha goofed up. He perhaps did not appreciate the meaning of your words. You said that you would marry someone who defeats you in battle. I think by 'battle' you meant sexual intercourse. Let me inform you that Shumbha understands the meaning of battle and is capable of winning you."

Hearing him speak rubbish, Kalika could not stop her sarcastic laugh and said, "O nincompoop! You, and not the messenger, seemed to have misunderstood Devi Kaushiki's words. You are twisting the meaning to derive an advantage that will neither help you nor your king.

Look at the Devi, who has a lion for her vehicle, and look at your master, akin to an ordinary jackal. How can there be a union between a lioness and a jackal or a female elephant and an ass or a Surabhi cow and an ordinary buffalo? Make haste and tell Shumbha to fight or go back to Patalaloka and save his life."

Dhumralochana was incensed with Kalika. He shot arrows and the battle turned ugly. All possible weapons like axes, clubs, musalas and shaktis were used. Kalika killed all the horses of Dhumralochana's chariot, thus forcing him to fight on his feet.

The enraged daitya threw the Parigha in his hand at Kalika, which made the Devi roar deafeningly. Her bellowing burnt the daitya alive. Seeing their general burnt to ashes, without even the usage of a weapon, the army of daityas was terror-stricken and fled.

While the devas rejoiced and sang praises for the Devi, she removed herself from the battleground to a distant place and blew her conch shell. It emitted a terrible sound so loud that Shumbha could hear it in his abode.

By the time he understood what had happened, he saw his tormented army, disfigured and haggard, bleeding and crying, returning to his camp.

The defeated army narrated to him the events of the war. They pleaded with the king to leave the thought of marrying the Devi.

Shumbha again consulted Nishumbha. He asked, "Kalika alone has defeated our great warrior Dhumralochana and a large part of his army. The other Devi is now defiantly blowing her conch. What shall I do? Do I quit the thought of consorting her? I ask you because you always counsel me as an elder, although you are my younger brother."

Nishumbha weighed his words and said, "We cannot flight from the battle. Fighting the lady is our only option. Let me go to the battlefield with our best generals. If I get killed too, reconsider the issue and then make the best decision as per the circumstances."

Shumbha considered the advice and said, "It does not befit using an elephant to kill a hare. Let Chanda and Munda first go to the battle."

He summoned the two warriors and told them, "Kill the tawny-eyed Kalika and bring Kaushiki to me. If that arrogant woman poses difficulty in coming with you, then kill her too." Chanda and Munda thus proceeded to the battlefield.'

Devi Chamunda

Vyasa continued, 'The fierce warrior brothers known for their valour, Chanda and Munda, led their huge army. The moment they came face to face with the Devi, they attempted diplomatic reconciliation.

While they spoke of the supremacy of Shumbha and Nishumbha, they veiled their threats in a sweet tongue. They goaded the Devi and said, "O beautiful one with eighteen hands! The devas are your friends for purely selfish reasons. Such friends should not be entertained. Therefore, you should look at the magnificent Shumbha, replete with all the qualities; he is handsome, strong, brave, intelligent, conqueror of Indra and expert in Kaamshastra[156]. What more can a woman want? He is the perfect match for you."

Though she had heard such statements before, the Devi was averse to such arguments. She had heard these in various yugas from numerous asuras. Her response had always been the same.

She said in a deep rumbling voice, "O ill-advised ones! I do not need a husband. I have destroyed asuras in different aeons to uphold dharma. This time it is the turn of Shumbha, Nishumbha and their daitya army. Now pick up your arms and fight to accept death as a warrior."

Comprehending that they had exhausted the peaceful option of talking with the Devi, the arrogant Chanda and Munda attacked her. As the war turned deadly, the Devi became enraged. At this juncture, Devi Kaali appeared from Devi Chandika's forehead. She was wearing tiger skin and a garland of skulls. Her body was covered with elephant skin. She had a belly like a dried reservoir. Her guise was dreadful as if representing a night of death and destruction. She held an axe, a noose, a trident and a sword in different hands. She licked her red tongue repeatedly and gobbled daityas on the battlefield in her wide mouth, killing them instantly with her grinding teeth.

She swallowed everyone coming her way. With the daitya army rapidly depleting, Chanda renewed his attack on Kaali and threw his chakra. Chandika cut it off with her arrows and hit Chanda back rendering him unconscious.

Seeing his brother falling to the ground, Munda confronted Devi Chandika. She launched a special missile-like weapon called Isika[157] that destroyed all the arrows in the sky. She followed it up with the Ardhachandra arrow that hit Munda unconscious too.

While Munda lay unconscious, Chanda regained his and attacked with a club. However, Kaali trapped him in paash, energised by mantras. Kaali sacrificed both Chanda and Munda lying at her feet by chopping off their heads with a sharpened axe. She then drank their blood.

Blessing Kaali, Ambika said, "As you have killed Chanda and Munda, you will be famed as Chamunda Devi."

With the felling of two of the top generals in the war, the daitya force ran helter-skelter to save their lives. The Devi's lion devoured the soldiers to his heart's content. The field became the source of a river of blood and marrow with corpses flowing in it like logs of wood in a river of water.

Those who fled alive reported back to Shumbha and requested him, "O King! You ought to recall that Brahma granted you a boon that you would not be killed by a male, be he a deva, daitya, human, naag, kinnara, yaksha or any other male being.

It seems that devas, aware of your boon, have sent this lady to kill you. Therefore, stop fighting and leave at once for Patalaloka and save your life along with those left in our contingents."

Shumbha was a valiant and intelligent asura. He responded, "The entire world and the happenings therein are controlled by fate. Why me, even Brahma, Vishnu and

Mahadeva are not immune to it. What is written shall come to pass.

But the brave do not think of fate, they perform their actions. Only the foolish and weak depend on fate. It is also used to console oneself after a defeat. If you take some material to a grinding mill, it will not grind on its own without exerting the required action. And the efforts will have to commensurate with the magnitude of the work required to be done."

Concluding his opinion, he summoned Raktabija and directed him to lead the army. A rather overconfident Raktabija mounted his chariot and left.

Seeing the new general on the battlefield, the Devi blew her conch shell, which created a ruckus in the daitya army. But Raktabija was unfazed. Instead, he came closer to the Devi and said in a soft voice, "O lean one! You think you can frighten me like you did Dhumralochana?

If you had the opportunity to be in the company of old and wise people, if you have studied political science and political economy, if you have knowledge of literature and tantras, then hear carefully what I have to say.

Two out of the nine rasas[158], sringara[159] and shanti[160], are considered to be the most important. Of the two, it is the first that is the chief among the rasas. It is the basis of creation as it bonds a female to a male. Do not be ignorant to this important emotion and accept to marry King Shumbha."

On hearing this, the three Devis, Ambika, Kalika and Chamunda, laughed. Ambika said, "O Asura of dull wits! I had said to the first messenger of your king that I would take a husband who can defeat me in a fight. So tell your king to fight and conquer me if he wishes to marry me."

Raktabija was left with no other option but to raise his bugle for war. The deadly battle began and Raktabija fell unconscious when attacked by the Devi.

Shumbha on hearing that Raktabija had become unconscious reached the war zone and ordered his entire army including cavalry, infantry, elephants and chariots to attack the Devi.

The Devi, on the other hand, was joined by all the other devis, the consorts of the gods and the devas. They came on the conveyances, holding the weapons and shaktis of their respective husbands. Brahmani, wife of Brahma, on a swan; Lakshmi, wife of Vishnu, on Garuda; Parvati, Shiva's wife, on Nandi bull; Kaumari Devi, consort of Kartikeya, on a peacock; Sachi or Indrani on Airavata and Yama's wife rode the buffalo.

Mahadeva blessed all of them, saying, "O shaktis behind the devas! The time has come for you to terminate the reign of Shumbha and bring back the world to its normal course. With this, not only the devas will get back their share in the sacrifices, but calamities like drought, floods, pandemics due to rats, bats, locusts and birds, will also end."

Devi Ambika greeted Mahadeva and said, "O Shankar! You be my emissary to Shumbha and give him a last chance to quit and go to Patalaloka."

Mahadeva went to Shumbha and said, "O King of asuras! I am the slayer of Tripura Daitya in ancient times. But I have come to you today as the messenger of Devi Ambika. You have the final chance to quit heaven and leave for Patalaloka where your clan of Bali and Prahlada live. Else, prepare to fight and die."'

Janamejaya interjected and asked, 'Is this why the Devi has one of her names as Shivaduti[161]?'

Vyasa nodded and said, 'Yes, because she sent Shiva as her messenger, she is also known by the name of Shivaduti.

Shumbha's time was too bad and he did not heed Shiva's words. He came prepared for the final battle. Meanwhile, Raktabija had also recovered and came back to fight.'

Vyasa paused here and asked his listener, 'Remember, Janamejaya, that Raktabija had an extraordinary boon?'

Janamejaya nodded in affirmative.

Vyasa continued, 'While the Devi also knew about the boon to Raktabija, she didn't appreciate the gravity of it till her Sudarshana Chakra struck the daitya. The moment blood came out of his body and fell on the ground, thousands of similar daityas came into being out of each drop of blood. They carried similar weapons to the original Raktabija and had the same energy to battle.

The daitya was struck by several women deva warriors. Brahmani attacked him with Brahma's staff, Maheshvari with Shiva's trident, Narasimhi with her nails and Varahi with her teeth. Each stroke caused a further cut, which complicated the battle scene by creating millions of Raktabijas filling the battlefield.

Sensing the situation, Devi Ambika asked Kaali, "O Chamunda! While I kill all the Raktabijas born out of the blood of the principal daitya, you open your mouth wide and drink their blood. You will have to make sure that not a single drop of blood falls on the ground. This is the only way of destroying these asuras."

Kaali did as she was told. As Chandika kept felling a host of daityas, Kaali gobbled their blood and devoured their bodies. Raktabija struck Kaali severely with his club but Kaali did not budge in spite of being hit hard.

Chandika destroyed the asuras and Kaali drank their blood. Finally, only the real Raktabija was left. Chandika cut him off in several pieces with an axe while Kaali ensured that his blood fell only into her mouth.

The rest of the army retreated to meet Shumbha. They recounted the horror of the war on account of the massacre by the devis.

Shumbha wished to join the war, especially after losing his illustrious warriors Chanda, Munda and Raktabija. But Nishumbha said, "You are the main pillar of your empire and, therefore, you shall not enter the battle until I am there to serve you."

While Nishumbha departed with all possible auspicious ceremonies, he knew in his heart that he would not come back alive.

Determined to win or die, Nishumbha arrived and began to shoot arrows from his bow made of horns. Seeing him, Devi Ambika said to Kalika, "Look at the extent of my maya. Even after witnessing the terrible end of Raktabija, they are still hopeful for a victory. Hope is the strongest ally and weapon of a man."

The Devi took up her bow and responded to Nishumbha's arrows. The Devi's lion too tore apart several asuras.

Meanwhile, a worried Shumbha could not resist joining the battlefield. He arrived in full vigour, struck Kalika and sped up to face the Devi. He saw Chandika, the most beautiful yet fiery at the same time. Her countenance dissipated the amorous feelings in Shumbha and filled him with fearsome thoughts of death.

The Devi again said to the brothers, "O vicious brothers! Go back to Patala or be killed fighting me."

Nishumbha responded not with words but by hurling his sword at the Devi and the club at the lion. The Devi skirted the attack and used her axe to chop off Nishumbha's head. The headless body fell to the ground like a mountain, making a violent sound.

The soldiers, who survived the massacre, made a bid to escape. They assembled around Shumbha and prayed to him, "O King! This lady has killed Nishumbha who had defeated the devas. She is no ordinary lady. There is still time for you to run away to Patalaloka."

Shumbha angrily said, "I do not care about death. Anyone who is born must die. Even Brahma dies and is born again. It is the fame of a person that lives permanently and not the person. Therefore, there is no way I can quit the war, especially after my brother Nishumbha and the great warrior Raktabija have been slain."

Shumbha arrived and again witnessed the Devi. This time she was composed and serene. In her peaceful state, she was the most gorgeous, with a lean body and excellent limbs. She was being attended by gandharvas, yakshas and kinnaras. This appearance of the Devi filled Shumbha with passion again. He wondered how come she had no amorous feelings and inclination to enjoy the pleasures of life.

He thought to himself that she was a woman only in name as she was more powerful than hundred devas. Yet, he contemplated, if he was killed by a woman, his fame would be tarnished.

With various arguments and counterarguments crossing his mind at the same time, he decided to go ahead with fighting the war and leaving the rest to fate. He spoke to the Devi, "O delicate one! Your actions are contrary to what is expected of a woman. A woman can use her eyes, her gestures and sweet words to win over a man. She needs no weapons and least of all, impertinence and immodesty.

O enchanter! I will not be able to fight a beautiful and delicate woman like you. If you really want to fight, then you will have to assume a fierce, repellent and hideous form. You shall also speak harshly with me, else how will I be able to strike you in war?'

The Devi roared, "O nincompoop! You are afflicted by misplaced passion. If you cannot fight me, then you pick Kalika or Chamunda. Both are superior to you in duel. I shall only be an observer."

Then turning towards Kalika, she sneeringly added, "O Kalika! Shumbha wants to fight someone fierce and your nature is fierce. He is your kill."

Kalika attacked the daitya with her club. The no-holds-barred battle between the two turned brutal. Shumbha struck Kalika on her chest. Before the daitya could hit again, she severed his left hand with her axe and right with her sword. In the next minute, she cut off both his legs too.

Shumbha, without hands and legs, limped towards Kalika. Showing no mercy, she beheaded him with ease. Indra and the devas began singing hymns for Devi Chandika, Kalika and Chamunda. All the celestial beings joined them in worshipping the Devis.

The few fortunate asuras, who were still alive, threw away their weapons and prostrated in front of the Devis before fleeing away to Patalaloka.'

Vyasa said, 'O Janamejaya! Those who hear this anecdote of the glory of Devi are fortunate. Their wishes are fulfilled besides wealth and prosperity accruing to them. It also helps them shed fear from all kinds of enemies.'

King Suratha

With the wish to understand the subject more deeply, a joyous Janamejaya requested Vyasa to describe who the first worshippers of the Devi were and whom she blessed and offered boons.

Vyasa replied, 'During Svarochisha Manvantara, a king called Suratha ruled. Suratha was an honest, just, truthful and liberal king as well as an expert archer too.

As everything comes to an end, so did Suratha's reign when he was attacked by the mlechchhas. The mlechchha army comprising elephants, chariots, cavalry and infantry came with full force and destroyed the capital city of Kola.

Though the king's larger and stronger army fought bravely, the course of events at the battleground turned out to be in favour of the mlechchhas. It was partly because the mlechchha army was ruthless and partly because several of the king's ministers had defected.

Suratha decided to flee his kingdom and, after travelling alone on horseback, reached a dense forest. He was aware that Rishi Sumedha had his hermitage in the forest. The purposeless and directionless king headed towards the hermitage.

The hermitage was exceptionally serene and beautiful. It was surrounded by trees and blessed with the presence of domestic animals. The sweet chirping of birds could be heard as background noise. As soon as the king entered the hermitage, he saw young students chanting Vedic mantras in unison, which created an atmosphere full of positive energy.

The king left his horse to graze and approached the rishi sitting on a deerskin. Rishi Sumedha had an aura indicative of his long years of tapasya. He received the king with honour. Offering a mat made of kusha grass to sit on, he enquired about the objective of the king's visit.

The fatigued and despondent king prostrated to the rishi and explained to him what all had happened in the war and thereafter. He requested the rishi to give him refuge at the hermitage.

The rishi gave him protection and allowed him to stay at the hermitage. He, however, imposed two conditions; first, the king could not kill an animal in the precincts of the hermitage and second, he would have to sustain himself on natural food from the forest. Suratha accepted both conditions and began to spend his time in peace at the hermitage.

Once sitting under the shade of a tree, Suratha brooded over the plight of his subjects, his family, his staff and even his pet animals like horses and elephants suffering under the rule of mlechchhas. He visualised how his corrupt ministers and the new rulers must be busy splurging his honestly accumulated treasury.

While the king was pensive, a man passed by. He looked distraught. Suratha enquired from him about his antecedents and the reason for his worried look. The man told Suratha that he was Samaadhi and belonged to the vaishya business community. He had earned a lot of money but eventually his ever-greedy family drove him out of the house on the pretext of him being stingy.

The king sympathised with Samaadhi and asked him to stay with him at the hermitage.

Samaadhi accepted but said that he was constantly disturbed by the question if he would be able to see his family and relatives ever again. As a result, he could not achieve quietude even in a calm place like this.

The king also shared that he too had been constantly concerned about his kingdom though it was ruled by someone else. They both decided to seek the muni's guidance in the matter.

The muni granted them a patient hearing while they explained their individual woes that were causing anxiety and sleeplessness.

Sumedha, full of wisdom acquired through hard penance of several years, said, "Everyone in the bodily form is under the influence of Devi Maha Maya. She is the basis of this creation and, therefore, called Mula Prakriti. In her, the three gunas – Sattva, Rajas and Tamas – are in equilibrium with each other. She creates maya, the delusion, of the existence of this world. Each being, from gods to devas to celestial beings to humans and to asuras, is under the effect of maya.

She has no beginning and no end, she is therefore eternal. She is formless, the unmanifested, but assumes manifest forms whenever she desires to achieve the purposes of gods. She, the shakti or energy, is the cause of life of each living being. Fate and time, which govern the lives of all living beings including the devas, have no effect on her.

Brahma, Vishnu and Shiva are her creations too. In fact, she bestowed to the three a part of her energy as their respective spouses – Sarasvati to Brahma, Lakshmi to Vishnu and Uma to Shankar.

Let me narrate to you an anecdote from the times of yore to further explain.

Once Vishnu undertook tapasya for ten thousand years. Around the same time, Brahma also performed meditation. Coincidentally, they both got up from their meditation simultaneously. They both were on the move to another place away from the place of their meditation when they met each other.

Brahma had no memory of Vishnu. He told Vishnu that he was Brahma, the creator of this universe. He then asked Vishnu who he was.

Vishnu was annoyed with Brahma's impudence and told him that he was Vishnu and superior to Brahma as he was predominantly Sattva Guna whereas Brahma consisted of Rajo Guna. Vishnu asked Brahma whether he had forgotten that Vishnu had fought for him and saved his life from the two terrible daityas, Madhu and Kaitabha.

An argument broke out between the two on who was superior. In the meantime, Shiva's lingam, an infinitely long phallus, appeared before them. A celestial announcement told them not to argue with each other. It said that whoever was able to reach either end of the lingam, would be the superior of the two.

Vishnu opted to go down parallel to the lingam towards Patala and Brahma went up towards the sky. Both travelled for a long time but could not find the end of it. An exhausted Vishnu decided to return. He came back to the same place where he had met and had arguments with Brahma. He began to wait for Brahma's return.

Brahma continued his journey upwards. While he did not find the end of the lingam, he encountered a ketaki[162] flower falling down. He presumed that it must have dropped from the head of the lingam and, thus, the end of the phallus was not too far. He was satisfied with this thought and caught the flower.

He proudly returned with the flower in his hand and presented it to Vishnu. Brahma presented it as proof of having been till the end of the lingam claiming that he got it from the head of the lingam.

Vishnu was not satisfied with Brahma's claim and the proof of the ketaki flower. He demanded a witness. Brahma cunningly said that as the place was too far to get someone as a witness, let the flower be the testimony. He then asked Ketaki to respond to Vishnu.

The flower said, 'O Lord of preservation! I was at the top of Mahadeva's lingam. Brahma has brought me down here.'

Though Ketaki spoke nothing but the fact, her words had camouflaged the whole truth. Vishnu was not convinced and said he would only believe this if Shiva said the same to him.

Shiva had already been paying attention to what was going on and became angry with Ketaki for revealing the masked truth. He announced, 'O Ketaki! You have lied. You had fallen from my head and Brahma caught you while he was ascending. You shall, therefore, be forbidden to be offered to me.'

Since then, Ketaki flowers are never offered to Shiva."

Rishi Sumedha then explained to Suratha and Samaadhi the power of maya causing delusion of grandeur. He added that while Devi Maha Maya could delude even Brahma and Vishnu, she also liberated by bestowing true knowledge to those who are fortunate to worship her.

The king and the vaishya were inspired by the muni's words and decided to worship Devi Bhagvati. They received the nine-lettered mantra, *'Aum Mahishamardinyai Svaha'*, from the muni and learnt how to meditate. Thus, they began their asceticism by living in the same forest.

They spent all their time in meditation and got up from their tapasya once a day to eat and meet the muni. Months passed turning into a year and the king and the vaishya continued with their asceticism. Their one meal a day was reduced to only fruits during the day and finally they lived on tree leaves.

Another year passed when Devi Bhagvati appeared in their dream. Motivated by her appearance in their dream, they spent the third year in even more severe tapasya subsisting only on water. As there was no sign of the Devi appearing to them in person, they decided to sacrifice themselves. They made a triangular kunda, a pit, each and lighted it with fire.

The king sliced off flesh from his body and offered them to the fire. The vaishya followed suit. Then they offered their blood as an oblation.

Seeing them in that state when they both were willing to sacrifice their lives, the Devi appeared, appeased with their extreme tapasya and asked to seek boons.

They were ecstatic on seeing the Devi. Suratha said, "O Devi! Make me conquer my enemies and regain my kingdom."

The Devi said, "I am pleased with you and thus withdraw my power from your enemies. They will be weakened and you will be able to defeat them easily. Thereafter, you will rule for ten thousand years."

She also blessed Suratha that he would be reborn from Surya in his next birth and be known as Savarni Manu.

The Vaishya said, "I neither wish to go back to my family, wife and sons, nor I wish any wealth. All these are temporary. I wish to be blessed with real knowledge. I have no desire to engage in this world, the Samsara, again."

The Devi blessed him too and disappeared.'

At this point, vyasa felt that he needed to explain an important intricacy here. He said, 'I hope you appreciate the implications of the Devi's blessings to King Suratha. While she infused strength in the king, she also withdrew the same from his adversaries. Therefore, the sum of both effects needs to be taken into account to comprehend the outcome in totality.

Having been blessed by the Devi, the king sought leave of Rishi Sumedha and prepared for his journey back home. No sooner than he did so, he was amazed to see his former ministers, accompanied by a large number of citizens from his kingdom, entering the hermitage.

They told the king that the invaders turned out to be vicious and, therefore, people revolted against them and killed them all. The kingdom was free of enemies and awaited his return.

King Suratha took the blessings of the rishi and left the hermitage. He returned to be reunited with his family, relatives and subjects. Samaadhi, on the other hand, achieved knowledge and became free from all attachments. He roamed like a vagabond ascetic spreading the light of wisdom and singing the hymns about the greatness of the Devi.'

Vyasa concluded, 'O Janamejaya! The worshipping of the Devi yields the desired fruits for all, irrespective of the fruits in the realm of dharma, artha, kaam or moksha. It fulfils all desires.'

Vritranihantari

Janamejaya asked the muni, 'O Vyasa! You have narrated the anecdotes of Mahishasura and Shumbha and Nishumbha. There was another famed asura by the name of Vritrasura, the son of heavenly architect Vishvakarma. I know that he was also killed by the conniving Indra with Vishnu's support. But you hinted in your narration that the Devi killed Vritra. I am confused and want to know the truth about the killing of the asura.'

Vyasa was happy with Janamejaya's intervention. He said affectionately to the king, 'O Son of Parikshit! You are a fortunate soul who has the opportunity to hear the Devi Purana. I am happy that you are paying excellent attention to my recitation. I am also delighted to note your growing devotion to it and eye for detail to understand the nuances of Devi Bhagavatam. Hearing of this Maha Purana with piety is akin to devas receiving nectar.

Let me now explain why I said that Vritra was killed by Devi Bhagvati.

Indra killed Vritra by deceit. Indra had entered into an agreement of peace with the asura, which earned him Vritra's trust and friendship.

But before killing Vritra, Indra killed his brother Trishira. Then, he obtained the help of Vishnu who entered his thunderbolt and killed Vritrasura. As you will remember, though Indra had sattva qualities, he was under Devi Maha Maya's influence which deluded him.

It is this influence that causes ahamkara and possessiveness for all. It leads one to believe that the mortal body, wealth, property, family, wife and sons are his own and forgets the transitory nature of everyone and everything.

Indra and Vishnu were, thus, under the influence of maya. This led them to kill Vritra. At the same time, the

Devi had withdrawn her blessings from the asura. But, despite this, Indra was made to pay an enormous price for committing this hideous act[163] .

Being the architect of heaven, Vishvakarma was considered superior to the other devas. He was widely respected. But within his heart, he had harboured enmity against Indra.

He decided to create a son superior to Indra and produced a handsome Trishira Vishvarupa. This deva son had three faces: one to study the Vedas, second to drink honey and with the third, he could see in all directions. Trishira, right from the inception, had no interest in worldly affairs and became an ascetic renouncing all the comforts of his father's palace.

He undertook severe penances. He hung himself upside down from a tree branch and practised Panchagni[164] tapasya during summers and remained in cold water during winters. Moreover, he did not eat any food.

Indra became insecure and worried when he saw Trishira performing such penances and able to control all his senses. He thought that Trishira would turn so powerful with his tapasya that he might replace him one day. Thinking of such an eventuality, he began to concoct plans to hinder Trishira's tapasya.

Indra summoned his trusted and most beautiful apsaras including Urvashi, Menaka, Rambha, Ghritachi and Tilottama. He asked them to go to Trishira and ignite his lust by all means of seduction so that his tapasya could be obstructed.

The apsaras used every trick in their book of Kaamshastra, from gestures to singing and dancing, to lure Trishira, but nothing worked. They failed miserably to even catch his attention. They returned without success but were thankful that Trishira did not curse them.

Left with no other option, an anxious Indra rode his elephant Airavata to Trishira's palace with the intention to kill him. He witnessed Trishira in meditational pose and realised that Trishira's body had turned effulgent, emitting light like the sun. Seeing this, Indra's worries were aggravated. He struck his unbeatable thunderbolt and the next moment, Trishira's body fell lifelessly.

Though Trishira had been killed, his corpse was lustrous as if he was still alive. Indra's fear had not dissipated. He took a woodcutter from nearby, by the name of Taksha, and requested him to chop off the three heads from the body of dead Trishira.

The woodcutter was first annoyed with Indra and tried to skirt his request. He told Indra that his axe was not big enough to perform the task. He also argued that Trishira was dead anyway and Indra should not compound the heinous crime by cutting off the heads of this great ascetic.

But Indra insisted and said that he did not want to take any chances and wanted to doubly ensure that Trishira was dead. He argued that dharma had prescribed that an enemy must be killed.

Indra then made an alluring offer to Taksha. "I will give you a share from each sacrifice from now on if you perform my task. You will be offered the head of the animals killed in a sacrifice."

The offer was too lucrative for Taksha to be rejected and he did as told by Indra.

The moment Taksha cut off the heads, three species of birds came out of them - kapinjala[165] from the head that used to study the Vedas, kalavinka[166] from the one used to drink honey and tittiri[167] from the head used to see in all directions.

Thus, a satisfied Indra and a happy Taksha returned to their respective homes.'

Vyasa paused for a moment to let the words sink in. He began again, 'O King! The effect of Maha Maya on

Indra's mind was so strong that it did not occur to him even once that he was guilty of brahmahatya[168].

On the other hand, Vishvakarma was enraged when he came to know that Indra had killed his son. He was even more indignant because Trishira had not offended Indra in any way. He decided to create another son capable of killing Indra. He initiated a sacrificial fire and recited mantras from the Atharva Veda for eight nights when a handsome and lustrous man emerged out of the fire. He looked like the fire itself.

Vishvakarma ordered him to grow big immediately and he became immense like a mountain. He looked at his despondent father and said, "O Father! The objective of my existence is to remove your sorrows. Kindly tell me the reason of your grief. If it helps to alleviate your grief, I could drink the ocean or destroy the mountain or stop the rising of the sun or even kill Indra and devas."

His son's words acted like a balm on Vishvakarma's wounds. He could not hide his pleasure and named him Vritra.

He then told the entire episode of the killing of his brother Trishira by Indra and unhesitatingly said, "I want you to kill Indra."

Vishvakarma, the designer and architect of devas, then crafted special weapons and armour for his son to equip him to kill Indra. He also created a chariot capable of moving at the speed of wind.

Vishvakarma performed the Svastyayana[169] ceremony for his son who left in the specially designed chariot to kill Indra. Hearing about Vritra's decision to kill Indra, the daityas, who had been earlier decimated by devas and were waiting to take revenge, also joined him.

Indra's scouts informed him of Vishvakarma creating Vritra through the Abhichara[170] mechanism and his impending attack on Devaloka at his father's instructions.

Indra called for an urgent meeting of the devas. The meeting noted all the inauspicious signs that had been taking place in the Devaloka in recent times. The crying of crows, vultures, herons and falcons, the shedding of tears by elephants and horses, the heart-rending sounds of the weeping of dark spirits in the night and the falling of flags without any blowing wind were all indications of something ominous. So much so that jackals were entering the premises of deva houses and screeching in the night along with lizards roaming freely inside the houses.

Indra was concerned. He asked Guru Brihaspati for advice. Brihaspati pensively spoke, "O Husband of Sachi! Those who trouble others, cannot be at peace and happy with themselves. Though you have killed the innocent Brahmin Trishira under the effect of maya, you have nevertheless earned bad karma. Vritra's coming to kill you seems to be the result of your karma. Vishvakarma had not only created Vritra as invincible for devas, but also equipped him with divine weapons. I feel that Vritra's death is unlikely any time soon."

As Brihaspati was articulating these words, Vritra advanced towards Devaloka, causing non-warrior celestial beings to flee to save their lives. Indra ordered an immediate attack. He himself mounted Airavata and led his army.

Vritra, accompanied by his asura forces, approached the divine lake, Manasarovara, in the high Himalayas from the northern side and met with the deva forces. An unrestrained war broke out, which lasted for one hundred years. With no end to the war in sight, the devas gradually began to take flight starting with Varuna followed by Vayu, Yama, Surya, Chandra and finally Indra himself.

Vritra, victorious in the war, returned to his father's abode and shared the great news that he had been waiting for. He presented Indra's elephant Airavata to Vishvakarma.

Vishvakarma was thrilled. He said, "I laud you my son as you have unburdened me today. But I warn you not to trust anybody, especially the wicked Indra. He is capable of hitting back with his crafty schemes. You should perform tapasya as it will bring you the desired prosperity, vigour and victories in wars. Go and perform austerities for Brahma to receive his boons and then kill deplorable Indra who is guilty of brahmahatya."

Heeding his father's counsel, Vritra went to Gandhamadan mountain and began the austerities. Seated on a mat of kusha grass, he first left food and then water too. He continued in the yogic position meditating on Brahma.

Indra was worried about Vritra's tapasya. He sent several celestial beings, such as gandharvas, yakshas, kinnaras, vidyadharas and apsaras to divert him from his meditation but nothing yielded the results that Indra wanted. Vritra continued to perform his asceticism without getting diverted.

After about a hundred years, Brahma was pleased. He came to Vritra and asked him to seek boons. There was no end to Vritra's joy. He bowed down with humility in front of the creator and asked what other demons before him had not thought of.

He spoke, "O Brahma! I wish that no weapon made of iron or wood or bamboo or wet or dry substance or any other weapon should cause my death. I gain more strength with each battle and, therefore, become invincible for the devas."

Brahma smiled at the intelligent and well-thought-of wish by Vritra. He granted Vritra the boons and disappeared.

Vritra informed Vishvakarma about Brahma's boon to him who said to him, "A son is truly a son if he follows the directions of his father, offers pindadaan at Gaya and feeds brahmins on his father's shraadh[171] after his father's death.

O Son! I am still tormented by the thought of Indra killing my sinless and ascetic son Trishira and I want you to kill the vicious Indra."

Vritra, hearing the desire of his father, again declared war on Indra. Once again, the asuras joined his army. Confident with Brahma's boon, Vritra led his army to invade Devaloka with the beating of war drums and blowing of conch shells.

The devas also geared up for the imminent war. An expert in warfare, Indra configured the army in Gridhra Vyuha[172]. But Vritra stormed into the formation and a terrible battle ensued. Both sides struck with all possible weapons.

The battle peaked causing din and anger on both sides. Vritra, getting furious by the minute, picked up Indra, stripped him of his arms and clothes and swallowed him.

The devas were terrified. Not knowing what to do, they ran back to Brihaspati and informed him what had transpired. They requested him to make use of his power of mantras or Abhichara[173] and save Indra.

Brihaspati closed his eyes and, as if visualising Indra in his thoughts, said, "Indra has been swallowed, but he is still alive inside Vritra. Let us do something to get him released from Vritra's mouth."

Then, as advised by Brihaspati, the devas together created a state of a yawn, an irresistible reflex. They immediately applied it on Vritra and his mouth opened wide. Seeing the mouth open suddenly, Indra collected himself and jumped out of the mouth of the asura.'

Vyasa blinked smilingly and said, 'O King! That was the first yawn in the world.'

He continued, 'The war began once again and this time lasted an Ajuta.[174] But Vritra had the boon that he would be more powerful with each battle. He, therefore, grew in strength during the course of the war. On the other hand, the devas became fatigued and thus enervated. Finally, the devas lost and fled.

Vritra took over the privileges and assets of Devaloka and began to enjoy the heavenly pleasures. He also started getting a share in the yagnas and sacrifices. Vishvakarma was extremely happy.

After some time, the devas reunited and went to consult Mahadeva at Mount Kailash. Mahadeva suggested that they should take Brahma and go to Vaikuntha to meet Sri Hari Jagannath.

As advised, they arrived at the abode of Vishnu and worshipped him with his favourite hymns. Vishnu was pleased. Looking at their distressed faces, Sri Hari asked the devas the motive of their visit.

The devas requested Vishnu to find a solution to this evil problem.

Vishnu said, "Brahma's boon has made Vritra unconquerable. Therefore, instead of waging a war, you ought to use other wise methods.

Go to Vritra and make peace with him. Do accept whatever conditions Vritra may impose to achieve peace. Gradually gain his faith and cultivate a deep friendship with him. When there is an opportune time coinciding with the end of his longevity, find an opportunity to kill him. I will be happy to help Indra in killing Vritra by entering into his thunderbolt."

After Vishnu had finished, one of them asked if the advice given by Vishnu was not equal to an act of betrayal and deceit.

Vishnu spoke again, "Deceit is a part of the stratagem used against a powerful enemy like Vritra who cannot be killed by ordinary means. No sin is committed when deceit is used in such circumstances. I too used deceit when I incarnated as a dwarf to fight Bali.

The time has also come for you to pray to Devi Maha Maya with the highest devotion. If she is appeased, she will delude Vritra thereby helping your cause. She had helped me in the same way when I meditated upon her during the fight with Madhu and Kaitabha. She deluded the two asuras and I was successful in killing them easily using a pretext."

The devas left for Mount Meru and began to meditate upon Devi Bhagvati. They chanted hymns in praise of the creatrix, preservatrix and destructrix of the world, the most merciful and the bestower of all desires.

Pleased with their devotion, the Devi appeared before the devas in her most gorgeous form and asked what did they want.

The devas spoke, "O Mother! We have been advised by Sri Hari to befriend Vritra. Do help us in deluding him and gaining his trust."

The Devi simply said, "That will be done," and disappeared.

A group of devas accompanied by devarishis[175] was constituted to see Vritra at his abode. They arrived there to find him engaged in meditation and his body emitting an aura that was suggestive of his prowess to be able to burn the three worlds and capable of devouring the devas.

Speaking in their sweetest words, they said, "O Lord of the asuras! Peace brings prosperity. Currently, devas, asuras and humans have no peace because everyone is constantly living under the fear of another war looming large due to continuing enmity between you and Indra. Therefore, we propose that both of you join hands in peace and amity. In order to do so, both of you should take a pratigya[176] and Indra would do it on the conditions obligated by you. It will bring calm and happiness for all."

Initially, Vritra resisted as he did not trust Indra but when the devarishis assured their backing for the treaty between both of them, he acquiesced. However, Vritra imposed a condition, reinforcing Brahma's boon, "Knowing the nature of Indra, you make sure that Indra does not kill me during day or night, nor with a dry or liquid substance, nor with a weapon made of wood, stone or any other solid material, nor with his thunderbolt."

The peace treaty between Indra and Vritra was sealed. Indra joined Vritra and began to live with him spending their time together, be it in heaven's Nandana Garden or in the hermitage at Gandhamadan mountain. As time passed, Vritra's trust in Indra grew whereas Indra continued to look for his shortcomings in order to find a way to kill him.

Vishvakarma learnt of the peace between the two and summoned his son. He cautioned Vritra, "If you had an enmity with someone, you should never place your trust in the same person. Indra is your foe and cannot be trusted because he is vicious, greedy, covetous, envious and insecure of others' positive attributes."

But Vritra had developed such affection and confidence in Indra that he did not heed the sane advice of his father.

Indra did not have to wait for too long for the fateful day to arrive. One evening, Vritra was taking a stroll at the beach. Seeing the dusk time, Indra recalled the conditions imposed by Brahma's boon on the killing of the asura; it was neither day nor night.

Indra, in his mind, chanted the name of Sri Hari who had promised him to enter his thunderbolt. Vishnu did oblige Indra immediately. Vritra was alone there and time was ripe but Indra still dallied thinking of his invincible power. While his mind was still contemplating, Indra saw the mountain of foam on the water. The foam cleared all his doubts instantly as it was neither liquid nor dry.

He paid obeisance to the Devi who permeated her energy into the foam along with the presence of Vishnu in the thunderbolt. Indra struck Vritra with his thunderbolt surrounded by the foam, killing him instantaneously. The body of Vritra fell on the wet beach like a mountain had been hit by an earthquake.

As Devi Bhagvati was instrumental in the killing of Vritra by first deluding him and then by energising the foam, she is also praised as "Vritranihantri", the slayer of Vritra. But, of course, the act was commissioned through Indra.'

Nahusha

Vyasa continued the anecdote, 'Indra returned to Devaloka and began to rule again. Peace returned to the universe but not to Indra's mind. He was constantly worried about the consequences of killing not one but two brahmins or two brahmahatyas; both the sons of Vishvakarma. The devarishis, who had always supported Indra as the personification of Sattva Guna and had forged the peace treaty between him and Vritra, pronounced him as sinful and that too with Vishnu's full complicity.

Vishvakarma was outraged to learn of this crooked and unpardonable act by Indra. He performed the last rites for Vritra and, in the same temper, cursed that since Indra had broken his oath and killed his son, fate would wreak extreme sufferings on him too.'

Janamejaya asked, 'What happened to Indra then?'

Vyasa was unfazed as he knew that destiny was inevitable. He said, 'As I had said earlier, fate takes its own course. The fruits of one's actions, whether auspicious or inauspicious, have to be faced. It is also true that when fate is in your favour, all the forces in the universe support you, just as Vishnu and Devi Maha Maya did to Indra to kill Vritra.

On the contrary, when it is unfavourable, everyone leaves you to your own, be it friends, family or advisors. The same happened to Indra when he underwent the ignominy and agony of brahmahatya.

Indra became a subject of jibes by munis and other people behind his back. But he was aware of these. It made him even more disturbed. He preferred to stay in his abode and stopped interacting with anyone. He felt that he had lost his sheen and knowledge.

Seeing her husband depressed and in fear, Indra's wife Sachi spoke to him, "O my lord! You have killed your most dreadful enemy yet you do not seem to be happy. I have noticed that you are constantly being withdrawn and fretful. What is the cause of it?"

Indra told her, "Since committing brahmahatya, I have not been able to find peace. The heavenly pleasures of this beautiful city, Nandana Garden, the exquisite trees including Kalpavriksha[177], the enchanting apsaras, the Kamdhenu cow and even you, Sachi, none appeals to me anymore."

The miserable Indra left his abode without informing anyone and went to Lake Manasarovara. There he entered the tubular shoot of a lotus flower and began to live like a snake trying to save his life in hibernation.

Indra's absence affected not only Devaloka, as it was left without its king, but also humans on earth as there was no rain. The rivers became dry and crops of grains, fruits and vegetables began to fail. There was anarchy everywhere.

The devas convened a meeting and decided to nominate Nahusha as the king in the absence of any news of Indra. Nahusha took over the throne of heavens and soon got infected by excessive Rajo Guna. He spent most of his time in carnal pleasures.

One day, he happened to see Sachi and became obsessed with the desire to possess her. He spoke to his advisors and the devarishis, "I have replaced Indra as the king. Therefore, his wife Sachi should be my wife."

The devas and devarishis tried to talk Nahusha out of his malicious desire, "O King of kings! Having illegitimate relations with someone's wife is prohibited according to the prescribed treaties. As Sachi is the chaste wife of Indra who is alive, she cannot become your wife."

But Nahusha was adamant. The devas informed Sachi who went to Guru Brihaspati and sought refuge. Brihaspati consoled her, "Stay at my hermitage comfortably, O Queen!

The one who forsakes one's refuge suffers for eternity. I shall never do so."

When Nahusha learnt of Brihaspati sheltering Sachi, he became angry. He threatened to kill the guru of the devas. The devas tried to convince him. They told him that he was the king of heavens and, therefore, the protector of religion and regulations. He couldn't behave in such an unreasonable manner.

They offered him to take any other woman or any apsara, all more beautiful and virtuous than the other.

Nahusha argued, "It is said that one should practise what one preaches. Where was this advice of yours when Indra and Chandra took away the wife of Gautama and that of Brihaspati respectively," and he insisted on Indrani coming to him.

The devas and devarishis, having failed to persuade Nahusha, went to see Brihaspati and requested him to let Sachi go. He stood firm on his words given to Indrani and refused to part with her. Fearful of Nahusha's anger, they asked the guru for his counsel.

Brihaspati thought about the problem and concluded that in the present circumstances, the best way would be to buy time from Nahusha. He said, "Let Sachi go to him and consent to marry him with the precondition that first it had to be ascertained if her present husband Indra was no more. Thereafter, she should make an all-out attempt to find Indra."

The devas went back with Sachi and the plan to Nahusha who was lustfully awaiting her. When Sachi proposed the condition, Nahusha accepted it.

Sachi returned to convene an assembly of devas and asked for their assistance in locating Indra. They all, led by Brihaspati, decided to meet the omniscient Vishnu and tell him about the problem.

Vishnu knew where Indra was. He said, "You will find Indra hibernating in Lake Manasarovara. You should go to him and ask him to undertake the Ashvamedha Yagna to please Devi Bhagvati. If she were pleased, she will destroy the most heinous sin of brahmahatya committed by Indra. And tell Sachi to worship the Devi too. When it is time, Devi Maha Maya will delude Nahusha appropriately."

As told by Vishnu, they found Indra in the debilitated condition in the lotus shoot in Lake Manasarovara. They comforted him and then convinced him to perform the sacrifice. Indra did as advised and was absolved of his sin. He, however, continued in the same place as he had been considerably weakened and demotivated.

On the other hand, Sachi worshipped the Devi with devotion and asceticism daily. The most gracious and most beautiful Devi was appeased and appeared before her. She asked Sachi what she desired.

Sachi, overwhelmed with joy, said, "O Mother Bhagvati! I wish to see the return of my husband and he regaining the title of the king of Devaloka. Also, I want to be rid of Nahusha whose trepidation looms large on me all the time."

The Devi blessed her, "So be it."

She then gave Sachi her duti, the messenger, and told Sachi to go with her duti to Lake Manasarovara where she would find one of Devi's idols known by the name of Vishvakama. There Sachi would also find Indra. In the meantime, the Devi would delude Nahusha so that he was forced to step down from the lordship of the heavens.

Sachi reached the lake and found Indra hiding there. Indra was amazed to see his wife and wondered how she was able to find him. Sachi told him about worshipping the Devi and receiving information about Indra as well as her assurance to deceive Nahusha. She also briefed him on Nahusha's stubbornness to take her as his consort.

Indra patiently heard her and told her to stay put and be patient till he found an opportune moment to return.

Sachi was annoyed. She reasoned with Indra, "Do you think it is possible for me? This man Nahusha is arrogant, lustful and beyond any reasoning. Though I managed to buy time thus far with the help of Brihaspati, I do not think Brihaspati would be able to withstand the pressures of the vicious and fake king for long."

An intelligent Indra considered various options and finally came up with a stratagem to dispense with Nahusha and his rule of Devaloka. He explained the plan to Sachi. She understood its nuances and gladly accepted it.

Thinking of the Supreme Goddess and chanting her mantra in her heart, she returned to Nahusha. She told him that she had no hope left to find Indra and, therefore, had come back to Nahusha.

Nahusha was ecstatic to hear this. Unable to control himself, he said, "O one with thin waist! I have no words to describe my joy. Let us get married the soonest."

Sachi enticingly said, "All my desires will be fulfilled by receiving you as my husband. But I have one small wish."

Sachi wanted to be extremely sure that Nahusha would do what she and Indra had planned. She kept steering him in the direction where he was bound to accede to whatever she imposed.

After a lot of adulation, she got Nahusha to swear on his words. Then she said, "Each deva has his own conveyance. But you as the king of devas have none. I want that you should be uniquely placed among them. Therefore, when you come to marry me, you should have munis and devarishis as your vehicle. This will elevate your stature to the highest level among the devas and munis."

Nahusha, deluded by Devi Maha Maya, thought that Sachi genuinely wished for his welfare and success as the highest king and most superior ascetic. He agreed to her suggestion.

He summoned all the munis and told them about Indrani's desire. He respectfully requested them to help him achieve it. They found the request to be disgusting but, considering this as a misfortune written by fate, they accepted it.

On the appointed day, Nahusha sat on a beautiful open palanquin crafted with gems and precious stones. It was carried by a battery of munis, each one of whom was capable of changing the destiny of the world on his own.

An excited Nahusha kept saying "sarpa, sarpa" signifying "move fast, move fast". In his heightened craving to marry Sachi, he even nudged the munis by his feet and, as if this was not enough, he whipped Agastya and prodded him to move quickly. The rishi was famed for not only demolishing the dreadful Asura Vatapi and drinking the ocean in one go but also his temper.

As "sarpa" also meant a "snake", Agastya, out of extreme annoyance and indignation, cursed him, "O Nahusha! As you have been repeating 'sarpa, sarpa,' you will turn into a terrible snake on earth. You will be released after several Ajutas when you will hear the words of wisdom from King Yudhisthira."

The turn of fate had gone against Nahusha. He got down off the palanquin and began to chant hymns to Agastya and other munis to please them. But it was too late. He fell to earth and turned into a snake.

No sooner than the news of this incident spread, Brihaspati went to Lake Manasarovara and informed Indra. Later the devas and munis too joined him. They motivated Indra to return and placed him on the throne of heaven.'

Vyasa added, 'Thus, Indra suffered the consequences of his karma but was remitted from it by the blessings of the Devi.'

Maharishi Vashishtha

Janamejaya was extremely pleased with the narration. He prayed to the Devi and asked Vyasa, 'O Son of Satyavati! Indra performed the Ashvamedha sacrifice and redeemed himself. He returned to Devaloka to assume the sovereignty. But why did he have to desert the kingship and suffer?'

Vyasa responded, 'O Scion of the Kuru family! I explained to you earlier about three types of karma. The eternal sages say that these are: Sanchita, Bhavishya and Prarabdha. Some term the Bhavishya Karma as Agami[178] or Vartamana[189] but they are the same. These are further subdivided into Saattvika, Rajasika and Tamasika.

The effects of one's karma get registered and form Sanchita. At the time of one's birth, a part of the Sanchita Karma that is ripe for fructification in that incarnation is called Prarabdha. The balance is carried forward and is settled in subsequent births.

This process of accumulation and expending of karmas, auspicious or inauspicious, good or bad, is true for all embodied beings including Brahma, Vishnu, Mahesh, devas, asuras, humans, yakshas, gandharvas and kinnaras. No one is immune to it irrespective of the period of their life span.

As the combination of sinful Sanchit Karma turned into Prarabdha when Indra committed brahmahatya, he had to suffer disgrace and pain.

While the qualities of people change with the change in yuga, there is an overall character of a particular yuga, called Yuga Dharma. It means that in Satya Yuga people had the dominant trait of dharma or religion. In the Treta Yuga, people mainly pursued dharma and artha. During the Dvapara Yuga, dharma, artha and kaam took prevalence. However, in the Kali Yuga, artha and kaam are dominant.'

Janamejaya had more queries. He asked, 'Where did the pious people of previous yugas go? And what will happen to the wicked people of Kali Yuga?'

Vyasa replied, 'People who performed virtuous acts, such as truthfulness, compassion, charity, faithfulness, non-covetousness, in earlier yugas rose to the level of heaven or Devaloka. They incarnated as high-souled devas or other celestial beings. They spent time in those incarnations and will return to take birth as humans or animals on earth when Satya Yuga begins again.

However, those who conduct wicked and malicious acts in Kali Yuga will have to suffer in hell and remain there till the end of the yuga. They will keep on incarnating back on earth during each Kali Yuga. This vicious cycle is broken only when they perform auspicious acts, which will upgrade them to be born in Dvapara Yuga. Similarly, those born in Dvapara Yuga take birth in Treta Yuga based on their virtuous karma. The same is true for those in Treta Yuga to be able to take birth in Satya Yuga. The cycle moves the other way around if one performs vicious karma.

The Yuga Dharma tends to prevail over the best of souls. For instance, Kali, the master of Kali Yuga, caused pain and problems for your father Parikshit. As a result, his mind was deluded and he insulted a muni. It is the nature of Kali to breed adharma.

As Kali moves forward, you will find men to be untruthful and wicked. Women will be lustful, rapacious and boorish. Our nature is also affected by the kind of food we take. More saattvika food clears one's mind and helps in observing dharma.'

Janamejaya became concerned and asked, 'O Muni! What is the way out of it?'

Vyasa explained, 'In the age of Kali Yuga, keeping good company and listening to the Vedas are certainly important. But meditating on Devi Maha Maya is the only way to steer oneself out of Kali Yuga. Chanting her name with devotion atones one's sins. Even if one chants her name unintentionally, one can achieve unimaginable fruits.

People recite the Gayatri Mantra without appreciating the complete significance of it, due to the effect of maya. This mantra signifies veneration to the Devi and its chanting ushers one's soul to liberation.'

Janamejaya asked Vyasa, 'Kindly enlighten me about pilgrimages and holy rivers? How should one undertake a journey to the places of pilgrimage and what rituals are prescribed for that?'

Vyasa said, 'Hundreds of rivers exist on earth. Out of these, the rivers that flow into the ocean are considered holy, while the others are considered less holy. In the former category, the rivers with a substantial flow throughout the year are considered holier. During the months of Shravana and Bhadra, the months during which the land of Bharat receives monsoon, the rivers receive much more water on account of rains and they overflow as if they are menstruating.

The principal rivers considered holy are Ganga, Yamuna, Sarasvati, Narmada, Gandaki, Sindhu, Gomati, Tamasa, Kaveri, Chandrahaga, Punya, Vetravati, Charmanvati, Sarayu, Tapi and Sabarmati.

The sacred places of pilgrimage are Pushkar, Kurukshetra, Dharmaranya, Prabhas, Prayaga, Naimisaranya and Arbudaranya. Similarly, there are mountains that are considered sacred. These are Shrishaila, Meru and Gandhamadan. Besides, Manasarovara, the lakes of Vindusarovara and Aksoda are also holy.

There are some hermitages that are more sacred than others, such as Badrikashram followed by Vamanashram and Shatayupashram. There are several other hermitages that are known by the name of the muni who performed tapasya there.

The Devi is worshipped in all these places. Just visiting these pilgrimages and complying with asceticism and observing vows are not enough to achieve the desired fruits. Dravya Shuddhi[180], Kriya Shuddhi[181] and Chitta Shuddhi[182] have to be performed too.

One should remember that travelling to pilgrimages can bring one into contact with undesirable people as well as lead to forsaking one's daily duties. Therefore, such journeys could culminate in accruing sins rather than earning good results. It is also said that if one follows one's duties and observes non-violence, truthfulness, non-stealing, purity of mind and heart and control of senses, then one can earn the same fruits as through pilgrimages.

While one can purify the bodies by the water in such pilgrimages, the water cannot clean the dirt in one's mind. Thus, the most difficult of all the shuddhis is Chitta Shuddhi. As you know, the mind is the most difficult to control. Therefore, purifying it by getting rid of lust, greed, anger and ahamkara is a challenge.

It is not easy to achieve even for seers who are the most knowledgeable. Without Chitta Shuddhi, visiting pilgrimages or taking a bath in holy waters or performing tapasya or doing charities will not bear any fruit. Chitta Shuddhi can be achieved through shraddha[183]. It is of three kinds too: Saattvika, Tamasika and Rajasika. It is Saattvika Shraddha, though rare, that fetches the best results.

As I said earlier, the holy water does not make a difference. Take the example of the great sage Vashishtha, the mind-born son of Brahma and an expert on the Vedas. He lived on the banks of River Ganga. He had enmity with another renowned seer, Vishvamitra, and both fought a bitter battle.'

Vyasa discerned curiosity written on the king's face and continued with the narration. 'Long before Sri Rama, a

Suryavanshi king by the name of Harishchandra reigned. He was Trishanku's son.

Harishchandra had no children. He made a vow to Varuna Deva, the lord of water and oceans, "If I am blessed with a son, I will perform Naramedha[184]."

It meant that he would sacrifice his son to Varuna. Varuna was pleased and in due time, the king's wife was pregnant. The king performed all the pre-delivery ceremonies and a beautiful son was born.

As soon as the festivities to celebrate the child's birth concluded, Varuna came to the palace guised as a brahmin. Unaware of his real identity, the king welcomed him. Varuna then revealed to the king his real identity and said that he had come to take the king's son as he had vowed.

The king was dejected. He was bound by the pledge but he did not want to part with his son. Deciding to buy time, the king said he would do as promised as soon as the boy's mother is out of her Sutak[185] period of one month.

Varuna, assured by the king's words, went away. Meanwhile, the boy was named Rohitashva or Rohit for short.

After the month was over, Varuna came back in the same guise as before. This time too, the king was reluctant to fulfil his vow.

This time Harishchandra gave another excuse, "Rohit is an infant. He will be treated like a child only after Chudakarana ceremony. Therefore, O Deva, kindly wait till that is over and I shall sacrifice him to you."

When Varuna turned up after the Chudakarana ceremony, the king came up with yet another plea. He said, "The boy has been born in the kshatriya family. He will be purified when he undergoes the Upanayana ceremony at the age of eleven. Till he is purified, he serves no purpose in a sacrifice."

Varuna again went back and returned at the time of the Upanayana ceremony. The king had yet another trick up his sleeve and said, "My son is now fit to be sacrificed but ifVaruna allows, I will perform a grand sacrifice as soon as he undergoes the Samavartan[186] ceremony."

This time Varuna clearly understood the king's intentions. But he accepted it with a final warning to him.

Rohit emerged as a brilliant student in all the streams of his studies. As he grew up, he learnt about his father's vow of sacrificing him to Varuna. To escape from being sacrificed, Rohit fled the kingdom and went to live in caves under the mountains.

Once again, Varuna came at the due time of the Samavartan ceremony. This time, the king told Varuna that he did not know where his son was since he had fled out of panic.

Varuna became furious. He cursed the king, "You have been deceiving me for too long. Let your body be afflicted by dropsy[187]."

The disease tormented the king. Rohit learnt about his father's condition and prepared to return to help his ailing father.

While he was on his way, he met Indra who had taken the guise of a brahmin. In his innocence, Rohit narrated his story to Indra. However, Indra discouraged him to return to his father.

Misguided by Indra's advice under the effect of maya, Rohit changed his mind and continued to stay in the cave. Whenever he thought of returning, Indra would talk him out of the idea.

Vashishtha, the family guru, came to visit the king when he heard about his extreme suffering. The king asked him if there was a remedy for his affliction.

Vashishtha suggested that the king could buy a brahmin boy and sacrifice him in lieu of Rohit. This would satisfy Varuna and, hence, the king would be cured.

The king ordered his ministers to find a suitable boy and offer his parents whatever they demanded. A thorough search began in the whole kingdom and ended with a penurious and greedy brahmin called Ajigarta. This brahmin agreed to sell Shunahshepa, the second of his three sons, in lieu of a hundred cows.

Elaborate arrangements were made for the sacrificial ceremony of the boy. When the ceremony began, Maharishi Vishvamitra's heart melted seeing the young Shunahshepa wailing with tears. He appealed to the king to spare the brahmin boy in accordance with the dharma of kshatriya kings. He assured the king that this act of compassion would not go waste.

The king was in pain and did not listen to Vishvamitra's counsel. The maharishi was miffed with the king and decided to give the Varuna Mantra to Shunahshepa. When the panic-stricken boy recited this mantra, it appeased Varuna. He arrived at the ceremony and freed the boy of the sacrificial captivity and also the king from the disease.

Though his objective was achieved, Vishvamitra bore a grudge against the king for not listening to him. In his annoyance, he disguised himself as a brahmin and met the king when he was passing by in a forest. He tricked the king to part with his kingdom and all the wealth.

When the family guru Vashishtha learnt of this, he detested Vishvamitra's act. In a subsequent chance meeting between both of them, he cursed Vishvamitra, "O kshatriya-turned-muni! You deceived Harishchandra to satisfy your false vanity. Since you behaved in a manner of a baka[188], you will be born as one."

Vishvamitra was enraged to hear the curse. He in turn cursed Vashishtha, "For as long as I will be a crane, you shall be a sarali[189]."

The two accomplished seers were thus born as birds near Lake Manasarovara, yet they remained hostile to each other. Both built their nests on different trees near the lake.

They fought daily with their beaks and talons making awful high-pitched shrieks. They continued to fight, bleeding each other, for an Ajuta.

Eventually, Brahma, joined by all the suras, came and negotiated peace between them, freeing them from their curses. Later Brahma also brokered the friendship between them.'

Vyasa paused to lay special emphasis on what he was about to say. He said, 'So you know now that Vashishtha, son of Mitra-Varuna, fought for so long just to satisfy his ahamkara. When such excellent sages cannot bring their ahamkara under control, how can we expect devas, asuras and ordinary mortals to do so?'

Janamejaya immediately interjected Veda Vyasa. He said, 'You just mentioned Maharishi Vashishtha as son of Mitra-Varuna. But he was the mind-born son of Brahma.'

Vyasa was happy with Janamejaya's attentiveness and said, 'He was, but he was also obliged to take a second body. He is, therefore, also known as Maitra-Varuni.'

The king could not stop from asking, 'I am confused, O Muni! Kindly explain this to me.'

Vyasa replied, 'King Nimi was the twelfth son born to the Suryavanshi king Ikshvaku. He was handsome, righteous, knowledgeable, just and loved by his subjects. He believed in truth and charities.

He created for himself a city called Jayantapur, near the hermitage of Rishi Gautama, and lived there to serve the brahmins. While continuing to do so, a thought crossed his mind that he should perform a yagna. He wanted it to last for a long time, during which he wished to give copious alms.

His father consented to the yagna. Nimi sent invites to the most accomplished seers to perform the sacrifices. Bhrigu, Angira, Vamadeva, Gautama, Vashishtha, Pulastya, Richika, Pulaha, Kratu and many others were invited with due honours.

Nimi requested Vashishtha, the family priest, to lead the yagna as he had resolved to perform the sacrifice for five thousand years and venerate Devi Ambika.

Vashishtha replied, "O Son of Ikshvaku! I would have gladly undertaken to execute your sacrifice, but I have committed to Indra to accomplish a sacrifice on his behalf for five hundred years. So, you will have to wait till I conclude Indra's yagna."

Nimi retorted,"I have already made all the preparations and invited everyone. Moreover, you are our family priest and performing my yagna is your primary responsibility."

But his arguments and goading did not cut ice with Vashishtha. Left with no choice, the king invited another priest, Rishi Gautama, to perform the task. The sacrifice began and Nimi continued to give generous alms to all the brahmins who took part in it.

Meanwhile, after completing Indra's sacrifice, Vashishtha returned. He wanted to see the king but the king happened to be sleeping at that time. Vashishtha waited for long but the king's attendants did not inform the sleeping king about the muni's visit. Feeling affronted, Vashishtha, in his rage, cursed the king, "As your family priest, I had asked you to wait for me to perform your sacrifice. Instead you opted to take another priest. Thus, you will be bereft of your body."

The attendants were frightened to hear Vashishtha's curse and rushed to convey the news to the sleeping king. Nimi, in all innocence, went to see Vashishtha and said, "Despite repeated requests, you chose to forsake my sacrifice in favour of Indra's. This did not befit a brahmin of your stature especially when you have the responsibility of being our family priest.

You have cursed me for no fault of mine, but possibly as a result of your own frustration and consequent anger. I too, therefore, curse you that your body, burning with anger, would be destroyed."

On hearing Nimi's curse, Vashishtha rushed to his father Brahma and narrated the incident. He requested a remedy by which he could have another body without losing his immense knowledge.

Brahma blessed him and advised him to enter into the tejas[190] of Mitra-Varuna, the rishi duo.

Vashishtha left his existing body forever and, turning himself into a subtle form[191], entered the body of Mitra-Varuna.

Once Mitra-Varuna saw apsara Urvashi and they were captivated. They requested her to spend some time at their abode. Urvashi happily agreed and stayed with them.

On an occasion, while they were engrossed in talking to Urvashi, Mitra-Varuna were overcome by their passion. Their semen fell into an open earthen pot. Soon two handsome boys were born out of their seed. The first was Agasti who took to asceticism in his early childhood. The second was Vashishtha, the same muni who had left his earlier body.

Vashishtha, in his second body, was again appointed by the Ikshvaku family as their priest.'

Vyasa looked at the king and knew that Janamejaya was wondering about King Nimi's body. To satisfy Janamejaya's curiosity, Vyasa continued, 'When the munis at Nimi's sacrifice came to know of the curse by Vashishtha, they discussed it among themselves. They decided to keep the body, already decaying due to the curse, intact by the power of their mantras till the yagna ended.

When the sacrifice was concluded, all the devas arrived to bless the successful yagna. They discovered the physical state of the king and offered to give him the body of a man, or even a deva, where he could assume the second body with all his qualities and appearance as did Guru Vashishtha.

But the king humbly refused and said he wished to live in the form of air on the top of everyone's eyelids.

The devas were heartened to hear about his wish but this was something beyond their capacities. They advised him to worship Devi Bhagvati and before departing, gave him a hint that the Devi was already appeased with his sacrifice.

Nimi lost no time in initiating hymns in praise of the Devi. She appeared before him and asked him to seek his desired boons. The gratified king repeated his request that he had made to the devas earlier and added, "Bless me with the awareness on how to achieve liberation from the cycle of birth and death."

The Devi granted him both his wishes and said, "When Nimi will reside on the top of eyes in the form of air, the eyes of all mortal beings will close and open in a blink like a twinkle. The immortals though will continue with a fixed gaze."

O Janamejaya! Now you understand why the unit of time, equalling the time taken by the flickering of an eye, is called Nimisha.'

Vyasa continued to complete his narration, 'After being blessed by the Devi, Nimi's soul left his body. The munis in the yagna performed the cremation by igniting the fire by placing arani wood pieces on his corpse. As the body burned, a beautiful boy of Nimi, looking exactly like Nimi, emerged from the funeral pyre.

The boy was named Mithi and later became renowned as Janak. He founded the city of Janakpuri on the banks of River Ganga. This city is also known as Mithila. Moreover, as King Nimi lost his body and became Videha, all his descendants were called by the same name of Janak and epithet Videha.'

The king could not help but ask a simple question, 'Isn't he the same king whom you had asked your son Shukadeva to meet?'

Vyasa said, 'Yes, Janamejaya. He was from the same lineage. You must have also noticed that neither the maharishi, the master of all knowledge, nor the king, knowing that the one cursing him was his family priest, could forgive. It is because of the effect of maya. It causes an imbalance of the three gunas on an individual due to his Prarabdha karma.

To conquer anger and to forgive, we need to not only acquire knowledge but also practise asceticism and yoga. All this is done to control the restless and irrepressibly moving mind. Once the mind is in control, all kinds of feelings are conquered.

Nimi was unfortunately not in the same state as Yayati who did not curse in return but forgave Shukracharya when the latter cursed him. On the other hand, the Haihayas, in greed and anger, annihilated the brahmins in the family of Bhrigu without an iota of consideration of brahmahatya.'

The Haihayas

Janamejaya's eyes widened when he heard about the new reference. He said, 'Kindly describe to me the anecdote of the Haihayas. Who were they? What was their enmity with the brahmins?'

Vyasa responded, 'In earlier times, a king called Kartavirya ruled. He belonged to a kshatriya clan by the name of Haihaya. The powerful king had a thousand arms and, hence, he was also called Sahastrarjun. He was a disciple of Maharishi Dattatreya.

The king loved to perform charities and undertook several sacrifices during his life. He lavishly gave away a huge amount of riches to the family priests who were brahmins of the Bhargava[192] clan. Consequently, the brahmins became filthy rich with not only gold, silver and gems but also other possessions like horses, chariots and mansions.

After the death of the king, his descendants found that the coffers had become empty. They went to the Bhargavas to seek money to manage the affairs of the State. The brahmins, though had accumulated excessive wealth, denied having any money.

Guilty in their heart, the brahmins thought that the Haihayas might take away their wealth by force and, thus, buried all their precious materials underneath their houses or shifted their wealth to distant places. Some gave away large amounts as alms to other brahmins. But they did not offer a single coin to the king's family.

Still, in fear, they fled to other places. On one occasion, a band of kshatriyas went to the house of one of the priests and found nobody there. Out of curiosity, they dug up the floor of the house and found the riches. Then they repeated the same in all the houses abandoned by the Bhargavas and were bewildered to find huge amounts of money.

The descendants of the king came to know about it and were extremely annoyed about being cheated. Their grudge against the brahmins for not helping them financially during their times of need turned into hatred. They began to kill the brahmins. First men, then children and finally even the unborn foetuses were mercilessly eliminated. The kshatriyas went around to find every member of the Bhargava clan and murdered each one, irrespective of his age.

When the Haihayas were dissuaded by other brahmins not to do such heinous and sinful acts, they argued, "The brahmins are not supposed to hoard wealth. They could have given it away as alms or charity after keeping an amount required for themselves.

Money has three culminations: charity, gratification and ruination. Some deserving people use their wealth for living comfortably and also give it away for charity. Some wicked people amass it without utilising it. Their wealth becomes a cause of ruination. Over and above, these Bhargavas turned out to be cheats and, therefore, their penalisation by the king is justified. Hence, the treatment was meted out to them."

After having extirpated all the males in the Bhargava clan, they went out to hunt for the females of those brahmin families. The terrified women folk fled to the Himalayas to take shelter from the vicious Haihayas.'

Vyasa wished to emphasise on an important learning at this point and, therefore, took a pause before beginning again, 'O King! Remember avarice is among the principal causes for a man to leave the path of dharma. Under its influence, one can kill one's own, cheat others and perform unimaginable heinous crimes.'

Janamejaya nodded his head in complete agreement. He asked, 'What happened to the families of those brahmins?'

Vyasa continued, 'Fearful of the Haihayas, the women hid in a small hamlet in the Himalayas on the banks of River Ganga. There they built and installed an earthen statue of Devi Gauri. They immersed themselves in worshipping the Devi and fasting for her.

One night, the Devi appeared in their dreams and blessed them, "One of you will bear a son from the thigh who will set things right again for all of you. This son will be my constituent."

Hearing this, one woman in the clan who, fearing the wrath of the Haihayas, had hidden her foetus in her thigh, became apprehensive and fled from the group. The Haihayas spotted and pursued her. She begged them to spare her life and wailed aloud.

Hearing her heart-rending cries, the womb ripped open and an effulgent boy, shining like the sun, came out. The Haihayas could not bear to see his lustre and lost their eyesight. With this, the realisation dawned upon them that they had committed atrocities on these Bhargava women and their plight was the result of their sins.

They fell to the feet of this woman who was still frightened to the core. They pleaded for mercy and the return of their eyesight. They assured her that the massacre of the Bhargava clan would end henceforth.

Seeing them blinded and hearing their prayers, the woman calmed. She said, "I am not responsible for your blindness but my son, Aurvya[193], who I carried in my thigh-womb throughout the time you were destroying the foetuses of the Bhargava women.

This child has been born with the blessings of Devi Gauri, the Supreme Goddess and, hence, effulgence emerged out of his body. He is not an ordinary soul and has been born with the knowledge of the Vedas. If you seek forgiveness from him, he might reinstate your eyesight."

The Haihayas prostrated in front of the boy and requested exoneration from their past acts. The boy spoke,

"Whatever was destined has happened. Go back to your kingdom with peace in your heart and forget all the anger you harboured against the Bhargavas."

By the time, the kshatriyas left the mountains, their eyesight returned to normal. Aurvya, with his mother, joined the other Bhargava women and created a hermitage there.

Janamejaya asked again, 'O Muni! Since the descendants of Yadu are called Yadava or Yaduvanshi, those of Bharat are called Bharatvanshi, similarly was there a king whose progenies came to be known by the name of Haihayas?'

Vyasa was happy to hear the king's logical question. He replied, 'In the days of yore, Devi Lakshmi had emerged from the churning of the ocean along with the best among the horses, called Uchchaishravas. While Lakshmi was taken by Vishnu as her consort, Uchchaishravas became the vehicle for Surya.

Once, Revanta, the son of Surya, was coming to Vaikuntha to meet Vishnu. He was mounted on Uchchaishravas. While they were approaching, Lakshmi saw her brother-like horse and was transfixed. Vishnu asked her what she was looking at so intently. But she was so engrossed in gazing at the magnificent horse that she did not respond to Vishnu even after he repeated the question a couple of times.

Vishnu became annoyed and cursed her that as she was so attracted to a horse, she would be born as a mare. Lakshmi was anxious and puzzled at the same time. She asked Vishnu, "O dear husband! What caused so much anger in you that you ended up cursing me whereas you have always showered me with love? I will, therefore, prefer to end my life rather than live as a mare without you," and further added, "tell me what I shall do to get rid of this curse."

Vishnu's anger had subsided by that time. He said, "You will come back to me after you have birthed a son like me."

Lakshmi took the birth of a mare in the hermitage of Devi Chhaya, the wife of Surya. The hermitage was located at a place called Suparnaksha whose north end had the confluence of River Yamuna and River Tamasa. Lakshmi meditated upon Mahadeva for one thousand years.

Her severe asceticism moved Mahadeva who appeared along with his consort Parvati. He spoke, "You are the wife of Sri Hari. Everyone chants his name and finds the path to liberation. Why should you meditate upon me when your husband himself is the lord of the three worlds?"

Lakshmi explained her situation and prayed to Mahesh, "O Mahadeva! Since I am alone here without my husband, how will I be able to bear a son and if that does not happen, I will never be able to go back and live with him. I learnt from my husband that if either of you is in distress or needs advice, one meditates upon the other. He had mentioned that there was no distinction between you two. I, therefore, meditated upon you. Kindly find a way out for me."

Mahadeva smiled as he knew that Lakshmi had understood something which no one else had. He blessed her, "O Devi! I will ensure that your Sri Hari takes birth as a horse and joins you in this hermitage to fulfil the condition imposed by him. The son born to both of you will be a great king by the name of Ekavira and he will establish the Haihaya lineage."

Mahadeva returned to Mount Kailash. He asked his trusted aide Chitrarupa to immediately go to Vishnu in Vaikuntha, convey Mahadeva's message asking Vishnu to take birth as a horse and, thus, fulfil his blessings to Lakshmi.

Vishnu took the form of a stunning horse and arrived at the hermitage where Lakshmi was practising austerities since her birth as a mare. They recognised each other instantly. They had met after a long time and, therefore, had been longing for each other. They spent time in each other's company at the serene hermitage.

In due time, the mare gave birth to a handsome boy. Both Lakshmi and Vishnu were pleased to see him. Vishnu lovingly told his wife, "O the most gorgeous one! It is time for us to go back to Vaikuntha. Let this child remain in this hermitage."

No sooner than both of them assumed their divine forms and were ready to mount Garuda, Lakshmi stopped him and said, "This child is too tender to be left behind. Who will take care of him? Let us take him along with us to Vaikuntha."

Vishnu said, "Everything happens in this world for a reason. This child has been born to be adopted by King Turvasu who is also known by the name of Hari Varma. Unfortunately, Hari Varma cannot beget a son. He has been performing sacrifices for the last hundred years. He will take care of our son."

Saying this, Vishnu joined by his wife left for their abode.'

Vyasa continued, 'The route for fate to achieve its result is, at times, torturous. In this matter, as soon as Vishnu left, a Vidyadhara called Champaka arrived there with his wife Madanalasa. They saw the child lying alone without anyone tending to him. They picked up the child. Madanalasa fell in motherly love with the child and embraced him closely. She expressed her desire to take the child along with them.

Champaka gladly agreed and they both took him to Devaloka to meet Indra. They sought his approval to adopt the child after due ceremonies. Indra stopped them from doing so and told them the true purpose of the birth of the child. He asked them to return the child to the same place.

Hearing this, Champaka hurried to the hermitage with the child. Meanwhile, Vishnu appeared to the meditating King Turvasu and said, "I am pleased with your tapasya. Go to the hermitage near the confluence of Yamuna and Tamasa. There you will find a child born from none other than Devi Lakshmi herself."

Turvasu's joy had no bounds. He rushed to the hermitage. He found the lotus-faced child and brought him to his palace. The child, resembling in appearance and traits to Lord Vishnu, was named Ekavira.

Ekavira was brought up with royal care. He grew up to be an intelligent and accomplished successor to his father Turvasu. He became the king when his father left for the forest to perform tapasya for the rest of his life.

Once King Ekavira went on a leisurely visit with his friends to the banks of the holy River Ganga. They were passing the hermitages of many munis when the king saw a beautiful young girl sitting alone and crying near a water body full of lotus flowers.

The king stopped by and asked her why she was alone and crying. She replied, "I come from the kingdom of King Raibhya and his wife Rukmarekha. The royal couple could not beget a child. Hence, they held a sacrifice with elaborate ceremonies. From the yagna, a magnificent girl emerged. The couple accepted her as their princess and named her Ekavali.

O handsome man! I, Yashovati, am the daughter of one of the ministers in the kingdom and a permanent companion to Princess Ekavali.

The princess is very fond of seeing lotuses and even travelled to distant places to see them. When the king learnt about this, he ordered his best guards to accompany the princess whenever she went out. At the same time, he created several lakes with lotuses in them around the city.

But the princess kept going out, especially to the banks of River Ganga to quench her desire to see padma[194] flowers.

Some days back, we both came here and were busy playing with each other when a daitya called Kaalketu saw her. He kept looking at her pristine youthful beauty and he abducted the princess.

While he took her away, I followed them to a distance towards the city of daityas in Patalaloka. Kaalketu noticed me but instead of turning me away or killing me, he allowed me to stay with Princess Ekavali. He perhaps thought that I would be able to comfort the princess.

Upon reaching their city, Kaalketu wanted me to convince the princess to agree to become his wife. When I did not agree to his demand, he went to the princess and proposed to her.

Ekavali told him that her father had wanted her to marry a prince named Haihaya. As she had mentally accepted the prince as her husband, she could not even think of anyone else."

At this point, Ekavira interrupted Yashovati, "I am that Haihaya. Tell me, O lean one, where the princess has been kept," and expressing surprise, added, "how did you manage to escape the daitya's captivity?"

Yashovati spoke, "O Prince Haihaya! When I was young, I had learnt the bijamantra of Devi Chandika. While in captivity, I chanted it all the time for a month. The Devi appeared to me in my dreams and asked me to go to the banks of Ganga where I would meet King Ekavira.

She also said that Ekavira also knew the mantra given by Muni Dattatreya. He is the son of Devi Lakshmi. He will help you to end the torment of the daitya and rescue Princess Ekavali. I then left the city incognito and found my way here."

Ekavira took Yashovati along and chanting the mantra of the Devi, they proceeded to the city of Kaalketu. They were followed by his vast army.

Ekavira attacked the impenetrable city, which was secured by an array of dreadful daityas and snakes. A terrible war ensued witnessing the valour of Ekavira having the blessings of Devi Chandika. Finally, Kaalketu was struck by the king's powerful gada and killed.

On Ekavali's return to her father, she told him about her abduction by Kaalketu and Ekavira rescuing her. King Raibhya gladly married his daughter to Ekavira with pomp and show.'

Vyasa said, 'O descendant of Bharat! This King Ekavira and his queen were blessed by a son named Kritavirya and his son was called as Kartavirya.'

Narada

Janamejaya said, 'O Muni! I am unable to fathom one aspect in so many descriptions that you have given. What happiness does one get by taking birth in this world? Each one, be gods, devas, asuras or humans, is affected by moha[195]. Why is it so?'

The question made Vyasa pensive. It probably touched a raw nerve. Yet he did not desist from replying. He said, 'O King! Once Muni Narada, during one of his world travels, visited me in my hermitage at Samyaprasa on the banks of the holy River Sarasvati.

I received him with respect. We had lunch and, thereafter, sat together for discussions. I asked him the same questions that you asked now. I also told him that I had failed to find happiness due to the attachments that existed in this material world.

I told him about the several worldly attachments that existed in my life, starting with my mother, two brothers and their families, the sons of Pandu and above all, my son Shuka. I wondered how even the high-souled persons having vast knowledge fell to the attractions of this world.

Narada said, "O Muni! You are among the high-souled persons. You have created the Puranas and divided the Vedas. Why are you asking me such a question?"

Having said so, he continued, "Nevertheless, let me share something with you that you know already. Every manifested soul in this world is affected by moha, whether it is for individuals or for material.

I, in spite of being the mind-born son of Brahma and adept in the knowledge of the Vedas, have been severely affected too."

I was surprised to hear that.

Narada continued, "In the days of yore, once Devarishi Parvata, who is my sister's son, and I travelled to the earth. Before we started from Devaloka, we agreed to be honest in conveying our feelings to one another, be it about wealth, food or women.

We visited several pilgrimages and took a dip in the holy waters. We had an opportunity to meet several rishis. We spent several months travelling to different places. When the monsoon season arrived, we happened to be in the magnificent city of a king called Sanjaya.

We decided to stay with King Sanjaya during those four months as it was difficult to travel during the rainy season. The king extended his warm hospitality and made our stay comfortable.

His beautiful daughter, Damayanti, took it upon herself to serve us. From providing water for our bath in the morning to serving us meals and washing our clothes, she did all of it with devotion.

We spent time in peace studying the Vedas. I also took to my passion for singing as I had my lute with me. Damayanti was enchanted with my recitals from the Saam Veda and fell for me. I too felt attracted to her.

As a result, she became more considerate towards me while taking care of both of us. Gradually, it became evident to Parvata too. Damayanti would give me warm water for bathing and warm food to eat while Parvata would receive relatively cold water and cold food. Her mannerisms and gestures also suggested amorous feelings for me.

One day Parvata finally asked me to reveal the truth and referred to our pact before beginning our journey. He said, 'It is evident that Damayanti wishes to take you as her husband and I can sense that you share the same feelings towards her.'

When I hesitatingly accepted the truth, Parvata became angry. Since I had hidden my feelings from him thus far, he cursed me, 'O Narada! Let your face turn into that of a monkey.'

The curse became effective immediately. I was furious as I thought that Paravata had cursed me out of proportion. I could not stop myself from cursing Parvata, in return, 'You spiteful Parvata! You would not be able to return to the heaven and will remain on earth.'

An annoyed Parvata left Sanjaya's city while I continued to live there. The princess' attraction towards me dampened when she saw my monkey face but her love for my singing did not.

Meanwhile, King Sanjaya had started consulting his ministers about his daughter's wedding. He asked them to suggest one prince who was of respectable descent as well as brave and kind.

Damayanti also learnt about this discussion. She took her maidservant into confidence. The maidservant, at Damayanti's behest, went to the king and told him that the princess was truly in love with my music and wished to marry me.

The king told his wife Kaikeyi about their daughter's choice. They were both concerned because while Damayanti was young and beautiful, I had the face of a monkey and was an aged ascetic. Moreover, Damayanti had been brought up with all the comforts whereas I always smeared my body in ashes and lived in austerities. They wondered how she would be able to survive with me.

They tried to reason it out with Damayanti. They told her that she was under the influence of moha for me and that the proposition was unworkable.

No argument, however, could budge Damayanti from her resolve to marry me. She argued, 'None in the three worlds, except Mahadeva himself, is as conversant with the Nada Rasa, the science of music, as Narada. A qualified and endowed man like him is a better option as a husband than an illiterate and wealthy man. I am glad that Narada loves me too.'

The royal couple was forced to accept their daughter's proposal. Finding an auspicious muhurtam[196], they gave their daughter's hand to me in a propitious ceremony."

Narada sighed and continued, "Thus, O Vyasa, I got married to Damayanti. But my appearance of monkey face was nibbling me inside and I could not find peace with myself. My only happiness was the ever-smiling gorgeous princess who served me with her pristine love.

Several years passed by when Muni Parvata arrived unannounced in the city. He had spent his time visiting many more places of pilgrimage, thereby earning punyas. And he was also calmer now.

We both sat together and exchanged pleasantries. We spoke with the same old love and respect towards each other. He saw me with a monkey's face and also noticed that I had married the princess.

He seemed to have grasped his foolhardiness in the earlier situation and was filled with regret for both Damayanti and me. He decided to withdraw his curse.

I regained my original face. Overwhelmed, I also withdrew my curse and blessed Parvata that there be no impediment to his return to heaven.

King Sanjaya, Queen Kaikeyi and Damayanti rejoiced to see that I had gotten back my original appearance. The king gave away a huge amount of alms to his people. He also presented Parvata and me with lots of riches.

Now you see, Vyasa, no one can be happy in body form. A body necessarily comes along with the three gunas. Their inherent imbalance in each being causes egoism, anger, covetousness and ahamkara. The moha is the result of these flaws. Also one should remember that all the embodied beings are subject to maya, which deludes everyone.

It is because of this maya that I was turned into a woman by Sri Hari. Not only that, I, as a woman, got married and gave birth to children." Narada thus concluded.'

Vyasa smiled and added, 'Besides unable to control my grin when Maharishi Narada was narrating, what he said also ignited my inquisitiveness.'

Janamejaya was intrigued too. He asked, 'O Dvaipayana! Kindly tell me in detail what Maharishi Narada told you about how maya turned him into a woman. How did he turn into a man again?'

Maya

Vyasa recalled what Narada had told him, 'Narada had explained that maya was incomprehensible to each being, moving and non-moving; whether it was Brahma or the smallest bacteria, gigantic mountains or a blade of grass.

He then recounted a story, "Once I desired to see Sri Hari. I travelled from Devaloka to his abode. I entered his chamber unannounced carrying my lute in hand and singing hymns from the Saam Veda.

Adorned with the most precious jewels, he was in an intimate moment with Devi Lakshmi. Noticing my sudden presence, she adjusted her clothes to cover herself fully and left immediately into the inner chamber. While she was leaving, her breast was partially visible through the fine muslin silk cloth.

After she had left the room, I said to Shri Hari, 'O Sri Hari! Devi Lakshmi is like a mother to me. My gaze was thus fixed on her feet. Moreover, I have always been an ascetic and brought all my passions under control. So much so that I have even conquered maya. Then why did she have to leave suddenly?'

Vishnu's eyes twinkled on hearing my words and he said, 'None in this universe, be him a yogi or a muni or even a deva, has been able to control maya. Knowledge of the Vedas or yoga or celestial music also does not enable anyone to conquer maya. All embodied beings are subjected to it. It has not even spared Brahma, Mahesh or me. Maya is unborn and thus incomprehensible to all. Therefore, your claim to have conquered maya does not befit you.'

His words left me flabbergasted. I asked him to show me this maya.

Vishnu smiled again and said, 'Alas, she is invisible. But she is acknowledged by all for her all-pervading presence and effect on each being. I will have you witness maya, if you insist, but I caution you beforehand not to be disheartened by your experience.'

He signalled me to join him and we both left Vaikuntha sitting on the back of his vehicle Garuda. Flying at an incalculable speed, Garuda reached earth in no time.

Garuda slowed down for us to enjoy the scenery of beautiful mountains and valleys, trees and forests, rivers and lakes, men and animals, cities and hamlets. We arrived near the city of Kannauj and stopped at a lake with shimmering clean water. Lotuses and lilies adorned the precincts of the lake. Several aquatic animals also lived in it.

Vishnu suggested that we bathe in the lake before we went to the city.

We both dismounted Garuda and rested for a while. He then asked me to bathe first. I kept my lute and deerskin aside on the banks and entered the lake.

I remember the ever-smiling face of Sri Hari before I took a dip into the water. However, when I came out of the water, I did not see the same face. Moreover, I had turned into a gorgeous woman.

Vishnu had disappeared with my lute, deerskin and every shred of my existence as Narada. I had no memory of who I was. I was a pretty woman standing in the water, absolutely naked and wearing exquisite jewellery.

I walked back to the edge of the lake wondering who I was. I came out completely lost and sat on a rock. It was not long before a king passed by the same way where I was sitting in that feminine form.

The king by the name of Taaldhvaja rode on his chariot followed by his retinue of security guards and royal servants. He was handsome like Kaamdeva. Before I could react, he stopped his chariot near me and lovingly asked, 'O most beautiful one with a thin waist! Who are you? Whence have you come from? What are you doing here at this lake?'

As I had no answer to any of his questions, I spoke cluelessly, 'O King! I have no idea who I am, where I am from and who my parents are. I seem to have lost all my memory and now I have nowhere to go.'

Taaldhvaja, who was smitten by my beauty and innocence, eagerly proposed to me, 'O charming beauty! Accept me as your husband and I shall strive to take utmost care of you.'

I immediately joined him in a specially crafted palanquin, not because I had no other option but because I was attracted to him too. We arrived at his palace. In a few days, at an opportune muhurtam, we got wedded in accordance with the rites in witness of the holy fire. He named me Saubhagya Sundari. We both began to enjoy our lives in each other's company.

Adept in Kaamshastra, Taaldhvaja was deeply in love with me. He immersed himself in enjoyment with me at the expense of everything else. Twelve years swung by and I became pregnant."

Narada continued, "All this while, O Vyasa, I had no inkling that I was ever a man and that too a muni. I had lost all my knowledge earned over aeons of tapasya. All I knew was that I was the wife of the king and my duty was to give him the best of companionship.

Then a very beautiful son was born to Saubhagya Sundari at a highly auspicious time. Two years later another son was born. The king was ecstatic. He named his sons Viravarma and Sudhanva, respectively.

Thereafter, I bore ten more sons. Gradually they all grew up to be handsome princes endowed with all the royal abilities. In time, they also got married and the family expanded with their wives and several of our grandchildren.

I was too occupied in taking care of all of them to think about anything else. I felt pain when anyone of them was hurt and pleasure when each one was joyous. Maya had deluded me to the extent that my sole objective was the welfare and prosperity of my family.

Every start has a finish. In this case, an inimical king from a faraway kingdom attacked the city of Kannauj. Taaldhvaja took his army to battle. He was joined by my courageous sons and grandsons. But destiny seemed to have another plan.

We lost the war with all my sons and several grandsons slain. When I learnt of this irreparable damage, I joined the king on the battlefield lamenting our misfortune. While we were crying our hearts out, a brahmin passed by. I, of course, had no idea that he was none other than Sri Hari himself in the guise of the brahmin.

Seeing me in such a miserable state, he stopped and explained to me in a soft voice, 'O enchanting lady! There is no point in crying over those who are gone. Remember that all this is nothing but a delusion of moha. Think beyond what has happened.'

He insisted, 'Now that all your sons and grandsons have passed away, you should perform Tilanjali[197] which is never done at home. You should take bath in a place of pilgrimage and perform the ceremony.'

Vishnu in the guise of a brahmin led us to a place called Pumtirtha, which had a tank of crystal-clear water. He asked us to bathe in the water and think of the millions of sons, fathers, brothers and husbands who had died in their previous births. He asked us who would we grieve for now and that all this was a delusion created by maya.

As advised by him, I took a dip and when I came out of the water, I was a man again. I was Narada again and I saw Lord Vishnu in his godly form wearing divine yellow attire.

At that point, I had complete recollection of what had happened in the past with me turning into a female and now back into my male form. Vishnu saw me brooding over my thoughts and called out, 'O Narada! What are you doing in the water? Come out quickly.'

On the other hand, the king was dumbfounded to see his wife Saubhagya Sundari entering the water and a male coming out in her place. The king wondered if she had been eaten away by fishes or crocodiles or if she had committed suicide.

He began to wail. Seeing Taaldhvaja in such a pitiable condition, Vishnu said, 'All the relationships in this world are akin to that of people travelling together in a boat. The companionships are thus transitory. In your case, you did not even know your wife before you met her at the banks of a lake. Now she has been lost the same way as you had found her. There is no point in lamenting what has happened. Calm yourself, O King. Go back and rule your kingdom again, according to dharma.'

The consoled king finished the last rites of his sons, took the blessings of Vishnu and returned.

After everyone had left and I was alone with Vishnu, he teased me. I also smilingly responded, 'O Prabhu! You really deceived me. But I now acknowledge what and how strong maya is. I had the same mind, soul and subtle body, yet I lost all the memory and knowledge. Kindly explain how and why it happened?'

Vishnu spoke, 'All embodied beings are subject to three states: awake, dreaming and deep sleep. However, there is a fourth state too, called Turiya[198]. While the body may change, it continues to be subjected to the four states. A person dreams about several things but once he gets up, he realises that all that he dreamt was not real. But the question arises whether what was seen in dreams was all untrue?

The incomprehensible maya acts in the same fashion. As long as there is the effect of the three gunas, no one can comprehend what is true or fictitious. Not even Brahma, Mahadeva and I can comprehend this.

One must live with the power of maya, which is not only incomprehensible but also inconceivable. There is no need to be sorry or be surprised or be bogged down by it. It is all-pervading.'

Saying so, Bhagvan Vishnu disappeared."

Narada then told me not to grieve over losses and live life in peace and happiness as everyone is born to enjoy or suffer the effects of past karma.'

Vyasa had revealed the Tattva Gyan[199] to the king. He said, 'The external traits in a person are caused by the combination of three gunas. They form the fabric of the existence of embodied beings much as a cloth consists of threads.

The only entity that is above maya is the Supreme Goddess. She is therefore called "Mayeshwari" too. If she decides to bless someone with her grace and mercy, that person can be free from the effect of maya. That is why, she is also known as "Devi Bhuvneshvari", the greatest lady in the three worlds.

Thus, the only way to combat maya is to leave moha and worship Devi Bhagvati.'

Chyavana Muni

Janamejaya knew that this was a lifetime opportunity for anyone to hear such discourse from Maharishi Vyasa. He did not want Vyasa to stop before he had satisfied his mind and soul with all the knowledge that he could imbibe.

Janamejaya asked, 'I am desirous to know about the Chandravanshi and Suryavanshi kings, the Lunar and Solar races, respectively. I understand that they were all devotees of Devi Bhagvati.'

Being equally keen to impart the knowledge of Devi Purana to the king, Vyasa continued, 'Let me start from the beginning. As you know, Brahma created seven mind-born sons, known as Marichi, Atri, Angira, Pulastya, Pulaha, Kratu and Vashishtha. Sanaka and his brothers were also born from Brahma's mind. Rudra appeared from Brahma's anger, Narada from his lap and Daksha from his right thumb. Daksha's wife Virini, also known as Asikni, was born from Brahma's left thumb. Narada, of course, had to be born again from the womb of Virini.'

Janamejaya was surprised to hear this. He interjected, 'I did not know that Narada was born from a womb.'

Vyasa said, 'This is the play of destiny. Let me tell you. Daksha was ordered by his father to procreate to bring mankind to the world. He, thus, produced five thousand sons with his wife Virini. When Devarishi Narada saw them, he mocked them saying if Daksha wished to populate the earth, he ought to know its size and limits.

Hearing his words, Daksha's sons left to explore the earth in various directions. Daksha became anxious as he could not see them around. He procreated more sons. But they were also advised the same way by Narada and they too spread around.

Daksha learnt of Narada's trickery and cursed him, "O wicked one! As you have destroyed my sons, you would be destroyed too. Since you instigated all my sons to leave me, you too would be born as my son."

Following the curse, Narada took birth again as the son of Daksha and Virini.

Daksha also had sixty daughters. Out of them, he gave thirteen in marriage to Marichi's son Kashyapa, ten to Dharma, twenty-seven to Chandra Deva, two to Bhrigu, four to Arishtanemi and the last four to Angira.

The sons and grandsons of Kashyapa became devas and asuras, the two classes completely antagonistic to each other. Not only them, but other species like yakshas, pannagas,[200] animals and birds also originated from him. This is the reason why this creation is also named after him as Kashyapi.

The Solar race was rooted in Surya whose son was called Vaivasvata Manu, giving the name to the present Manvantara.

Manu had ten sons: Ikshvaku, Nabhaga, Dhrishta, Shrayati, Narishyanta, Pranshu, Nriga, Dishta, Karusha and Rishadhra.

Shrayati was blessed with a son called Anarta and a daughter Sukanya. She was wedded to the old and blind Chyavana Muni.'

Janamejaya was amazed and asked, 'How come a beautiful daughter of a king like Shrayati got married to a blind muni? Why did the king agree to such an alliance?'

Vyasa replied, 'The king had four thousand wives but only one daughter, Sukanya. The charming girl was the apple of everyone's eye in the palace.

A lake was situated close to Shrayati's capital city and not far from there, Chyavana Muni had established his hermitage.

He took to severe meditation. Controlling his thoughts and breath, he gave up food and finally water too. He stayed in a position for so long that an anthill covered him. Over time, it was covered with creepers.

Once the king went picnicking at the lake with his family. Princess Sukanya roamed around the lake with her companions, her anklets making a sweet musical sound.

She saw the anthill amid a tree grove and noticed two holes in the anthill. When she peeped through the holes, she found something shining through them. These were the eyes of the meditating muni. But she had no inkling that there was a muni meditating inside.

Presuming those shining objects as fireflies, Sukanya decided to catch them. She picked up two long twigs and pricked through the holes. The muni saw the beautiful princess before his eyes were hit and cried out in a faint voice, "O gorgeous one! Don't do it."

But his voice was too muffled to be heard by the princess, partly because of the anthill around him and partly because of the frailty caused by years of tapasya. As a result, his eyes were permanently damaged. The excruciating pain in muni turned him wrathful.

Meanwhile, everyone in the king's entourage, from family members, attendants and soldiers to even the animals like horses, camels and elephants, immediately stopped excretion. There was a sudden panic. Everyone rushed to Shrayati who pondered the cause of it.

Later, they all returned to the city where the king began to consult all the wise people to discern the cause for such a calamity on the entire entourage. He learnt about the muni living near the lake and assessed that it had perhaps something to do with him.

He enquired from everyone who had travelled to find out if anyone had caused harm to the muni. Finally, his daughter came up to him and told him what had transpired. She admitted that she had probably heard an indistinct voice too. But she recalled that when she pulled out the twigs from the holes, they were wet on the other end.

The king at once returned to the same place and removed the anthill. There he found Chyavana Muni in deep suffering. He had the muni nursed and brought him to a comfortable state to talk. Then he folded his hands and prayed, "O Muni! Though unintended, it is my daughter who is responsible for this sin. I seek your mercy for the innocent girl."

Chyavana spoke, "I have neither anger nor ill-feeling towards your daughter. I did not curse her or your entourage. Nevertheless, given my old age and now the blindness too, I wonder who would take care of me."

The king offered to send palace servants to serve him. The muni replied, "O King! I do not think that your servants would care as they wouldn't be my family. However, if you are serious about my welfare, then marry your daughter to me so that she takes care of me."

The king was stunned by muni's outrageous proposal. The numbed king did not react.

After returning to the palace, he kept brooding, "It would not be fair for young Sukanya to marry an aged and blind ascetic. She has been brought up with a lot of affection and indulgence. She would be unable to adjust to the frugal living of the muni. Having been used to attendants around her for the smallest of chores, the girl would not be able to take care of the old man single-handedly. Moreover, being a young girl, how she would satisfy her passion."

The king called for the counsel of his wise ministers. Even they did not recommend the alliance in spite of the calamity that had befallen.

Sukanya heard about the deliberations and understood the gravity of the situation. She went to see her father and said, "It was my fault. Therefore, I shall go back to the muni and seek his forgiveness. I am willing to serve him all my life."

The king tried to reason her out of her resolve emphasising that she was a young princess and it would be difficult for her to settle with the aged and blind muni. But he could not shake Sukanya's steadfastness. She assured her father that no matter what, she would be a chaste wife to the muni.

The king relented and arranged for the immediate betrothal of Sukanya with Chyavana. The muni accepted only the princess and refused to take any of the presents and servants along with her. No sooner than the wedding took place, the entourage members were able to excrete again.

Sukanya gave up her silk clothes and exquisite jewellery. She transformed into an ascetic's wife and began to live as a chaste wife, serving her husband and taking care of him like a mother.

She got up before sunrise and prepared warm water for his bathing. She helped him in getting ready for his morning routine of venerations and served him breakfast of sweet fruits. Later, she would serve him lunch and fan him while he took a nap.

In the evening again, she prepared his seat made of kusha grass on which he would sit and complete his evening homa ceremony[201]. She would cook a delicious supper of rice and make his comfortable bed of soft leaves. Only after he slept, she would finish her day.

Life was moving at a steady pace when, one day, the Ashvin twins, the sons of Surya, came to visit the lake where the hermitage was situated. At the same time, Sukanya was returning from the lake after taking a bath. The Ashvin brothers' sight fell on her divine beauty.

They were swept off their feet instantly and asked her a barrage of questions. Sukanya explained to them who she was. She then invited both guests to bless their hermitage.

Instead, they tried to woo her.

They said, "O moon-faced one! You are wasting your youth with an aged and blind ascetic. We will give you a place in Devaloka. Choose either of us as your husband."

Their words left the princess shaking like a leaf. She begged them, "Do not speak to me in this manner. You are the sons of Surya and I am the incorruptible wife of a maharishi. Your father is a witness to all your actions. What you are saying is adharma. If you don't stop, I will have to curse you."

The two brothers were taken aback by the threatening words of Sukanya. They became afraid of the powers of the muni too. To assuage her, they changed tack and said, "O sinless one! We are pleased with your virtuosity and wish to grant you any boon that you want from us," and added, "we are the physicians of the devas, we could turn your husband young and handsome. He will be the same as two of us, in age and looks."

At this, they returned to their earlier wish and offered, "Thereafter, you could choose one of the three as your husband."

Sukanya was shocked. She did not know how to respond. She rushed to her husband and told him everything that had just transpired between her and the Ashvin twins. She sought his wise counsel.

Chyavana, however, did not vacillate and said, "O immaculate one! Accept their condition and bring them here at once."

Sukanya went back to the Ashvins and told them that she agreed with their stipulation, that is, her husband becoming young and healthy again. The brothers came to the hermitage and took the muni to the lake. All three took a dip in the lake.

In a few moments, three bodies emerged out of the water and there were not two but three Ashvins, the exact replicas of each other. They were equally handsome, bright, youthful and lustrous as well as wearing the same attire and ornaments. They also spoke in the same voice at the same time.

Sukanya had not expected this. She was perplexed and wondered if it was a spell cast by the Ashvin brothers. In this confused state, she began to meditate upon the Supreme Goddess. She sang hymns in her heart to praise the Devi and sought refuge in her to resolve the puzzle.

The Devi was pleased. She infused into Sukanya a special power to help her identify the muni out of the three. In the next moment, she looked at them and knew exactly who her husband was.

The Ashvin twins were also pleased with her chastity. But before they could leave, Chyavana offered to them, out of his indebtedness towards both, a boon in return.

The brothers told him that as they were physicians, Indra had forbidden them from drinking Soma at the sacrifice performed by Brahma at Mount Meru. The brothers asked for the muni's help in obtaining the right to drink Soma.

Chyavana gladly accepted their request.'

Janamejaya intervened and asked, 'O Vyasa! Was Muni Chyavana so powerful that he could go against Indra's wishes to fulfil his boon to the Ashvin brothers?'

Vyasa explained, 'While this episode was taking place in the hermitage, Shrayati's wife was getting anxious about her daughter's welfare. She demanded the king to go and find out if Sukanya was doing fine with her frail and blind husband.

Shrayati, accompanied by his retinue of bodyguards, reached the hermitage. There he did not see the old Chyavana. Instead, there was a young and handsome man living with her daughter.

He lamented why he got his daughter married to an old man at all. He presumed that his daughter had betrayed the muni and killed him with her young paramour to satisfy her lust.

As the king was engrossed in his scandalous thoughts about his daughter, she spotted him and came running to her. She said lovingly, "O dear father! I am so glad to see you. Come and meet your son-in-law."

Shrayati was simmering with anger and guilt owing to his presumption. He said, "O Sukanya! How could you do such a vicious act of killing your husband and accepting someone else to fulfil your desires?"

Sukanya understood that her father had misread the situation for the right reasons. She smilingly introduced the young muni to her father and explained what had transpired. The astonished king greeted Chyavana and took his blessings.

Chyavana told the king about the Ashvin twins' request and asked the king to allow him to perform Agnishtoma[202] Yagna for him. This way, Chyavana would be able to fulfil the boon granted to the Ashvin brothers. The king readily agreed.

Shrayati began the preparations for the yagna and on the appointed day, Chyavana initiated the sacrifice. Vashishtha and several other munis were in attendance. Indra, joined by other devas, arrived at the yagna to partake in Soma juice.

When Indra found the Ashvin brothers present at the yagna, he annoyingly asked, "Who has invited them? Doesn't one know that they are prohibited to have Soma?"

Chyavana spoke, "O Lord of Sachi! These two have been born to Surya. They are also devas. Why shouldn't they drink Soma? I have granted them the boon that I would make them drink it."

Indra said, "They were appointed as the physicians of devas and have been looked down upon. Thus they have been forbidden to drink Soma."

The muni replied angrily, "You have performed several vicious acts, including treacherous killings and abducting Ahalya. If you have the right to drink it, so do the Ashvins."

With these words, Chyavana made them drink Soma juice accompanied by the recitation of relevant mantras.

Indra was enraged. He took out his powerful thunderbolt and launched it to kill the muni.

The muni stopped Indra's weapon in mid-air. He then initiated the yagna and created Kritya[203] out of the sacrificial fire with the power of mantras from the Atharva Veda. From Kritya, a gigantic demon, called Mada, emerged.

Mada was so frightful that even the devas were terrified to see his dreadful size and appearance. At muni's signal, he rushed to devour Indra.

Indra closed his eyes and prayed to Brihaspati who immediately arrived there.

The guru advised the lord of devas, "O Indra! This demon has been created by Chyavana with the shaktis he acquired through devotion to the Supreme Goddess. I am afraid that neither you nor even Brahma and Vishnu can kill him. The only recourse is to ask Chyavana to pacify Kritya, from whom Mada has originated."

An intelligent Indra immediately discerned the situation and surrendered to Chyavana. He said, "O Muni! I accept your words. The Ashvins will henceforth be able to take a share of Soma," and added the following to pacify the muni, "I deliberately provoked you to appraise the power of your tapasya. Now forgive me and withdraw this demon."

Chyavana agreed to Indra's request. He divided the demon into four vices, namely, addiction to sex, consumption of alcohol, gambling and hunting of animals. These vices were then sent off to different destinations.

Thereafter, Chyavana completed the yagna seeking the welfare of his client, Shrayati, to rule peacefully.'

Trishanku

Janamejaya asked, 'What happened to Suryavanshi King Shrayati afterwards?'

Vyasa continued, 'The king had a son called Anarta whose son was Revata. Revata established a city, Kushasthali, in the middle of the ocean and ruled from there. He was blessed with hundred sons, of whom Kakudmi was the eldest, and an auspicious daughter named Revati.

When Revati grew up, the king wanted the most suitable match for her. He thought of taking Brahma's advice in his quest for the most suitable husband for his daughter. Thus, both the father and the daughter went to Brahmaloka.'

Janamejaya was amazed, 'How could mortal beings go to Brahmaloka?'

Vyasa was always ready for such queries. He smiled and continued, 'You recall that your great grandfather Arjuna went to Devaloka and spent five years with his father Indra. I also mentioned earlier about King Mahabhisha who went to Brahmaloka and met Ganga there.

Even asuras have gone up to heaven, conquered and ruled it. Thus, mortals can travel to such places inhabited by devas and gods, though such privilege is earned through good karma and asceticism.

When Revata and Revati arrived at Brahmaloka, a session of dance and music by the gandharvas was in progress at Brahma's court. Both sat there captivated till it concluded.

When Brahma became free from the court, the king presented to Brahma his daughter and his concern regarding her nuptial alliance.

The king and his daughter had little realisation that the concept of time was very different in Brahmaloka vis-à-vis that on earth. While they had spent a short while watching dance and chatting with the lord of creation, the earth had moved through several aeons.

Brahma was not oblivious to this reality. He could not control his laugh and said, "O Revata! Not only all the possible bridegrooms that you may have had in mind but several generations of theirs have also gone by on earth. Currently, the earth is in the twenty-eighth Dvapara Yuga.

Now go back to earth and visit the city of Dwarka, the city built by Krishna, the incarnation of Vishnu. His elder brother Balarama, who is part-incarnate of Ananta, is the most appropriate bridegroom for your daughter.

Thus receiving Brahma's counsel, they returned to earth. After giving Revati in marriage to Balabhadra[204], the king left to perform tapasya at Badrikashram.'

Janamejaya could not stop himself from interrupting, 'You mentioned that a hundred and eight yugas passed by while King Revata and Revati performed the journey to Brahmaloka and returned. How is it that they did not have the effect of ageing? Did they turn immortal in the meanwhile?'

Vyasa loved such interventions. He responded, 'O King! The Brahmaloka is free of all vices, old age, hunger, thirst and fear of death and, hence, its dwellers have such longevity. I had earlier told you about the concept of time for various lokas. So, while one is in Brahmaloka, he experiences the same amount of time as its inhabitants. Hence the father and daughter did not age.[205]

While both were away, the king's descendants were destroyed by daityas. Thereafter, a sneeze by Vaivasvata Manu produced a powerful son from his nose who came to be known as Ikshvaku. He founded the Solar dynasty in the city of Ayodhya. On Maharishi Narada's advice,

Ikshvaku turned into a devout devotee of the Supreme Goddess.

Vikukshi was the eldest of his hundred sons. Ikshvaku sent fifty sons to the established kingdoms in the north and forty-eight to the south.

Vikukshi was also known as Shashad and his son was named Kakutstha. The son also earned other names of Indravaha and Puranjaya.'

Janamejaya stopped Vyasa at this point and asked, 'How is it, O Muni, that several of these kings were given names other than their formal name?'

Vyasa replied, 'Each sobriquet earned subsequently had a reason. In the case of Vikukshi, he was once directed by his father to get meat that was untainted[206] to conduct shraadh. He went to the forest and hunted several animals but in the process, he was fatigued and forgot his father's instructions.

Since he was starved, he partook a portion of hare meat and brought back the rest. When Vashishtha, the family priest, saw it, he knew that a portion of it had been eaten. That made the meat unfit for the ceremony.

Ikshvaku, in his anger, banished his son from the kingdom. Thus, he was also named Shashad. However, he succeeded as the ruler after his father's demise and his son Kakutstha took over from him.

During Kakutstha's reign, the devas were decimated by the asuras. They, on Vishnu's advice, went to seek the help of Kakutstha. He agreed to fight the daityas on one condition that he would ride into the battle zone on Indra's back. Indra acquiesced reluctantly and assumed the form of a bull.

Owing to riding a bull's hump called kakud, the king was named Kakutstha and as he was carried by Indra, he was also known as Indravaha. The third title of Puranjaya was earned as he won the battle against the daityas.

Kakutstha's lineage was carried on by Prithu, then Vishvarandhi, Chandra, Yuvanashva, Shavanta, Brihadashva,

Kuvalashva, Dridhashva, Shriman Hrayashva, Nikumbha, Vrahanashva, Krishashva, Prasenajit, Yauvanashva and Mandhata.

Mandhata built one thousand and eight palaces to venerate Devi Bhagvati. He who was born from his father's belly and not mother's womb.'

Janamejaya was surprised to hear this. He inquired, 'How is it possible?'

Vyasa saw the amazement written on the king's face. He explained, 'King Yauvanashva had a hundred wives but no child. He tried several ways but nothing could yield a son for him. Finally, he went to the forest and began to live like an ascetic.

The other ascetics around him took pity on his troubled condition and asked him the reason for his sacrifices. He narrated the reason and asked for their advice on the appropriate sacrifice to achieve his objective.

They helped him to perform a particular sacrifice to appease Indra. After the ceremony, they filled a jar of water energised with mantras. It so happened that the king woke up thirsty during the night and searched for water.

He could not find any other utensil with water except the energised jar. It was kept specifically for his queens to drink but he drank it unknowingly during the night.

When the other ascetics did not find the energised water in the jar, they enquired and came to know the reason. As the water was charged to bear a son, the king was impregnated. After due time, the royal doctors cut out his belly to take the son out. With the grace of the devas, the king also survived.

When the issue of whose milk the newborn would drink came up, Indra offered his forefinger to the child to suck and, hence, the name Mandhata.

Mandhata also earned the title of Sarvabhauma as he had conquered all other kings on earth. Moreover, afraid of his rule, all the thieves and bandits left the cities to live in caves. Thus, he is also called Trasadasyu.

His wife Bindumati bore him two sons, Purukutsa and Muchukunda. Purukutsa was blessed with a son Anaranya or Brihadashva who had a son called Haryashva. The next in line was Tridhanva and his son Arun.

Unfortunately for Arun, his son Satyavrata turned out to be greedy, vicious and impious. Once Satyavrata stole away a daughter of a brahmin. His outraged father, Arun, exiled him and asked him to go live with the chandalas[207].

While he was living in the company of chandalas, it did not rain for twelve years causing a severe drought. At the same time, Maharishi Vishvamitra also left his home to practise austerities.

Unable to look after the basic needs of their children in those difficult times, Vishvamitra's wife decided to sell off one of their sons. She thought that the money that she would get from selling could support her other sons, lest they all would die from hunger.

When she went out to undertake the trade, holding the son's neck by a rope, she encountered Satyavrata. He enquired the reason for her doing so. The lady cried and introduced herself. She then told him that they had no food in the house and the children could not bear to be hungry anymore.

Satyavrata, of his own volition and kindness, offered to supply her with food daily. He told her that till her husband was back, he would leave some food under a tree near her hermitage.

The child with fastened neck came to be known as Galaba and became a renowned saint.

Satyavrata hunted wild animals in the forest and provisioned the kill for the family. The family was grateful for the help.

One day, Satyavrata could not find a hunt. However, while traversing the nearby area, he came across Guru

Vashishtha's cow. He had always grudged that Vashishtha had deliberately not helped him by not assuaging his father's anger towards him.

Thus, under the effect of resentment and partly under delusion, he killed the cow and supplied a part of it to Vishvamitra's family. Oblivious to the fact that it was beef, the family ate it.

Soon Vashishtha learnt of this. He cursed Satyavrata, "O immoral one! First, you committed the sin of abducting a brahmin's daughter, then the wrath of your father and now you have killed a cow. Therefore, you will now be a pishacha[208]. For the three heinous crimes you have committed, you will have three shankus[209] on your head. Henceforth, you will be known as Trishanku."

Wandering in the forest, Satyavrata-turned-Trishanku became an ardent devotee of the Devi. He learnt the nine-lettered mantra of the Devi and recited it rigorously. Once he approached the brahmins to assist him in performing the Purashcharana[210] ceremony of the mantra.

The brahmins refused as he was in the pishacha state and, thus, not entitled to perform the ceremony.

Finding no redemption for himself, he decided to sacrifice his life. He lit a pyre. As he was about to enter the fire, the majestic Devi Bhagvati appeared there. She blessed him and said, "Your father will now take to performing austerities. You will succeed him as the next king."

With the Devi's grace, Trishanku was exonerated from his state of pishacha and all his previous sins. He regained his earlier handsome appearance of a prince.

Meanwhile, Narada reached Ayodhya and briefed King Arun. The king heard of his reformed son and his attempt to end his life. His heart changed. He directed his ministers to fetch his son.

The king welcomed his son back and before handing over the kingdom to him, gave him a set of advice. He said, "O Son! Continue to worship Devi Bhagvati. If she blesses you, you will have a successful life and eventually, you will be rid of the cycle of birth and death. Follow the path of dharma that obliges you to respect elders, ascetics, brahmins and gurus. Be charitable to them always. Perform your daily routine of sacrifices and venerations.

Always speak the truth. Control your senses. Never get addicted to hunting, betting, intoxication of any kind and harlots. Do not ever trust those who are habituated to any of the foregoing. Accumulate wealth in your treasury only through just means."

Saying so, Arun anointed Trishanku on the appointed day with due rites and mantras. The king, thereafter, left for the forest with his wife to enter Vanaprastha, the third stage of life.

In time, Satyavrata was blessed with a bright and promising son who was named Harishchandra. The son, after attaining adulthood, was named the crown prince.

Satyavrata felt the desire to leave the kingdom to his son and ascend to heaven while he was in his mortal body. He went to Vashishtha and expressed his wish. He sought the guru's counsel on the kind of sacrifice that would enable him to go to Devaloka.

Vashishtha explained to him, "It is not possible to go to Devaloka in the human body. When a person dies and leaves his body, he can then go to heaven provided he has earned it through good deeds by performing his duties and sacrifices."

But the king had made up his mind and was not willing to heed to right counsel. He warned Vashishtha, "If you are unwilling to perform an appropriate sacrifice for me to achieve my objective, I would engage another priest."

Vashishtha did not like his impertinence. The memories of various sins committed by the king came to his mind. He cursed Satyavrata again, "O wicked one! Your thoughts are akin to being a chandala. Therefore, you will live like one and never be able to go to heaven even after leaving this mortal body."

The curse changed everything for Trishanku so much so that he lost his lustre and his appearance turned dreadful. He thought to himself that he could not go back to that state of wretchedness.

He considered the option of suicide but, that being the most heinous crime without atonement, decided to leave for some unknown place and live the life of a chandala till he met a person who could help his restitution. With a repentant heart, he went to live near the banks of River Ganga.

When the king did not return, scouts were sent out looking for him. They learnt of the curse from Vashishtha and returned with the news to the prince. Harishchandra sent the ministers to go and convince his father to come back home.

The king, now a Chandala, did not agree to their request. He asked them to go back and coronate his son instead.'

Janamejaya became sad. He commented, 'Satyavrata perhaps is the only king to have been cursed twice. How did he manage to get rid of it the second time?'

Vyasa nodded in agreement and said, 'Destiny has strange ways of compensating. In Satyavrata's case, while he spent his time meditating on the Supreme Goddess, Maharishi Vishvamitra returned to his hermitage after concluding his tapasya.

He was pleasantly surprised to see his family in good health. He asked his wife how they managed to survive during the time of famine.

The wife narrated the dire conditions in which she had decided to sell off one of their sons and how Satyavrata had rescued them from the situation. She also told him that because of him committing the sin of killing a cow to save their family from hunger, he faced the wrath of Vashishtha's curse.

After listening to his wife, Vishvamitra consoled her and readily offered, "I will do all that is possible in my power to remit the sins of King Satyavrata."

He soon discovered that the king was living in a colony of chandalas as a result of being cursed by Vashishtha again. Vishvamitra met the king and said, "O King! You have gone through hell in the process of saving my family. I am indeed indebted to you. I shall help you to fulfil your desire."

The king took his blessings and revealed to him what he had requested Vashishtha to help him with.

Vishvamitra gave it careful thought and decided to perform a sacrifice for the cursed king. He began the preparations and invited all the other munis. But the news of Vashishtha's curse had also reached everyone and no one turned up for the sacrificial ceremony.

But Vishvamitra had already made up his mind. He took water in his hand and energised it with the recitation of the Gayatri Mantra. He said, "I give away all my punyas earned till now to Satyavrata. With the power of these, let him rise to heaven."

Propelled by the power of Vishvamitra's accumulated punyas, the king ascended through the air without wings and sped towards Devaloka. When the gatekeepers saw someone with an ugly appearance approaching heaven, they stopped him and informed King Indra.

Indra saw him and understood immediately what was happening. He said, "O cursed King! You are not fit to enter here. Go back to earth."

Indra's words caused Satyavrata's free fall towards earth. But the king was not one of those to give up. He shouted out for Vishvamitra's help.

Vishvamitra halted him wherever he was. While he was immobilised between heaven and earth, Vishvamitra initiated a grand sacrifice to fashion another creation with its own heaven.

Indra learnt of it and rushed apprehensively to Vishvamitra. He pleaded, "O Vishvamitra! Cease your sacrifice. Tell me what shall I do to satisfy you?"

A mollified Vishvamitra smiled and said, "I want King Satyavrata to go to Devaloka and spend his time there. Take him with you."

Indra was forced to accept Vishvamitra's wish as his command. He took Trishanku in his aerial car to his abode and changed his appearance to a lustrous divine form.

Vishvamitra returned to his hermitage and family. The city of Ayodhya continued to be ruled by a virtuous king, the son of Trishanku, Harishchandra.'

Harishchandra

Vyasa said, 'Harishchandra was overjoyed to learn that his father had been accepted in Devaloka. He was at peace and thus began ruling Ayodhya with happiness that was reflected among his populace. But the issue of not having an offspring became a persistent cause of worry.

He went to Vashishtha for advice. Vashishtha told him to worship Varuna, the best among the devas to grant a son.'

Janamejaya interrupted Vyasa. He asked, 'O Dvaipayana! Isn't Harishchandra the same king who had offered to perform Naramedha of his son to Varuna Deva? I distinctly recall the anecdote.'

Vyasa was pleased to see that Janamejaya was such an attentive listener. He smiled and continued, 'Yes, the great-grandson of Arjuna. The king was blessed with a son with Varuna's blessings and then tried to stall the sacrifice of his son, Rohit.

He first took the plea of the Sutak period and then sought time till the child had a tonsure ceremony. He extended it up to the Upanayana ceremony. Finally, he requested Varuna to wait till the Samavartan ceremony.

By the time of Samavartan, the boy had gone missing. Harishchandra was cursed and eventually found another boy, Shunahshepa, to be sacrificed in place of his son.

During the sacrificial ceremony of the brahmin boy, Vishvamitra intervened and gave the Varuna Mantra to the boy. The appeased Varuna who came and saved the boy as well as freed the king from his disease caused by the curse.

O King! I narrated to you the above in detail earlier. Now hear what happened thereafter.

When the Rajasuya Yagna was concluded, Shunahshepa raised a question in that assembly of wise persons. He asked, "Whose son am I now?"

The sages, brahmins and ministers present at the yagna began to argue. Some said he was the son of his biological father, Ajigarta while others thought that as Ajigarta had sold the boy, he was not entitled to be the father and, therefore, the buyer, that is, the king was the father now.

Yet some others contended that once the boy was given away by the king for the sacrifice, he could not be the father either. Since Varuna had saved the boy, he should be considered the father of the boy.

The assembly turned to Vashishtha, the guru of the royal family, and sought his counsel. He said, "There is no doubt that the boy had been bought by the king but he gave him away for sacrifice. Varuna saved the boy but he honoured the boy's veneration for him and, therefore, acted as a deva should. But in reality Shunahshepa had been saved by Vishvamitra as it was he who gave the boy the mantra. Thus, Vishvamitra is his father."

Vishvamitra agreed with the prudent words of Vashishtha and took the boy along to his hermitage.

Meanwhile, Rohit, who was living in a cave, heard about what had happened in Ayodhya and returned. The king welcomed him back and showered all his love on his only son.

In some years, the king performed a Rajasuya Yagna in which Vashishtha was the chief priest.'

Vyasa continued, 'Once Indra convened an assembly in which both Vashishtha and Vishvamitra were invited. Upon their arrival, Vishvamitra felt that Vashishtha, the family priest of the Suryavanshi kings, was being conferred more respect and care.

Vishvamitra could not curb his curiosity and he directly asked Vashishtha the reason for it. Vashishtha told him that King Harishchandra had given him great honour and made him the chief priest during his Rajasuya Yagna.

Vashishtha also praised the king for being virtuous, truthful and altruistic.

As Vishvamitra did not have the same experience with the king as Vashishtha had, he felt disgusted and said, "How could the king be considered virtuous? He first cheated Varuna on several occasions. Then he bought a young innocent boy to be sacrificed. He is a liar. And I shall prove it. If I do so, all of Vashishtha's punyas will be destroyed and if I don't, mine will be negated."

Both maharishis went their way after this altercation.

Sometime later, Harishchandra was on a hunting expedition in the forest where he found a fine-looking woman crying. The king stopped and asked her the reason and assured her that she was safe in his kingdom.

She said, "I am Siddharupini, the success. Maharishi Vishvamitra is currently practising austerities to control me. Save me from being possessed by him, if you could."

The king went to meet Vishvamitra and interrupted his meditation. He asked, "Why are you performing such severe austerities? I will give you whatever you desire."

The agitated maharishi returned to his hermitage and constantly thought about why the king had disturbed his tapasya. An already aggrieved Vishvamitra, harbouring anger towards the king, which was exacerbated since his encounter with Vashishtha in Indra's court, turned into vengeance against Harishchandra.

Vishvamitra directed a dreadful demon to take the guise of a gigantic boar. The boar entered the kingdom of Harishchandra and created havoc. He uprooted beautiful trees and trampled flowers. The workers and florists ran away frightened.

The city guards attempted to drive the boar away with stones, arrows and spears but he could not be controlled. He continued his rampage.

The king became furious when he learnt about it. He took his armoury and left on his horse in the direction where the boar had been spotted. An army of palace guards and soldiers followed him.

The king attacked the boar with his arrows. The boar dodged and ran away into the forest with the king trailing him. In this process, the soldiers were left behind and the king became alone.

As the sun went up and the day became hotter, the king and his horse were fatigued. He lost sight of the boar and his way too. He decided to take a short break and gather himself.

While he looked around for a place to relax, he found a rivulet with clean water. He dismounted the horse. The freshwater gave him and the horse much-needed relief.

Meanwhile, a passer-by brahmin saw the king and asked him for his introduction. Unbeknownst to the king, this brahmin was none other than Vishvamitra.

The king introduced himself and explained to him what had happened from the moment when the huge boar entered his kingdom till he lost sight of him in the forest.

Vishvamitra seemed to have a plan. He said, 'O Son of Trishanku! You are standing at a place which is highly auspicious. Take a bath and offer tarpan[211] in the name of your forefathers. You can also make charities as you may afford. This will earn punyas for you and your manes. Once you are done, I shall show you the way back to Ayodhya."

Harishchandra did as he was told and with folded hands said to the brahmin, "O high-born Dvija[212]! I have performed Rajasuya Yagna and I am capable of giving anything. Ask me whatever you desire."

So as not to show haste, Vishvamitra paused for a moment and said, "I have arranged for my son to get married, but I am a poor brahmin. All I want is some wealth to accomplish his wedding."

While uttering these words, the muni also cast a spell of gandharvi maya on Harishchandra and simultaneously created a young boy and girl as the young couple to be married.

The brahmin took the king and the young couple to his hermitage in a nearby city. After a wait of a couple of hours, he declared to Harishchandra that the wedding ceremony was over and asked for a grant of charities.

The effect of his maya had numbed the king's mind. Without asking for the amount, the king committed to giving whatever was required for the wedding.

The brahmin said, "O King! Give your entire kingdom with all its accoutrements of wealth, jewellery and the royal insignia as charity to the bridegroom."

Without the slightest hesitation, the king accepted to give away everything. But Vishvamitra went a step ahead. He said, "Daan[213] is not complete without dakshina[214]. Now give me a gift."

The king was shocked. He was left with nothing to offer. But he asked, "What do you want as dakshina? You fix the amount and I shall pay."

The brahmin fixed two and a half loads of gold. The king agreed to pay this too.

The king returned to his palace and, by this time, regained his lost senses. He told his wife how he had been deceived by a brahmin. He told her that he had given away everything and, therefore, they would have to leave the kingdom.

Before the king's subjects could bid farewell to the king and his family, the brahmin appeared at the palace and asked for the committed amount of gold. He added, "You have lost everything, the kingdom and the wealth. Where will you get the money to buy the gold? If you acknowledge that you cannot give it to me, I shall go away."

The king folded his hands again and pleaded with him, "O Muni! I have already given away everything in charity.

All I am left with is my wife Madhavi, son Rohit and me. In the past, I had the privilege of completing the Rajasuya Yagna and giving whatever everyone desired. Thus, give me a month and I shall give you the gold."

Harishchandra with his family went to Benares, the oldest city on earth and protected by Shiva himself. On the last day of the time limit of one month, Vishvamitra appeared in front of Harishchandra.

Harishchandra offered to give away his wife, son or himself to serve the muni but the latter was adamant that he only wanted his dakshina. As the thirtieth day was still not over, Harishchandra asked the muni to wait till the end of the day.

Harishchandra weighed all options including begging, stealing and borrowing and disregarded them as these were not according to the dharma of a kshatriya. He knew there would be unbearable consequences of these in future births. But not paying dakshina was not an option either.

Seeing his miserable condition, Madhavi suggested to him, "O dear husband! It is the play of time that we humans are in different states of happiness and sorrow. Time determines when one would get fame and respect or opprobrium. Time makes one a patron or a recipient. So, do not grieve about the deprivation of your kingdom and wealth.

To bear this difficult time, the best path for you would be to sell me and satisfy the brahmin with due dakshina. It will not fetch you any sin since the selling is neither for personal gain nor for obtaining any enjoyment."

Accepting the wise words of his wife with anguish, Harishchandra took her to the city's central plaza. With a heavy heart and choked voice, he cried out for buyers to take her as their maidservant.

Meanwhile,Vishvamitra assumed the form of another old brahmin and went to the same place. He asked for her price and without waiting for an answer, offered, "According to prescribed regulations under the Dharma Shastras, the price of a male servant is equivalent of one arbuda[215] gold mohurs[216] and that for a female servant is one koti[217] gold mohurs."

Harishchandra was too distressed to speak. Taking his silence as acceptance of the price, the brahmin placed the money and dragged Madhavi by her hair.

Seeing his mother's plight, Rohit clung to her and cried. The old man tried to whisk him away but failed. Madhavi begged the brahmin to buy her son too so that he remained with her. The brahmin agreed and threw another sack of gold mohurs in front of the king.

Madhavi, before leaving, circumambulated her husband and prayed that if she had earned virtues by performing yagna and charities as well as by serving brahmins, then she should get married to Harishchandra in her next birth too.

Witnessing the cruel behaviour of the brahmin towards his wife and son, Harishchandra lamented his fate in spite of having been born in the Ikshvaku dynasty.

Meanwhile, Vishvamitra, as the earlier brahmin, arrived there and asked Harishchandra for his dakshina. When Harishchandra offered him the gold that he had earned by selling his family,Vishvamitra did not accept it as it was still not enough.

Harishchandra prayed to the brahmin to further wait till the end of the day. The brahmin agreed to come back later at dusk.

Harishchandra now presented himself for sale at the same spot where he had earlier traded his wife and son. He begged to be bought before sunset.

Dharma Deva disguised as a hideous-looking Chandala, by the name of Pravira, arrived there. He offered to buy Harishchandra as a slave, but the latter hesitated and said that he wanted to be purchased by either a brahmin or a kshatriya.

Meanwhile, Vishvamitra came back again. He asked Harishchandra to sell himself quickly as there was hardly any time left before the day ended. Harishchandra begged him to take him as his slave instead of the balance dakshina rather than being sold to a Chandala.

Alas, there was no end to Vishvamitra's tricks. He accepted Harishchandra as his slave. But before Harishchandra could sigh with relief, the muni addressed the only buyer, "O Chandala! Tell me how much will you pay for my slave. I do not need him. I only want wealth."

Dharma-turned-chandala offered one thousand gems, one thousand jewels, one thousand pearls and one thousand gold mohurs to Vishvamitra, who gladly accepted them.

When the transaction was completed and Harishchandra was preparing to accompany the Chandala, a voice from heaven announced, 'O Harishchandra! You are now free of Vishvamitra's debt of dakshina.'

The Chandala dealt with Harishchandra in an as cruel a manner as possible. He chained him and kept him starved. But Harishchandra kept himself immersed in thoughts about his family.

After four days, the Chandala unchained him. He tasked Harishchandra to hold an old club in hand and guard the shamshan[218] in the southern part of the city. Besides, he was asked to collect the clothing of the corpses.

In spite of the dreadful smell and ambience, the cremation ground was a busy place. It was not only frequented by a large number of people accompanying the dead bodies for the final rites but also by jackals, dogs and vultures.

Harishchandra did as instructed. He disrobed the corpses and collected the valuables. Keeping a small portion of those for himself, he kept the major stake for his master. He worked day and night with little time to eat. A year passed by and Harishchandra was unrecognisable in his soiled rags over a skinny frame.

On the other end of the city, Rohit was growing up serving their master, the brahmin who had bought him and his mother. One day he went out with his peers to the forest to play and also to collect kusha grass for the veneration by his brahmin master. He also collected palash wood for homa before returning.

On his way back, he stopped to drink water and kept his headload on an anthill. Suddenly, a venomous snake came out and bit him. He died instantly.

The other boys ran to inform the brahmin. When Madhavi heard of this unfortunate news, she fell unconscious. When she regained her senses, she started wailing. The brahmin scolded her for crying during twilight hours.

She begged the brahmin to allow her to go and cremate her young son. But the brutal master wanted the work at home to be completed before she could leave.

It was well into the late evening when Madhavi finished all the chores and the brahmin allowed her to depart, with the condition to come back in the morning to continue with the work routine the next day.

With a grieving heart of a doting mother, she found the body of her dead son and cried her heart out. She deeply regretted the absence of her husband.

She recalled the prophecies by astrologers at the time of Rohit's birth that he would be a famed king and have a long life full of luxuries. She lamented that none of the predictions had come true.

While she was wailing with the head of the lifeless Rohit in her lap, she was spotted by the alert guards in the city. They mistook her to be a rakshasi feeding on young children and raised an alarm. They dragged her to the Chandala.

The chandala praised the guards for arresting the rakshasi and bringing her to him. He told them that they would accrue virtues in return and asked them to return to their respective places.

The Chandala tied Madhavi in a corner of his house and began to lash her. He simultaneously summoned Harishchandra. Telling him that she was a children-eating demon, he handed him a sword to kill her.

Harishchandra's soul trembled to hear the instruction. He withdrew from executing her. He said, "O Master! I can kill anyone for you, be him a deva or asura or human or a heavenly being. But I have vowed not to kill a woman. The killer of a woman has to suffer in the terrible Raurava[219] hell. I shall, therefore, do anything else that you desire of me."

The Chandala furiously said, "You will suffer in hell in any case for not following the orders of your master."

He forcibly gave a sharp scimitar to Harishchandra to execute the woman.

Harishchandra reluctantly went closer to Madhavi and said in a low voice, "O Devi! Forgive me for this monstrous act."

Madhavi gathered all her energy and requested him, "I have lost my young son due to a snake biting him. Allow me to get his dead body for the final rites. Once that is done, I am willing to die."

Harishchandra, out of pity, allowed her to get the body. She brought the dead body to the cremation ground and began to cry aloud. Till such time, both had been oblivious of each other's identity due to their piteous condition making them unidentifiable.

Harishchandra, out of curiosity, removed the sheet from the face of the corpse. When he carefully focused on the face, he recognised the beautiful features of his son. His suspicion was corroborated by the lamentations of his wife calling out his and his son's names.

He was aghast. Harishchandra screamed for his son and wife and let her know that it was him, her husband, in that appalling state. His grief was beyond words after realising the distressed condition of his wife over and above the pain of the death of their son.

Then it was her turn to be horror-struck, seeing the distraught condition of Harishchandra turned into a Chandala. She could not fathom the depth of contrast between a lustrous, healthy and handsome man who ruled earth with access to every luxury and the man in front of her in tattered clothes, matted hair and emaciated body living in such a penurious state.

She wondered if it was really her husband. Or was she dreaming? She prayed that if it were a nightmare, let it come to an end immediately.

But it was no dream. She gasped and said, "O King! You have always stood by dharma and truth. You now must follow your master's order. Go ahead without any hesitation and sever off my head."

Harishchandra was frozen and wished time would not move ahead. He contemplated, "As a slave to the Chandala, I do not even have control over my body and actions. I, therefore, cannot even end my life. If I do so, I will have to go to hell and be born again as a Chandala.

But the deepest sorrow for a man is to see his dead son. Irrespective of what happened to me, I shall immolate myself in the burning pyre of my son."

He told his resolve to his wife and asked her to go back to the brahmin's house. Madhavi insisted that she would join him in hell by entering the funeral fire.

Harishchandra readied the pyre and lit it. Then he and Madhavi, preparing to immolate themselves, began to meditate upon the Supreme Goddess. In no time, Indra and the devas along with Dharma, discarding the guise of Chandala, appeared in front of them.

Dharma stopped them and said, "I am pleased with your truthfulness, patience and immutable resolve to the path of dharma. I will grant you whatever you desire."

Indra added, "You with your karma have transcended this mortal world. I have come to take you, your wife and your son to Devaloka."

A few drops of nectar by Indra over the burning pyre extinguished it. The young Rohit became alive. The next moment, along with Rohit, Harishchandra and Madhavi too had regained their healthy appearances and royal attire.

Indra invited them to join him on the journey to heaven.

Harishchandra said, "How can I join you till I am a slave of the Chandala?"

Dharma smiled and said, "I am the Chandala. I also disguised as the snake that bit Rohit. For me, you have passed all the tests. Now you will join us by virtue of your karmas."

The king lived up to his fame again. He said, "A king is what he is because of the affection and respect of his subjects. I cannot go with you without them joining me. If I do so, it will be as grave a sin as the killing of a cow or a brahmin or a woman as well as addiction to drinking."

Indra replied, "All of them are not entitled. Some may be too sinful to be taken to heaven."

The king requested, "Allow me to distribute to them all my punyas earned throughout my life. One day of living with them in heavens will be superior to spending all my life there without them."

His arguments pleased the devas even more. They arrived in Ayodhya and informed the populace of their king's decision to take them along to Devaloka.

Before departing, Harishchandra crowned his son as the next king. He joined the aerial car sent by Indra with a large number of his subjects from the city willing to travel to heavens.'

Vyasa concluded, 'O Janamejaya! Seeing the king travelling to heavens in the divine aeroplane, Shukracharya commented, "The glory of Titiksha[220] and the fruits of daan have no comparison. It is because of these that Harishchandra has ascended to heaven today."

Therefore, O King, those who get to listen to this episode of King Harishchandra attain joy in their life.'

Shakti Pithas

Janamejaya asked, 'O Vyasa! Who did the great King Harishchandra and his wife meditate upon? Who helped them?'

Vyasa smiling replied, 'They remembered the name of Shatakshi Devi. To describe to you who she is, I will have to take you back to the days of yore.

Once there was an evil daitya called Durgam, son of Ruru and descendant of Hiranyaksha. In his evil mind, he wanted to know the source of devas' strength. He deciphered that the brahmins worshipped devas according to the manner prescribed in the Vedas by offering sacrifices. He deduced that the best option to weaken the devas would, therefore, be to annihilate the Vedas.

Durgam initiated severe penance to appease Brahma. He continued for one thousand years surviving only on air.

Finally, Brahma appeared to him and asked him to seek boons. The cunning Durgam asked for two wishes. He told Brahma, "O Grandsire! Let all the knowledge of the Vedas be with me only and also grant me enough strength to defeat the devas."

Brahma had no option but to grant Durgam what he desired.

As soon as Brahma granted Durgam the boons, there was chaos all around. The brahmins were devoid of mantras, hence they could not recite any. It led to a situation where their daily routine, full of distinct mantras, came to a halt. The brahmins were unable to comprehend the reason for the sudden disappearance of knowledge of mantras that came from the Vedas.

As there were no homa, japam and yagna to feed the devas, the latter gradually enervated. In the absence of devas' strength and energy, the cycle of nature was also disrupted. Rains stopped and the earth was parched with men, animals and plants losing their lives.

This was the apt time for the daityas to strike. They dislodged devas from Devaloka who ran away to Mount Meru to save their lives.

The devas decided to meditate upon the Supreme Goddess. The brahmins also joined them as they too wished to seek the Devi's forgiveness.

In time, the Devi appeared in her majestic form. Her dark blue appearance had the brilliance of millions of suns. Her four hands were holding arrows, lotus, bow and prasadam for her worshippers.

She was moved by the sufferings of her devotees. It caused water to flow out of her countless eyes. The water turned into continuous rain on earth for nine days and nine nights, which washed away people's misery.

The devas and brahmins bowed down to her and said, "O Devi! You have blessed us with water from your thousand eyes reviving this creation, therefore we will call you by the name of 'Shatakshi'."

The Devi then distributed the prasadam of fruits, vegetables and roots to all her devotees, which satisfied their thirst and hunger. Since then, she has also been given the title of Shakambhari.

Meanwhile, Durgam's spies informed him of the happenings on earth. He immediately gathered a humongous daitya army of one thousand Akshauhini and attacked the gathering of devas in the presence of the Devi.

The Devi first created a ring of protection around the congregation of her devotees and then came out to battle.

She created, from her body, thirty-two principal shaktis, with various names of Kalika, Tarini, Bala, Tripura, Sodashi, Bhairavi, Kamala, Bagala, Matangi, Tripura Sundari, Kamakshi, Tulaja, Jambhini, Mohini, Chhinnamasta, Guhya Kali, Dashsahastra-Bahuka and others. These shaktis doubled, followed by a multitude of shaktis arising out of the Devi.

A ten-day war followed in which the shaktis destroyed Durgam's huge army. Finally, Durgam himself joined his depleting forces on the eleventh day. He was decked up in red clothes and red garlands and was smeared in red sandal paste.

Fighting bravely against several shaktis simultaneously, he came face to face with the Devi herself. The battle continued for several hours. Eventually, the Devi shot fifteen dreadful arrows at him, which killed the charioteer and his four horses and pierced Durgam's arms and eyes. The arrows finally struck his heart and killed him. With this, the Vedas were released from his captivity.

The devas sang hymns praising the Devi. Addressing them with affection, she said, "The Vedas, the absence of whom created havoc for devas and humans alike, have originated from my body. Preserve and safeguard the knowledge of the Vedas. Henceforth, I shall also be known as Durga, the slayer of Durgam."

Devi Durga disappeared after delivering the words of wisdom.'

Vyasa's face showed a hint of pride as he narrated this anecdote because much later, it was he who had divided the Vedas into four and made them comprehensible for mankind. He continued, 'I was able to accomplish the enviable task of writing the Vedas only because of the blessings of Devi Bhuvneshvari.

She is beyond and above Brahma, Vishnu, Mahesh, Ishvara[221] and Sadashiva[222]. Her seat has the first four gods as the pillars and Sadashiva as the canopy above. Remember, these are also the presiding deities of the earth, water, fire, air and akash[223].'

Janamejaya felt privileged to be in the august company of Vyasa. He asked, 'O Muni! You had earlier explained that the trinity of gods was granted their respective energies in the form of consorts by Supreme Goddess at the Mani Dvipa. But in your narration, you have described Shiva's consort as the daughter of Daksha and Himalaya and Maha Lakshmi emerging out of the churning of Kshir Sagar. I am confused. Kindly remove my doubts.'

Vyasa was happy to hear this logical query from the king. He said, 'You are very right. The Supreme Goddess, the Mother of all, had given Sarasvati, Lakshmi and Gauri to Brahma, Vishnu and Shiva, respectively.

Later, it so happened that a daitya named Halahal, intoxicated by the boon from Brahma, invaded the abodes of both, Vishnu and Mahesh. The war between his forces, on one side, and Vishnu and Shiva together, on the other side, lasted sixty thousand years before yielding a victor, the gods.

On return to their respective places, they began to crow about their prowess, little realising the role of Shakti in their victory. Lakshmi and Gauri laughed at their bragging which irritated them profusely.

In their anger and as a result of the effect of maya, they disrespected their respective consorts who left them. As both became devoid of their shaktis, they lost their powers and lustre.

Brahma was worried to see this. Not able to find a solution on his own, he meditated upon Para Shakti, the ultimate power. He learnt that both Vishnu and Shiva were suffering due to her ire.

While he obligingly undertook the roles of Vishnu and Mahesh too, he called his sons Manu, Daksha, Sanaka and others to perform meditation to appease the Devi so that Lakshmi and Gauri could reincarnate.

After long years of tapasya, the Devi appeared to them. They prayed to her to reunite Hari and Hara with their respective consorts so that they could revert to their natural self.

The Devi said, "They had insulted my shakti and, therefore, are suffering. They will now reclaim their powers through Gauri, to be born in the family of Daksha, and Lakshmi who would arise out of the ocean of milk."

Accordingly, Devi Gauri was born to Daksha Prajapati. She, being the true part of Devi Bhagvati, was named Sati. In due time, she was married to Shiva, although she immolated herself later due to an unfortunate incident.'

Vyasa paused to read the mix of amazement and curiosity written on the face of Janamejaya. He continued, 'Once Maharishi Durvasa, on the banks of River Jambu, meditated upon Devi Bhagvati. She was pleased and blessed him with an exquisite garland. The garland attracted bees due to the sweet smell of its makranda[224].

While Durvasa was wearing it, Daksha saw him. He enquired about the extraordinary and fragrant garland. When he explained how he got it, Daksha asked for it.

Given Daksha's stature and his being a devotee of Shakti, Durvasa happily parted with the Devi's prasadam. Daksha brought it home and kept it on his bed. In the night, he made love to his wife on the same bed.

This animal-like action by Daksha caused his mind to harbour enmity towards Shiva and Sati. Consequently, when he abused Shiva at his grand sacrifice, Sati could not bear it and immolated herself.

Shiva was enraged to no limits. Bhadra Kaali and Virabhadra destroyed Daksha's sacrifice and wreaked havoc. Daksha was beheaded and his head was replaced by that of a goat.

An extremely distressed Shiva, with Sati's burnt body in his hands, began to crazily roam around. Vishnu cut the body into several parts with his arrows to stop

Shiva's madness. These parts fell in one hundred and eight places where Shiva's shrines were established as he spent time in them meditating on the grief of being separated from Sati.

Known as Siddha or Shakti Pithas[225], these are home to Shiva and Sati. These places of pilgrimage[226] are recommended for visiting and worshipping by all the devotees of Devi Bhagvati.'

The Virat Form of the Devi

An indefatigable Vyasa continued, 'While an anguished Shiva was aimlessly carrying the burnt body of Sati all around the world, the world was in pain too. It seemed that peace, joy and prosperity had left earth. So much so that planets moved in retrograde.

Coincidentally, a daitya called Taaraka gained supremacy in the three worlds. He had received a boon from Brahma that he could be killed only by Shiva's son. Since Shiva had lost his wife, the devas were unable to discern how the daitya would be killed.

The devas gathered at Vaikuntha and presented the cause of their anxiety to Vishnu. He explained, "As a mother may rebuke her children but never abandons her love and blessings on them, similarly Mother Goddess has no reason to be upset with you. She must have a plan in all this, eventually for a good reason and lesson for all of you to learn. Go and meditate upon her and seek her refuge."

The devas went to the Himalayas and practised various meditational forms to appease the Devi. They engaged in sacrificial ceremonies, yagna, meditation, Purashcharana[227], Tritiya Vrat[228], recitations of Devi Sukta[229], Antarayagas[230] and Pranagnihotra[231].

On the ninth day in the month of Chaitra, the Devi appeared. She was like an endless fire radiating like millions of suns yet having the serenity of millions of moons. She was adorned in red attire, with divine ornaments from head to feet.

The devas were overwhelmed by her grace and sweet smile. They prostrated to her and chanted hymns. They eulogised her several acts and forms in the past.

She asked them what they desired.

The devas explained the situation to the Devi. They told her about Brahma's boon to Taarakasura that he would be killed only by Shiva's son. On the other hand, Devi Sati had given up her body and Shiva was without a wife. As the devas could not understand how Shiva would beget a son to kill the daitya, they begged the Devi to take birth as the son of Shiva and deliver them from the vagaries of Taaraka.

The Devi blessed the devas, "A part of my shakti will incarnate as Gauri and be born as a daughter of Himalaya. She would marry Shiva and her son will eliminate Taarakasura."

Himalaya, the king of mountains, was overwhelmed with joy to hear this. He folded his hands in front of the Devi and said, "I must have earned many punyas in previous births that I am getting the privilege of becoming your father. I know that this is far bigger than any Ashvamedha or Rajasuya Yagna.

O Mother! I pray to you to reveal your real self to be able to understand you."

Devi Bhuvneshvari was pleased. She said, "There was nothing before this creation but I. I am known by several names but I cannot be described. I am beyond mind, thought, birth, death or any kind of mutation.

Maya originated from me. No one can define maya. It is neither existent nor non-existent. It cannot be a combination of both due to inherent contradictions. Everyone is subject to maya till one attains emancipation.

Maya is as natural as the light of the fire and the rays of the moon. It is my manifestation. It causes the cycle of birth and death. When the Pralaya[232] arrives, all beings, living and non-living, dissolve into maya. Several names are ascribed to maya – Pradhaan, Prakriti, Aja[233] and Shakti.

Maya is of two kinds: pure or Shuddha Sattva and impure or Avidya united with the gunas. The first is all-pervading, omniscient and omnipotent. Joined with the

Supreme Self, it is called Ishvara. When the Supreme Self joins Avidya, it forms Jiva. Impurity clouds Brahma, the knowledge, and causes all the miseries in the form of maya.

Ishvara as well as Jiva, both have three forms of bodies: causal called as Praagya, subtle as Taijasa and gross as Vishva. Ishvara in these three forms is known as Isha, Sutra and Virat, respectively.

Ishvara creates the universe through my shakti and is, therefore, implicit in me. Ishvara, on the one hand, creates worldly pleasure for Jiva and, on the other hand, helps him to liberate himself.

Remember, I am Nirguna. But when I am joined by maya, I assume various traits and become Saguna.

One must also remember that I am not the doer either, rather I am a witness to all the acts performed by Ishvara and Jiva. I, in the form of maya, discern one Ishvara from the other. I, in the form of Avidya, create the differences so as distinguish a Jiva and give him a distinct identity. Everything, living or non-living, moving or non-moving, exists because of a substratum and that is me."

Seizing this opportunity, the devas requested the Devi to demonstrate her virat[234] form in the fourth-dimensional space. She obliged them with the mesmerising form where Satyaloka[235] was her head, sun and moon her eyes, directions her ears, the Vedas her words, the universe her heart, earth her loins, Bhuvarloka[236] her navel, Maharloka[237] her neck, Janaloka[238] her face, Taparloka[239] her head, Svarloka[240] her arms, the Ashvin twins her nose, Brahma her eyebrows, Yama her teeth, oceans her bowels, mountains her bones, rivers her veins and trees her hair.

Her form was completed by maya as her smile, modesty as her upper lip, covetousness as her lower lip and unrighteousness as her back, moon as the mind, Hari as her knowledge and Rudra as her destroying power.

In that cosmic form, she licked the universe with her lips with her teeth making deafening sounds and her eyes emitting fire. Suddenly, the devas saw innumerable heads and eyes in that dreadful form. They shuddered and many swooned with fear. The Vedas, which were on four sides of the Devi, helped the devas to become conscious again. In the process, the devas also received the Vedas.

The devas prostrated to the virat form and sang hymns in praise of her. Then the Devi displayed her pleasant familiar appearance holding the noose and goad.

It was clear to all that the exhibition of the virat form by the Devi was a privilege, which could not otherwise be achieved by the knowledge of the Vedas or yoga or by any kind of austerities or meditation. It could only be granted by the Devi herself.'

Vyasa paused to let his words sink in and resumed the narration of what the Devi had told the devas, 'The cycle of birth and death, caused by Avidya, is incessant. It cannot be terminated with karma alone. One needs to acquire gyan too.

It is clear that karma ties more knots for a Jiva in contrast to the acquisition of knowledge, which is meant to open these knots. The karma, therefore, should be continued till one achieves Chitta Shuddhi.'

Janamejaya interrupted, 'What do you mean by Chitta Shuddhi? What happens after attaining it?'

Vyasa continued, 'The Devi answered the same question for the devas.

She said, "It means a combination of Shum, Dum, Titiksha, Vairagyam and Sattva Sambhava. It signifies control of the inner and outer organs of senses, the ability to equally endure physical dualities of life such as heat and cold, having dispassion and filling one's heart with Sattva Guna.

As one performs them, one is able to decipher the meaning of '*Tat Tvam Asi*'. Tat denoted Me and Tvam, the Jiva. Asi unifies the two opposite entities.

Similarly, my bijamantra 'Hrim' is also then understood. The sounds of Ha, Ra and I signify gross, subtle and causal bodies whereas Ma indicates the state of Turiya."

Himalaya then asked the Devi, "It is said that it could be achieved through yoga. How does one do it?"

The Devi replied, "Yoga is nothing but an instrument to unify the Jiva with Parmatman. But it is impaired by six adversaries: avarice, anger, covetousness, ignorance, ego and envy. A yogi or a practitioner of yoga utilises eight tools of Yama, Niyama, Asana, Pranayaam, Pratyahara, Dharana, Dhyana and Samaadhi.

As part of these tools, a yogi observes ahimsa and ensures no harm to others, Asteyam or non-stealing, truthfulness, brahmacharya or celibacy, mercy, honesty, compassion, cleanliness and frugal eating. This is in addition to the physical and mental exercises and postures that he is required to perform.

The yogi also focuses on the three most prominent nadis[241] of a total of seventy-two thousand. These are Sushumna, the central one with Ida on its left and Pingala on the right."

Thereafter, the Devi also explained other forms of yoga as well as Kula Kundalini and the seven chakras in the body. She finally said, "Yoga accompanied by mantras is an excellent route to realise knowledge which is nothing but me, the Devi."

O King! This knowledge is not easy to comprehend. It is important to have a guru to impart it and the guru ought to be served with due care. It is said that if gods are angry, the guru can salvage but if he becomes annoyed, even god cannot save.

This is how the two Ashvin brothers obtained the Brahma Gyan, the knowledge that was delivered by the Devi to the devas after showing her virat form.'

Janamejaya requested Vyasa to narrate this anecdote.

Vyasa obliged, 'Once Muni Dadhichi belonging to the Atharvana family wanted to obtain Brahma Gyan. He went to Indra and requested him. Indra agreed to teach him on one condition that Dadhichi would have to sever his head if he parted the knowledge with anyone.

After Dadhichi was enlightened by Indra, the Ashvin twins went to him and prayed to be delivered of the ultimate knowledge. He told them about Indra's warning.

The Ashvin twins were no ordinary beings. They were the physicians of the devas. They told Dadhichi that his head would be replaced with that of a horse and he could impart the gyan from the horse's mouth. When Indra, as his prerequisite was, would chop off his horse head, they would again replace it with his original one.

It happened as it was planned and the Ashvin twins were able to receive Brahma Gyan.'

Janamejaya never ceased to seize an opportunity to ask a question, 'If knowledge, accompanied by karma, is the path to salvation and ends the cycle of birth and death, then what is the role of bhakti, the worshipping?'

The muni continued, 'The Devi also explained this to the devas. Let me tell you what she said.

The three routes to liberation or moksha are karma, gyan and bhakti. The latter is the easiest for humans, especially during Kali Yuga. Bhakti is also of three kinds owing to the three gunas.

It is Tamasika if someone worships to inflict harm to others; Rajasika if worshipping is intended to quench a desire for oneself, be it fame or material objects; and Saattvika if it is done to purify oneself with no other objective. The last one leads to Para or Supreme Bhakti.

In Para Bhakti, one is completely devoted to the Devi and does not think himself to be separate from her. This devotion transforms into gyan leading to liberation or moksha. Gyan is not outside but resides in each human being like ghee potentially is in the milk. Gyan is achieved through the merits of several births like the sharpening of an arrow on a stone.

In order to perform bhakti, the Devi also described places of pilgrimage where visits earned a man punyas. The best of these are Vindhyachala Vasini, Annapurna and Kanchipuram. Then there are Sri Guhya Kaali, Meenakshi Devi, Bhuvneshvari, Mallari and Kamakhya.

In addition to these, there are other places such as Kolhapur, Matripura in Sahyadri mountain, Tulajapur, Saptashringa, Hingula, Jvala Mukhi, Bhima Devi, Vimala Devi, Sri Chandrala Devi, Nilamba, Pushkar, Amarkantaka, Naimisharanya, Pushkareshini and Prabhas.

O Janamejaya! The Devi also mentioned the names of several other places in the land of Bharat.

Not only the pilgrimages, but she also pronounced two ways of worshipping her: external and internal. External worshipping is again of two kinds: Vaidik and Tantrik.

In the Vaidik custom, one worships the Devi's virat form after casting aside ego and arrogance, based on the mantras from the Vedas and its derivatives like Shrutis and Smritis.

The Tantrik form makes use of certain mantras that do not originate from the Vedas but are contrary to them. These, known by the names of Vama, Kapalak, Kaulak and Bhairava, were created by Mahadeva and utilised by the daityas and other negative forces.

External worship eventually takes one to the next stage, that is, internal. It occurs only after one's heart constantly meditates on Para Brahma[242].

The Devi also prescribed the mode of external worshipping. It begins by waking up early morning and meditating upon Brahmarandhra[243], the thousand-petal lotus of the colour of camphor. Thereafter, remembering his guru, one should practise Kundalini[244] and then meditate on the Kundalini fire in the Muladhara[245] lotus.

After completing the daily routine, one should perform Agnihotra Homa and puja for the Devi. Following this, Bhuta Shuddhi of the elements of the body and Martika Nyasa[246] should be performed.

Subsequently, visualising the Supreme Goddess sitting on Panchmahapreta[247], one should meditate upon her along with japam. After performing arghya and purifying all materials in the puja, one should place the deity on the aasana and invoke her through Praan Pratishtha[248]. The worshipping of Devi Bhuveshvari as the chief deity yields all the desired results.

After the homa, feeding of brahmins and young virgin girls, who represent the Devi, should be done with devotion.'

Vyasa paused before completing the narration, 'The Devi after delivering the Brahma Gyan to Himalaya and the devas disappeared. In due time, Gauri was born to Himalaya and married Shiva. Their son Kartikeya killed Taarakasura. Lakshmi also emerged out of the churning of the ocean and was presented to Vishnu.

Hence both, Shiva and Vishnu, received their shaktis back.'

Creating the Creation

Janamejaya asks, 'O Vyasa! I am keen to know how this creation came into being. I feel if one knows it, it would help avoid the sharp effects of maya.'

Vyasa smiled at the king's natural inquisitiveness and responded, 'O King! This has been a perpetual quest. Once Narada himself had asked this to Maharishi Narayana. Though Narada knew that all the causes of this creation eventually merge into one and only Devi Maha Maya, he still requested Narayana to describe the origin and the end of creation.

To this, Narayana said, "Brahma had asked Svayambhuva Manu, his son and the lord of Manvantras, to bring creation into existence. Svayambhuva Manu sought Brahma's advice so that it could be done unimpeded. Brahma told him to worship Devi Bhagvati, the Mother Goddess, and seek her blessings.

Manu meditated upon the Devi and eulogised her. She appeared and asked for his wish. Manu's desire was simple yet encompassing everything possible. He said, 'If you are pleased, then bless me that my mission would be accomplished without any obstacles.'

Manu received his desired boon and went to Brahma and asked for a place to begin his work of creating. Brahma fell into deep thought as earth was still submerged in eternal waters. He thought of seeking the help of Vishnu whose navel he himself had arisen from.

While Brahma was still contemplating and discussing this with his son, a young boar emerged out of his nostril. His size was as big as a thumb. While it was still in the air, it began to grow bigger. In no time, it turned bigger than an elephant. By the time it came on the ground, it had taken a gigantic form.

Everyone understood that the boar was none else but Sri Hari himself. They all chanted hymns in his praise.

Vishnu, in the incarnation of a boar, dived into the endless ocean in search of earth. While the ocean was frightened, the boar went deep inside trying to find earth through her smell. The moment he found earth, he picked her up on his protruding teeth. He placed her outside the waters in her due position, but not before killing Daitya Hiranyaksha who resisted him.

Brahma then asked Manu to go about with his assigned task of creation.

Manu had two sons, Priyavrata and Uttanapada, and three daughters, Akuti, Devahuti and Prasuti. They were given in marriage to Maharishi Ruchi, Prajapati Kardam and Prajapati Daksha, respectively.

While Akuti gave birth to Yagnapurusha, a part of Sri Hari himself, Devahuti was blessed with Kapila who conceived the Samkhya Shastra, a treatise on spiritual philosophy and Dhyana Yoga.

Prasuti and Daksha were blessed with several daughters whose progenies were responsible for creation.

Priyavrata married Vishvakarma's beautiful daughter Brahishmati and had ten sons and one daughter. Three of them, Mahavira, Savana and Kavi, renounced worldly affairs. The others were Agnidhra, Idhmajibha, Yagnabahu, Rukmashukra or Hiranyareta, Dhritprishtha, Medhatithi and Agnihotra.

Priyavrata also had three more sons, Uttama, Tamasa and Raivata from another wife. Each of these three became the lord of one of the Manvantaras.

Priyavrata ruled earth for a long time. He once noticed that while one part of earth had sunshine at a particular time, the other part was engulfed in darkness and vice versa. To rectify this, he mounted his chariot, as lustrous as the sun, and circumambulated earth seven times.

During this process, seven oceans came into existence on earth by the touch of the wheel of his chariot with the intervening land turning into seven continents. These were named Jambu, Plaksha, Shalmali, Kusha, Krauncha, Shaka and Pushkar.

The seven oceans, called Kshar Sagar consisted of salt water, Ikshu Sagar of sugarcane juice, Sura Sagar of wine, Ghrita Sagar of ghee, Kshir Sagar of milk, Dadhimanda Sagar of curd and Shudho Sagar of pure water.

Priyavrata made his son Agnidhra the lord of Jambu Dvipa, which is surrounded by Kshir Sagar. He also made Idhmajibha the lord of Plaksha surrounded by Ikshu Sagar, Yagnabahu the lord of Shalmali surrounded by Sura Sagar, Hiranyareta of Kusha surrounded by Ghrita Sagar, Dhritprishtha of Krauncha surrounded by Kshir Sagar, Medhatithi of Shaka surrounded by Dadhimanda Sagar, and Agnihotra of Pushkar surrounded by Shudo Sagar.

He gave his daughter Urjasvati in marriage to Shukracharya who bore the famed daughter Devyani.

Narayana further described that Jambu Dvipa was divided into nine varshas[249] of which the central one was called Ilavrita. Mount Meru is in the middle of Ilavrita Varsha. The northern territory of the varsha has three mountains, Nilagiri, Shvetagiri and Shringavau, which divide it from the Ramyaka, Hiranmaya and Kuru varshas, respectively.

The southern part too has three mountains, Nishadha, Hemakuta and the Himalayas whose further south is the territory of Bharat Varsha. The west has Malyavan and the east has Gandhamadan with Nilagiri and Nishadha mountains extended into it.

The four main mountain ranges of Mandar, Merumandar, Suparshava and Kumud are considered the four pillars of Mount Meru. From the Mandar range, a river by the name of Aruna flows down towards the east. Here Devi Bhagvati is worshipped as Aruna Devi. Another river from Mandar flows towards the south of Ilavrita called Jambu. The Devi acquired another name at this river, Jambadini.

The golden mountain Meru is surrounded by Jathara and Devakata on the east, Pavamana and Pariyatra on the west, Kailash and Karaveer on the south and in the north, Trishanga and Makar. Brahma's abode is in the centre of Mount Meru while eight lokpalas of Brahma have their cities encircling it.

Thus, the nine cities on Mount Meru are known as Manovati, Amaravati, Tejovati, Samyamani, Krishnaganga, Shraddhavati, Gandhavati, Mahodaya and Yashovati. Brahma and other devas inhabit these cities.

River Ganga flowed above these cities through a hole created by the toenail of Vishnu's incarnation, Vamana, when he was circumambulating the universe. Therefore, Ganga is also known as Vishnupadi.

From Brahmaloka, Ganga gets divided into four streams: Sita, Alakananda, Bhadra and Chaturbhadra. Alakananda flows through Bharat Varsha and confluences into the ocean.

Narayana also described various mountains and rivers flowing out of them in the land of Bharat. He emphasised that only the fortunate ones were born in Bharat as this land had the grace of gods.

It is for this reason that even the devas and the rishis who have to necessarily serve in lower births of humans to redeem their karmas, wish to be born in Bharat Varsha. It is here that mortal beings get the opportunity to devote themselves to worship Sri Hari Vishnu and achieve Moksha.'

Vyasa continued, 'Rishi Narayana also explained to Narada the significance of other continents. Plaksha Dvipa, deriving its name from the plaksha tree of golden colour, was given to Idhmajibha. He divided it into seven varshas and gave them to his sons.

Shalmali, twice the size of Plaksha, again took the name of the tree there. The tree is the abode of Garuda. Yagnabahu also gave its seven parts to his sons.

Next is Kusha Dvipa, where kusha grass grows. Its ruler Hiranyareta divided it into seven parts. The inhabitants of this dvipa worship the fire god.

Krauncha is twice the area of Kusha and inherits its name from the gigantic mountain in that land. Varuna is the presiding deity of this dvipa.

Shaka continent is known by the name of the tree existing in that dvipa. The people in this land are known for worshipping Sri Hari through the practice of Pranayaam.

Pushkar, also known by the name of the tree, is Brahma's seat. It is divided into two varshas.

Beyond the ocean of pure water, a mountain called Lokaloka exists where nobody lives because anything that comes in contact with the land there turns into gold.

Further away from Lokaloka, there lies the ellipsoidal or egg-shaped space between heaven and earth, called Antariksha. As the sun in the form of Vairaja is in the middle of this otherwise dead space, it is also called Martanda. The sun is like a soul for all living beings, both moving and non-moving. The sun also assumed the name of Hiranyagarbha as it was born from this golden egg.

The sun is on constant move, from uttarayana to dakshinayana and then back. This movement changes the span of daytime vis-à-vis the night. During the move, the sun traverses twenty-seven nakshatras[250]. Three nakshatras form a vithi[251] and three vithis form a marg[252].

Ashvini, Krittika and Bharani form Naga Vithi, Rohini, Ardra and Mrigashira form Gaja Vithi and Pushya, Ashlesha and Punarvashu make Airavati Vithi. These three vithis define the Uttara Marg when the days in Bharat are longer.

Purvaphalguni, Uttara Phalguni and Magha are called Arshabhi Vithi while Hasta, Chitra and Svati are called Go Vithi and Jyeshtha, Vishakha and Anuradha are known as Jaradgavi Vithi. They form the Madhyam Marg.

Mula, Purvashadha and Uttarashadha are named Aja Vithi. Shravana, Dhanishtha and Shatabhisha are known as Mriga Vithi. Uttara Bhadrapada, Purvabhadrapada and Revati are called Vaishvanari Vithi. These three vithis make the dakshina Marg during which the days are shorter than the nights.

Besides, Abhijit Nakshatra was specifically created to revolve around Mount Meru and is termed the twenty-eighth nakshatra.

The city of Indra and devas, located in the east of Meru, is known as Devadhanika. The city of Varuna is in the west of Mount Meru and is called Nimnochani. The city of Yama, Samyamani, is in the south while the city of Chandra, called Vibhavari, is in the north.

What various cities term as the rising and setting of the sun, means that the sun appears and disappears for these cities. But the sun always exists and is visible to the inhabitants of Meru.

Narayana also explained to Narada the motion of other planets and their effect on the destinies of humans. He said that the sun and all the planets move through twelve rashis[253] with Mount Meru kept as the axle. The sun and all the planets have three kinds of movements: Shighragati[254], Mandagati[255] and Samgati[256].

The time the sun takes in traversing over two rashis is called a ritu[257]. Thus, there are six seasons in a year.

The moon travels past one nakshatra in thirty muhurtas[258]. The moon has several sobriquets because of its properties. It is called Manomaya, the giver of all desires; Annamaya, the lord of all aushadhhis; Amritdhara, full of nectar; Sudhakara, the one that gives Nirvana and Sarvamaya, nourisher of all beings.

Also present is planetVenus or Shukra and further away is Mercury or Buddha. When Mercury, the son of Moon, is away from Sun, then natural disasters like hurricanes or droughts or showers of meteors occur.

Located higher than earth is another planet Mars or Mangal, the son of Earth. It takes three fortnights to travel through one rashi. Planets Jupiter or Brihaspati and Saturn or Shani are located higher than Mars. Consequently, their movement is even slower.

Jupiter takes about a year to pass through one rashi and Saturn takes about thirty months. Shani, the son of Sun, is the slowest planet and is the cause of turbulences and grief to all.

The farthest is the Saptarishi[259] mandala, the seven stars. They circumambulate Dhruvloka[260], the abode of Dhruva, located the farthest. It is also known as Vishnupada signifying the highest place of Bhagvan Sri Hari.

O King! Each deva, planet, star or any of the celestial body continuously revolves around Dhruvloka untiringly.'

In an attempt to explain an endless subject in as succinct a manner as possible, Vyasa continued, 'Muni Narayana also mentioned Rahu which is situated below the sun. The vengeful Asura Rahu, son of Simhika, hits the sun and the moon on various occasions due to an old enmity, which results in eclipses.

Siddhas, charanas and vidyadharas inhabit the regions below Rahu. Under these regions, other places existed that are occupied by yakshas, rakshasas, pishachas, pretas and bhutas.

He also described that there are seven nether regions under earth called Atala, Vitala, Sutala, Talatala, Mahatala, Rasatala and finally Patala. There exists a world filled with prosperity for asuras and serpents who live a resplendent life.

These regions are no less than heaven in their comfort and affluence. So much so that many snakes carry such gems on their crest, which brighten the night like a day leaving no darkness anywhere.

They have drinks that are of medicinal variety and save them from all kinds of diseases, old age, sweats, malodours and usual fatigues. They only fear the brilliance of Sri Hari and his Sudarshana Chakra.

The powerful Daitya Bal reigns the Atala region. He is the son of the famed Asura Maya, the creator of ninety-six forms of maya. No other being knows so many forms. A yawn by Bal created three kinds of women: Pumshchali or unchaste woman, Svairini meaning an adultress and Kamini signifying a lovely woman.

The second region Vitala is below Atala where Hatakeshvara, a form of Shiva, lives with his consort Bhavani. Also, a place called Sutala exists where Sri Hari settled Daitya Bali after taking away the three worlds from him, in the form of Vamana.

Right below Sutala is Talatala where the city of the famed Daitya Tripura is located. Under that is Mahatala, the city of descendants of the serpent Kadru. Going down further is Rasatala where Pani asuras live.

Finally, Patala, the abode of Vasuki, the chief of snakes, exists. His band of dreadfully poisonous snakes have multiple heads, even up to a thousand. Some of them have crests on their heads illuminating the nether region.

Below Patala, there is a region of infinite darkness. There exists a form of Sri Hari with thousand heads called Shankarsana or Ananta.'

Hells

An untiring Vyasa continued, 'Narada had more queries. He asked Narayana to explain why so many diversities had been created when the karmas performed by living beings were the same.

Narayana said, "The karmas bear the results depending on their nature or shraddha, which is of three kinds: Saattvika that always bears happiness, Rajasika that causes pain and Tamasika that leads to wretchedness and loss of wisdom. The innumerable permutations due to the varying degrees of these in the performance of karmas lead to different results.

Based on these results, Yama calculates the net outcome for a dead who is brought to the southern region between Prithvi and Atala. This region is cohabited by Yama, his ganas[261] and the pitris. Here, the pitris called Agnishvaata continue to meditate and offer blessings to their descendants.

If the analysis of karmas leads to net sins committed by a being, then one is sent to one of the twenty-eight tormenting hells where one suffers according to the karmas committed in a lifetime. These hells are Tamisra, Andha Tamisra, Raurava, Maharaurava, Kumbhipaka, Kaalsutra, Asipatra Kanana, Shukramukha, Andhakupa, Krimibhojana, Taptamurti, Sandamsha, Vajrakantaka-Shalmali, Vaitarani, Puyoda, Pranarodha, Vishasana, Lalabhaksa, Sarameyadana, Avichi, Ayahpana, Ksharakardama, Rakshogana Bhojana, Shulaprota, Dandashuka, Avatarodha, Paryavartana, and Suchimukha."

Narada then asked, "O Narayana! Kindly enlighten me on the correlation between karma and the corresponding hell."

Narayana explained, "Tamisra is the destination for those who purloin possessions, wives or sons of others. If one deceives a man and illicitly enjoys with his wife, he is sent to Andha Tamisra where, upon reaching, he turns blind, hence the name Andha.

The one who is only bothered about 'I', 'me', 'myself' and 'mine' meaning that he only reared himself and his family, goes to Raurava. There he is tormented by the Ruru animals who are more savage than serpents.

If someone takes advantage of others, he is sent to Maharaurava where the beings who were tormented by him take the form of Rurus and feed upon his flesh. One who cruelly kills other animals and birds is broiled in hot oil in Kumbhipaka hell.

One who squabbles with his pitris and brahmins is taken to Kaalsutra hell where he is incinerated by fire and Surya. One who violates dharma and leaves the path of the Vedas is sent to Asipatra. There, upon being whipped, he runs helter-skelter and is cut by the sharp asi[262] leaves.

The kings or courtiers whose punishments are not in accordance with dharma are sent to Shukramukha. Those who do not appreciate the pain of those being tormented by them go to Andhakupa where they are haunted by beasts and cruel animals.

A man who amasses wealth and does not perform acts of charity to feed the devas or honour his guests is considered akin to a crow. Such a person is sent to Krimibhojana, a reservoir of worms.

One who thieves gold and jewellery is taken to Sandamsha. Those who maintain illicit cohabitation are brought to Taptamurti where they are made to embosom blazing hot iron statues of the other sex.

A person who commits unnatural sexual acts with other species goes to Shalmali, which is full of thorns made of iron.

O Narada! When anyone from royal lineage or in the service of royalty walks the unrighteous path, he is thrown into Vaitarani. It is like a ditch full of aquatic animals ready to eat his flesh.

Those who marry Vrishalis, girls under the age of puberty, or remain unclean by not caring about shame on account of breach of established customs are thrown into Puyoda. It is filled with pus, mucous, excreta, urine and such abhorrent things.

The twice-born[263], who maintain dogs and donkeys or are fond of hunting or killing deer and birds are shot arrows at by the ganas in Pranarodha hell. Other twice-born who copulates with a woman of the same gotra[264] are taken to Lalabhaksa, filled with semen and made to drink it.

Those with vanity and temper to kill an animal as a vain sacrifice are whipped ruthlessly in Vishasana. Others who plunder or arson or poison someone or are deceitful as well as those kings or courtiers who misappropriate or destroy their own people are all destined for Sarameyadana. This hell has seven hundred and twenty ferocious sarama[265] ready to devour them."

Narayana continued with the description, "Those who falsify transaction of money or a testimony go to Avichi hell. There, they are dropped from a great height with their head downwards towards the ground that appears to have waves.

A man who turns negligent due to drinking alcohol is thrown into Ayahpana where he is made to drink molten iron. One who does not respect seniors or elders in age, rank, birth, knowledge, etc., out of misplaced ego is made to rot in Ksharakardama.

Those who perform human sacrifices suffer in Rakshogana Bhojana where they are made to eat human flesh like a rakshasa. Yet those who kill innocent humans by piercing shulas[266], particularly in breach of their trust, go to Shulaprota.

Someone who brings distraught or misery to others like a serpent does is sent to Dandashuka hell to be eaten by five- and seven-headed worms. Those who torture others by forcing them to stay in dark places are taken to Avatarodha, which is filled with poisonous smoke.

A sinful eyeing of one's guests leads one to Paryavartana hell where one is tormented by crows and vultures who take out one's eyes. Lastly, someone who distrusts everyone due to greed for money and is involved in making and hoarding it is sent to Suchimukha.

O Narada! These hells further have excruciating kundas[267], eighty-six of which are prominent although there are many more."

Narayana also told Narada that these kundas are manned by ruthless servants of Yama. The sinners are tormented in these through various means depending upon the kind of sin committed.

Thus, a sinner suffers in various hells and pays for his deeds whereas a virtuous one goes to other realms of pleasure and happiness. Besides avoiding sin, worshipping various forms of the Devi also helps in crossing the ocean of existence, maya.'

Prakriti

Vyasa further recalled, 'Narada also requested Narayana to describe various forms of the Devi and the manner of worshipping them to get over this tide of maya.

Narayana replied, "The Devi's worshipping removes all obstacles and fulfils one's desires. Though no one can fully comprehend Prakriti, simply knowing them leads to liberation. Therefore, I will now tell you about the five aspects of the Devi called Prakriti Panchaka, as I heard from my father, Dharma.

While 'Kriti' means creation, the prefix 'Pra' adds 'excellent' to it. At the same time, the three parts of the word, 'Pra', 'Kri' and 'Ti' signify Sattva, Rajas and Tamas gunas, respectively. While the Devi has always existed, even before the creation, she is termed as Devi Prakriti after the creation was created or, in other words, maya was manifested.

At the time of creation, the eternal Brahma divided himself into two halves: the right side as male called Purusha and the left side as female termed Prakriti. The Purusha and Prakriti are inseparable like the fire and its burning ability.

The Devi or the Shakti, post-creation, has five principal forms: Durga (the mother of Ganesha), Radha, Lakshmi, Sarasvati and Savitri.

The first, Mula Prakriti, called by several names, Maha Maya, Durga, Devi Ishvari, Narayani and Vishnumaya, is the consort of Shiva. The most auspicious one, she is the presiding deity of all the devas. She possesses all eighteen siddhis and when pleased, bestows all auspiciousness, bliss and happiness to her devotees.

The second is Padma or Lakshmi or Maha Lakshmi. Her nature is Shuddha Sattva, the purest form of Sattva Guna, which means she is free from all kinds of avarice, anger and vanity. She rules wealth and prosperity and, therefore, is the source of life.

The third, Devi Sarasvati, is the deity of learning, speech, knowledge, intelligence and wisdom. Her nature is also of Shuddha Sattva.

Known by the names of Devi Savitri as well as Gayatri, she is the mother of all four varnas[268], the Vedas, the seed of mantras and tantras and the embodiment of all samskaras. This fourth Shakti is the presiding deity of Brahma Teja[269].

The fifth Shakti is Devi Radha or Radhika, who is the presiding deity of five praan[270] by virtue of which she exists everywhere and in everything, as well including in the rasalila. She is Nirguna, devoid of the three gunas, Nirakara, without a shape and Nirlipta, without any attachments. Therefore, she is not afflicted by ahamkara. On the one hand, she bestows bhakti towards Krishna and on the other hand, affluence and fortune."

Narada interjected, "O Maharishi! How do these five Prakritis manifest into other forms of the Devi?"

Narayana continued, "O Narada! Each female is a part or part of a part of these five supreme forms.

The first among all rivers, Ganga, originating from the lotus feet of Vishnu, purifies each being and liberates everyone who takes a dip in her holy waters. The holy tulasi, who dwells at the lotus feet of Hari, is the foremost among all the flowers. She helps in performing all acts of veneration.

Devi Manasa, the daughter of Ananta Deva and the sister of Vasuki, also known as Jarat Kaaru or Naagmata, is the presiding deity of mantras. Mangal Chandika originated from the face of the Devi and bestows bliss, prosperity and happiness.

Devi Shashthi, the giver of male progenies, is the sixth Mula Prakriti and, hence, called Shashthi. She is like a foster mother to all children and is, thus, worshipped on the sixth and twenty-first day after the birth of a child.

Kaali, who appeared from the forehead of Durga, is the foremost of all Shaktis. While she grants success to all, she can destroy the universe in one breath. Vasundhara, is the cradle of civilisation and, thus, the mother since her surface gives birth to all kinds of food and her womb is the source of all precious metals.

Devi Svaha is the wife of Agni and without whom no oblation to any god can be performed. Dakshina and Diksha are the wives of Yagna without whom the latter cannot provide fructifying results.

The utterance of Devi Svadha's name is a must while making an offering to the pitris. She is the wife of pitris. Devi Svasti, fructification of action, is the wife of Vayu while Pushti, nourishment, is the wife of Ganesha. Tushti, contentment, is the wife of Ananta Deva. Sampatti, wealth, is the wife of Ishaan Deva.

Dhriti, patience, is the wife of Kapila Deva. Sati, truth, is the wife of Satya Deva. Daya, mercy, is the wife of Moha Deva. Pratishtha, the wife of Punya Deva, bestows merit while Kirti, the wife of Sukarma, gives fame.

The honourable Kriya, effort or action, is the wife of Udyoga, diligence.

Mithya, falsehood, is the wife of Adharma. She was virtually non-existent in Satya Yuga but started developing in subsequent yugas and gained complete impudence and all-pervasiveness with her brother Kapat, deceit, in Kali Yuga.

Shanti, peace, and Lajja, modesty, are the wives of Sushil, good behaviour. Buddhi or intelligence, Medha or genius and Dhriti or fortitude are the wives of Gyan, knowledge.

Murti, personification through an idol, is the wife of Dharma without which the deities would not have a place to rest. Yoga Nidra or sleep is the wife of Rudra

Deva. Nidra's daughters – Tandra or lethargy and Priti or affection – are the wives of Sukha, bliss.

Kaal, time, has three wives, namely, Sandhya, twilight, Ratri, night and Din, day. Not even Brahma can reckon time without them. Kaal has two daughters – Jara, senility, and Mrityu, death – both married to Jvara, fever.

Kshudha or hunger and Pipasa or thirst are the wives of Lobha, covetousness. They are essential as without them, the world would be submerged in anxiety.

Prabha, splendour, and Daahika, combustion, are the wives of Tejas, the essence of fire.

Shraddha, faith, and Bhakti, devotion, are married to Vairagyam, dispassion.

Then there are Aditi, the mother of devas; Surabhi, the mother of cows; Diti, the mother of daityas; Kadru, the mother of serpents; Vintaa, the mother of Garuda; and Danu, the mother of danavas[271]. Each of them has a role in the creation. All these and many more are kalaas[272] of Mula Prakriti.

Rohini, the wife of Chandra; Sanjana, the wife of Surya; Shatrupa, the wife of Manu; Sachi, the wife of Indra; Tara, the wife of Brihaspati; Arundhati, the wife of Vashishtha; Anasuya, the wife of Atri; Devahuti, the wife of Kardama; Prasuti, the wife of Daksha; Menaka, the daughter of Ambika; Bhadra, the wife of Kubera; Varuni, the wife of Varuna; Vindhyavali, the wife of King Bali; Sita, Lakshmi's incarnate; Yojana Gandha, the mother of Vyasa; Usha, the daughter of Vana and her companion Chitralekha; Renuka, the mother of Parashurama; Rohini, the mother of Balarama; Sati Durga, the sister of Sri Krishna; Lopamudra, Kunti, Damayanti, Yashoda, Devaki, Gandhari, Draupadi, Shaivya, Satyavati, the mother of Radha, Mandodari, Kaushalaya, Kauravi, Subhadra, Revati, Satyabhama, Kalindi, Lakshmana, Jambavati, Nagnajiti, Mitravinda, Rukmini, Kaali, Prabhavati, Bhanumati, Mayavati, Ekananda and many other manifestations are parts of Prakriti.

Each attribute of the Devi is worshipped, to the extent of any female deity in a village, forest or city.

The three gunas define the nature of a woman; Sattva gives virtuousness, Rajo the average nature with an inclination towards worldly pleasures and Tamo gives the worst of the kind, scurrilous. A hermaphrodite is also part of Prakriti but has Tamo Guna.

Every female in the universe is a part of Prakriti. It is, therefore, said that an insult to a woman is an insult to Prakriti and that worshipping an eight-year-old virgin girl is deemed as worshipping Prakriti Devi," said Narayana.'

Vyasa recounted, 'Narada was still gazing at Narayana's face when the latter finished. It took him some time to fathom the details and collect himself.

He further asked, "O Muni! Kindly tell me why Mula Prakriti precedes the creation of five elements. How did Adya Shakti, the prime energy, evolve into five parts?"

Narayana replied, "O Rishi! Mula Prakriti is as eternal as the Atman, the Kaal, the ten directions, the Goloka[273] and Vaikuntha Dham. The Atman cannot create without the support of Prakriti as a potter cannot make earthen pots without earth.

She is called 'Shakti' after combining 'Sha' denoting 'Aishvaryam', which means prosperity, and 'Kti', meaning might. She is also called 'Bhagvati' as 'Bhaga' indicates knowledge, prosperity, wealth, fame and strength. Atman in conjunction with Bhagvati is, thus, called 'Bhagvan'.

When Bhagvan decided to manifest, he took the form known as Sri Krishna. 'Krish' signifies everything and 'Na' means the root. Thus, he is the root and creator of all. He is the one who created the universe.

On his own volition, he let himself be divided into two halves: the left became female with the most exquisite traits of femininity and the right turned into male.

Both were in sexual union for an incredibly long time, which resulted in the female part perspiring and creating water, Varuna, submerging the whole universe in a deluge and breathing, thus fashioning air, Vayu. A female sprung from the left side of Vayu and through their mating, five sons were born, namely, Praan, Apaan, Samaan, Udaan and Vyaan.

The female part, Shakti, conceived and after remaining pregnant for one hundred Manvantaras, gave birth to a golden egg. Unhappy to see the egg, and not realising that it had the capacity to bear the whole universe, she threw it in the water.

Witnessing such an act, Sri Krishna turned angry and cursed her. He told her that as she had abandoned her newborn, she would not be able to bear any more children. Moreover, all the women emerging out of her parts would also be deprived of birthing a child.

While Sri Krishna was uttering these words, a splendid daughter in all white and holding a lute, sprung out of the Devi's tongue. She was Devi Sarasvati, the presiding deity of all Shastras.

Next, Mula Prakriti, the Vamanga[274] of Sri Krishna, was divided into two: the left became Kamala or Lakshmi and the right was called Radhika. Radhika wanted Krishna as her consort and Lakshmi also wished the same.

At this point, Sri Krishna also divided himself into two, a two-handed form of Krishna from the right and a four-handed Narayana or Vishnu from the left. Both were equal to each other in all respects.

He requested Sarasvati and Lakshmi to be the wives of the four-armed Narayana and follow him to Vaikuntha, while he requested Radha to be his wife. Due to the curse, Lakshmi and Sarasvati remained issueless.

From Narayana, arose a multitude of four-handed attendants, all equal to him in appearance and characteristics. Similarly, millions of female attendants emerged out of the pores of the body of Kamala, all similar to her.

On the other hand, innumerable gopas or cowherds and gopa kanyas, cowherdesses, emerged from the pores of Sri Krishna and Radhika, respectively.

Following this, arose Durga from Sri Krishna and Savitri along with her husband Brahma from Vishnu's navel.

At this moment, Krishna again divided himself into two. The left turned into Mahadeva, holding a trident and spear, wearing a tiger skin, body besmeared with ashes, blue neck, serpents around his neck as ornaments and bare loins, thus called Digambara as the sky was his clothing."

Narada was curious about the other thread in the description presented by Narayana and asked, "O Maharishi! What happened to the golden egg?"

Narayana smilingly continued, "It kept floating in eternal waters for long, as much as the life of Brahma, and then broke on its own giving birth to an effulgent child. The orphaned and hungry child looked up and cried aloud. Sri Krishna blessed this child and said that his hunger and thirst would vanish and that he would not be affected by any infirmities such as age, death, disease or sorrow.

The blessed child became the grossest possible assuming one-sixteenth power of that of Sri Krishna and came to be known as Maha Virat or Maha Vishnu. He received the maha-mantra '*Aum Krishnaya Svaha*' and also the fifteen-sixteenth of the offerings to Sri Krishna in every universe.

Each of the countless pores of his body holds a Brahmanda[275], having its trinity of Brahma, Vishnu and Mahesh. Thus, there are an infinite number of universes with their trinities and with similar compositions from Patala to Brahmaloka.

Everything in each Brahmanda is transient and is destroyed at the end of its time cycle except Goloka and Vaikuntha which are eternal," told Narayana to Narada.'

Sarasvati and Ganga

Vyasa had no hesitation in sharing with Janamejaya everything that he knew. So he continued, 'Narada asked Narayana, "Can you explain to me the methods of worshipping, mantras and hymns to please the Devi originating from Mula Prakriti, as described in the Vedas and Puranas?"

Narayana continued, "O Son of Brahma! Sri Krishna recognised the amorous feelings of Devi Sarasvati towards him and advised her to marry the four-armed Narayana. He explained to her that Radha would always remain closest to him and that Radha was more powerful than her as she was equal to himself in every aspect. Moreover, Radha was the presiding deity of his own life.

On the other hand, Sarasvati was as gorgeous and able as Lakshmi and both were not afflicted by covetousness, anger and envy. Therefore, both would be able to live with each other delightfully.

Krishna blessed Sarasvati that she would be worshipped and meditated upon by all those who sought knowledge in accordance with the description in Kanva Shakha of the Yajur Veda. In particular, the fifth day of Shukla Paksha of the month of Magha would be dedicated to her and marked as the day of commencement of learning.

The mulmantra to invoke Sarasvati is '*Aim Klim Sarasvatyai Namah*'. A devotee could also offer everything to her by uttering '*Aum Shrim Hrim Sarasvatyai Svaha*' and seeking whatever one desires. A man turns siddha like Brihaspati if he recites this mantra four hundred thousand times."

Narada then asked Narayana to describe the Vishvajaya Kavach[276].

Narayana said, "In times of yore, Bhrigu requested Brahma to give him this kavach. Brahma told him that he had received it from Sri Krishna. Later, this kavach enabled Brihaspati, Shukra, Valmiki, Svayambhuva Manu,

Gautama, Kanva, Panini, Daksha, Katyayana, Yagnavalkya and even Vyasa to master their skills and intelligence.

Brahma is the rishi of this kavach, Brihaspati is its chhanda[277] and Devi Sharada Ambika is the presiding deity. It is applied in acquiring knowledge, be it spiritual, literary or analytical, or success of any kind. If the kavach is recited half a million times, one becomes a siddha."

Narayana, while explaining these mantras, was deep in thought and continued, "Let me also tell you the stotram of Devi Sarasvati that Rishi Yagnavalkya recited to her. It so happened that the rishi forgot all the Vedas due to a curse of his guru.

The disheartened muni started practising austerities to appease Surya. In due course, Surya was pleased and taught him the Vedas again. However, he advised the muni to worship Devi Sarasvati to get his memory back to retain the knowledge.

Surya recalled the incidents when Brahma became speechless once in front of his son Sanatkumara, when Ananta Deva was dumbfounded in front of the earth, when Valmiki could not explain some sutras of the Puranas to Vyasa and when Brihaspati could not respond to Indra's query on the Shabda Shastra; each one prayed to Devi Sarasvati, the shakti behind speech, memory, knowledge, intelligence, talent and imagination, and received the desired help.

Yagnavalkya too devoted himself to meditating upon the Devi and sang hymns to praise her. Finally, the Devi appeared and granted him the boons by which he turned into an eloquent poet."

Narayana was immersed in the Devi's thoughts. He spoke again, "O Narada! It is the same Sarasvati who came down to earth as a river in the land of Bharat and let her holy waters sanctify the sinners."'

Vyasa told the king, 'The attentive Narada asked surprisingly, "Why did Devi descend to earth as a river?"

Narayana told Narada, "It was because of a curse from Ganga after a quarrel between the two of them," and continued, "Lakshmi, Sarasvati and Ganga were the three wives of Sri Hari and equally loved by him.

Once Ganga continued to cast amorous glances towards Narayana. He in turn responded with a smile. While Lakshmi noticed this and did not react, Sarasvati turned furious. She accused her husband to be partial towards Ganga and even Lakshmi too. She alleged that she was being neglected.

Narayana sensed the sensitivity of the situation and left the room. His absence made Sarasvati even more indignant. She used foul language and tried to catch hold of Ganga by her hair. Lakshmi intervened causing Sarasvati to curse her. Sarasvati said that Lakshmi did not intervene to stop the unacceptable behaviour of Ganga as if she was a tree or a river, so she would turn into one.

A calm Lakshmi did not respond to the curse and instead tried to pacify Sarasvati by holding her hands. Meanwhile, Ganga was enraged. She challenged Sarasvati to show her prowess.

She did not stop at this and cursed Sarasvati, 'Since you have imprecated Lakshmi, I too curse you to turn into a river where mortals would shed their sins.'

Sarasvati was too infuriated to stop her from reciprocating. She cursed Ganga to also become a river on Prithvi.

By this time, Narayana returned and held Sarasvati close to his chest. He learnt of all the curses pronounced on his three wives.

He took amends immediately. He told Lakshmi that she would be born, without any womb, as the daughter of King Dharmadhvaja and called Tulasi. She would turn into a tree there due to an evil twist of destiny. Then, Asura Shankhachuda, born out of his parts, would marry her. However, she would currently proceed to earth as a river with the name Padmavati.

He told Ganga that she would be taken by King Bhagirath, and, hence, the name Bhagirathi, to Bharat as the most sanctifying river in the world capable of purifying every being of their sins. She would marry King Shantanu, born of Hari's parts.

Similarly, Sarasvati would also be a purifying river in the land of Bharat.

Sri Hari then directed Sarasvati to proceed to become the wife of Brahma and Ganga to Shiva. He retained the Saattvika Padma as his wife.

Hari's words left the three Devis in tears.

O Narada! Thus, the women born of the parts of Padma are religious and devoted to their husbands. Further, the Vedas forbid keeping together three wives or three servants or three friends of different nature.

The repentant Devis pleaded with Sri Hari to not separate them from their lord, their husband and their love. Sarasvati and Ganga even threatened to end their lives.

Lakshmi also had foreboding questions in her mind, such as the length of their stay on earth due to the curses taking them away from their husband and how they would rid of the curses. She requested Hari's forgiveness for the other two and asked him to take back both of them as his wives.

Sri Hari could not have denied Lakshmi's request. He had to find a balance between his words, the curses and what was being demanded by his beloved Lakshmi.

He allowed a part of Sarasvati to have the form of a river, one-half part of her to go to Brahma and yet remain with him in Vaikuntha in her full parts. For Ganga, he let a part of her go to Bharat as Bhagirathi and another part remain in the matted hair of Mahadeva and yet let her remain with him in full parts.

He also said that the curses would come to an end after five thousand years of Kali Yuga. He added that his true bhaktas would help the three of them in ridding the curses through their ablutions in their respective rivers and by reciting his mantra, the Vishnu Mantra.

O Narada! When that transpires, the sanctifying rivers and tulasi will disappear from the face of earth. It will lead to the extinction of the Vedas and related practices, practising of austerities, dharma, assembly of virtuous people and blessings of devas. The world will be afflicted with falsehood, deceit, ego, greed, licentiousness and lies.

It will result in non-committal marriages, husbands obedient to their wives, unchaste women rebuking their husbands, parents-in-law serving the daughters-in-law, brothers of wives managing the household affairs, brothers of master of the house appearing as strangers, kings' powers getting diminished and subjects will be overburdened with taxes. People will donate for name and fame and ultimately take it back what they had provided.

In the Kali Yuga, all humans will be of short stature, diseased, have shorter lives and of little youthful virility. So much so that at the age of sixteen, a person's hair will turn grey.

Finally, after the full life of Kali, Vishnu will incarnate as the son of a brahmin called Vishnuyasha. He will free earth from the unrighteous mlechchhas in three nights and disappear.

A deluge will drown the earth followed by the rising of twelve suns to dry up the water. This will lead to Kali Yuga giving way again to Satya Yuga."

This is what Narayana told Narada,' said Vyasa.

The king was mesmerised after the long description by Veda Vyasa. He recalled the concept of time for humans, devas and gods explained earlier during the narration.

He waited for Vyasa to catch his breath and asked, 'O Dvaipayana! What is then Pralaya?'

Vyasa said, 'The deluge takes place every time a Chatur Yuga ends. But the Prakrit Pralaya happens when Brahma dies. The entire Brahmanda is dissolved. Even Vishnu, Mahesh, other rishis and Devi Prakriti diffuse in Para Brahma. This lasts just a Nimisha, after which a new creation begins.

No one knows how many Brahmas have been born and how many will be. But the Para Brahma remains one and only one. This supreme power is Mula Prakriti from whom emerges Sri Krishna.'

Prithvi and Ganga

Vyasa told Janamejaya that Narada had more questions for Narayana. He wanted to derive the most from this excellent opportunity.

Vyasa thus continued, 'Narada asked Narayana about what happened to earth when such Pralaya took place.

Narayana smiled and said to Narada that there were many theories about the creation of earth. Some said that it was created by the marrow of the daitya duo Madhu and Kaitabha, but that was not true.

What happened was that they both requested Vishnu to kill them on the part of earth that was not underwater. Therefore, it is clear that earth was already existing, though it was perhaps not visible as it was immersed in infinite water. After earth was taken out of the water and post-killing of the daityas, their marrow got mixed with earth. Hence, she is also called Medini.

Narayana asked Narada whether he knew the process of Panchikarana. It also produced a Mahaprithvi, the Great Earth. This was broken into pieces and placed in each pore of the Maha Virat. Thus, each pore hosting a Brahmanda had an earth. She disappeared at the time of Pralaya and reappeared during creation submerged in water.

Narada asked Narayana whether earth was also called Varahi.

Narayana answered in affirmative and said that this was because she was rescued from the nether region of Rasatala by Vishnu incarnated as a boar or Varaha. After doing so, he was enamoured by the magnificent form of the presiding deity of earth.

He then converted himself into a gorgeous form and spent a passionate one full year with Earth. Earth was

Vishnu's wife in his boar form, hence the name Varahi. This reunion gave birth to Mangal or Mars as her son.

After being exhausted from love-making, Vishnu resumed his boar form and worshipped Devi Prithvi, as prescribed in Kanva Shakha, with her Mula Mantra "*Aum Hrim Shrim Klim Vasundharayai Svaha*".

Earth has a pious connotation. By gifting a piece of land measuring one vitasti[278] to a brahmin one can achieve Shivaloka and by gifting a brahmin a piece of land full of corn entitled one to live in Vishnuloka. Conversely, if one took back the gift or stole the land from a brahmin, then one would go to Kalasutra hell. Even the person's progenies would suffer in Raurava hell.

Hell is also prescribed for those who cultivated grazing land or an enclosure designated for cows and reaped a harvest of grains from such land. Releasing one's semen on earth out of amorous passion also lands one in hell. Digging ground during Ambuvachi[279], when the earth is supposed to be unclean and agriculture is prohibited, is an unpardonable offence that can lead to spending time in hell.

The importance of earth is also highlighted during the Shraadh period[280]. The food that is offered to the manes ought to be accompanied by an offering to the owner of the land on which the ceremony is performed.

Similarly, the lamp of light, conch shell, yantras, the phallic emblem of Shiva, image of Shivani[281], the shaligram[282] stone in addition to pearls, gems, diamonds, gold and jewels, ought not to be placed directly on the ground. The same is advised for all materials used in worshipping, from flowers to books to tulasi leaves.

Narayana then recounted to Narada the complete story of Ganga.

King Sagar of the Solar dynasty had two lovely wives - Vaidarbhi and Shaivya. The latter bore a brilliant son called

Asamanja. Vaidarbhi worshipped Shiva and became pregnant with his blessings. After a hundred years of pregnancy, she delivered a lump of flesh.

The queen was distraught and again took refuge in worshipping Shiva. Disguised as a brahmin, Shiva appeared and divided the flesh into sixty thousand pieces. These pieces turned into handsome and powerful sons. However, they were all burnt to ashes due to a curse by Muni Kapila.

The king could not bear the grief and left for the forest, while his other son Asamanja began tapasya to bring Ganga to earth for the deliverance of his step-brothers. He passed away after one hundred thousand years of meditation and his son Anshuman continued it till he also left for his heavenly abode.

Anshuman's son, Bhagirath, a great devotee of Sri Hari, continued the legacy of his father. Finally, Krishna appeared and granted Bhagirath what he wanted.

Since then, Ganga has been washing away the sins of humans committed over multiple births. Bathing in River Ganga gives more fruitful results if done with a sankalpa or on a day when the sun changes its raashi[283] in the zodiac or on a new moon or full moon day.

Such plentiful results are also achieved when bathing is done through the Chaturmaas[284] or during Akshaya Navami, Akshaya Trittiya, Manvantara tithi, Yugadya[285], Shukla Saptami of Magha, Bhishmashtami, Ashokashtami, Rama Navami, Vijayadashmi, Maha Varuni day and during a solar eclipse.

The worshipping of Ganga is prescribed in the Kauthuma Shakha and was performed by Bhagirath accordingly. To begin with, he worshipped Ganesha for the removal of all obstacles, Sun for health, fire for purification, Vishnu for prosperity and power, Shiva for knowledge and Shivani for liberation. Then he meditated upon Ganga and sang hymns praising her, followed by an offering of sixteen items.

Narada could not stop interjecting, "O Muni! How did Ganga originate and how did it reach the earth?"

Narayana continued and said that Ganga, originating from the body of Sri Krishna and enriched by the perspiration of Radha, first appeared in Raas Mandalam[286]. A long time ago, Sri Krishna was playing raas with Radha on Kartik Purnima. They were accompanied by all the devis that appeared from Mula Prakriti as well as Brahma, Mahadeva, devas and rishis besides gopas and gopis.

The august gathering was enthralled by the singing of Devi Sarasvati. On Brahma's request, Mahadeva sang in praise of Sri Krishna on this special occasion, mesmerising everyone. When he finished and everyone awoke from the trance, they could not find Krishna and Radha. At the same time, Raas Mandalam was submerged in water.

Brahma immediately meditated upon Krishna and realised that both had immersed themselves in water for the deliverance of people at large. He asked everyone to join him in singing hymns.

Pleased with the praises of the gathering, a heavenly voice said, "I and my Shakti Radha pervade all. Nothing separates us from you except the bodily forms. We assume various forms to show favour to our devotees. Thus, kindly request Maheshwara to create Tantra Shastra[287] in accordance with the verses of the Vedas.

This shall include mantras, kavach for protection, strotram, hymns and rules of worshipping, but in a hidden form so that sinners do not get them. All my devotees who recite the Shastra will be blessed with witnessing my form."

Mahadeva, hearing of this direction in the form of a request, took water from Raas Mandalam in his hands and committed to doing so. Pleased with Mahadeva's resolve, Krishna and Radha appeared and resumed their raas.

In due time, Mahadeva prepared the Tantra Shastra.

This water that Mahadeva took in his hands was the liquid form of Ganga, which sprung in Goloka from Sri Krishna.

Traversing Goloka through Vaikuntha, Brahmaloka, Shivaloka, Dhruvaloka, Chandraloka, Suryaloka, Tapoloka, Janarloka, Maharloka, Kailash, Devaloka where she is known as Mandakini, Ganga reached earth after assuming varied forms and dimensions in various lokas.

Upon reaching earth, Bhagirath took Ganga to the ashes of Sagar's sons and with her touch, they were released from the curse and moved to Vaikuntha.

Narada then requested Narayana to enlighten him as to how Ganga came to be the wife of Sri Krishna.

Narayana replied that once Ganga had joined Sri Krishna in her exquisitely enchanting form capable of enticing anyone. Sitting by his side, she could not help but continue to gaze at him with passionate desire.

At some point, the eternal Radha, as beautiful as millions of moons put together, arrived there. But before Sri Krishna could get up to welcome her and offer her arghya, she noticed Ganga by Krishna's side and was so angry that her face became red and her lips quivered.

While Radha took her throne in the room, she was worshipped by Krishna. Ganga too joined in, fully aware of Radha's perceptible annoyance causing a chill in her spine.

Sri Krishna was well aware of how Radha and Ganga felt. Yet Radha was his soul and thus overpowered him. A delicate glance from Krishna, however, calmed the frightened Ganga.

Radha, who had collected herself by now, did not mince words in enquiring Krishna about Ganga.

She recalled how she had forgiven Krishna on previous occasions when he had been involved with other women. She remembered how she had caught Krishna with Virja Gopi who, out of shame, assumed the form of a river near Jagannath Puri. Not only that, Krishna still went after her and seeded her womb, which gave birth to the seven oceans.

Then he was found to be passionately involved with another gopi called Shobha. She too quit her body and joined the sphere of the moon giving a cooling effect to the moon's appearance.

Later, he was caught with Prabha Gopi in Vrindavan who left for the solar atmosphere giving luminosity to the sun. After that, Krishna was with Gopi Shanti in the Raas Mandalam who, out of fear, disappeared in him and is recognised as one of the noblest qualities. Next, Krishna was found sleeping with Kshama[288] who left for earth.

Concluding that Krishna had, thus, given away several of his attributes, Radha turned towards Ganga preparing to reproach her. Ganga, aware of what was coming next, disappeared from there and turned into water.

It did not take Radha long to figure out through her yogic powers the whereabouts of Ganga. She decided to drink the whole of Ganga's water in one gulp. Nowhere else to go, Ganga took refuge in Krishna's feet.

Radha looked around for Ganga everywhere from Goloka to Vaikuntha to all the lokas. But she was nowhere to be found. Meanwhile, in the absence of Ganga, the gods, devas, rishis and munis all turned very thirsty as there was no water anywhere.

They all went to Goloka to appeal to Sri Krishna to save the universe. Brahma was requested to take the lead to present the matter.

The omniscient Krishna knew about the matter. He described to them the situation and told them that he was willing to hand over Ganga to them, but they would have to appease Radha to spare Ganga from her wrath.

The group of highly accomplished beings went to Radha and sang hymns to worship her. Brahma explained to her that Ganga was born of liquid from Raas Mandalam, which was nothing else but Radha and Krishna. Therefore, she was like Radha's daughter.

Brahma assured that Ganga would be four-armed Vishnu's wife in Vaikuntha and take the ocean as her husband on earth. His words pacified Radha who granted protection to Ganga who then reappeared from Krishna's feet. Since then, Ganga is also known as Vishnupadi.

Brahma brought Ganga to Vaikuntha and requested Narayana to marry her. Thus, Lakshmi, Sarasvati, Ganga and Tulasi became the four wives of Vishnu.

Maharishi Narayana then sighed and said that this was not the end of it all. While Ganga spent her days happily with Vishnu, Sarasvati became jealous of her. Narayana recounted to Narada that he had already narrated that episode,' concluded Vyasa.

Tulasi and Shankhachuda

Vyasa continued, 'Thus Narada understood why envy and jealousy ought to be avoided. He then asked Narayana to narrate to him the anecdote of Tulasi and how she became Narayana's wife.

Narayana continued as if he already knew the next question. He asked Narada if he had heard about the ninth Manu, Daksha Savarni. It was in the previous kalpa that he and his successive descendants Brahma Savarni, Dharma Savarni, Rudra Savarni, Deva Savarni and Indra Savarni were all great devotees of Vishnu. However, Indra Savarni's son Vrishdhvaja became Shiva's devotee.

His devotion received reciprocation from Shiva who loved him like his own son. This devotion reached such an extent that Vrishdhvaja stopped worshipping Narayana, Lakshmi and Sarasvati.

This infuriated Surya who cursed him that he would lose all prosperity in no time. Shiva learnt of the curse and ran after Surya with his trident. Surya sought refuge from his father Kashyapa who took him to Brahma, Kashyapa's father. Meanwhile, Shiva continued to chase Surya.

Afraid of Shiva's rage, they all went to Vishnu in Vaikuntha and obtained his Abhaya[289].

Following close on Surya's heels, Shiva arrived. He paid his humble respects to Vishnu. Simultaneously, Brahma, Kashyapa and Surya bowed down to Shiva and praised him.

Shiva explained the situation and said that even those who recited Hari's name are protected, what to speak of Surya who had taken personal refuge. At the same time, Vrishdhvaja was like his son. He asked Vishnu what would happen to his cursed devotee.

Vishnu smiled and said while they were talking, twenty-one yugas had elapsed on earth within this half ghatika[290] in

Vaikuntha. Meanwhile, several generations had passed over and Vrishdhvaja and his son Rathadhvaja had passed away.

His grandsons Dharmadhvaja and Kushadhvaja, devotees of Vishnu, were in a penurious state. They both would worship Lakshmi who would bless them through their wives. Thus, they should all go back to their respective places and let fate take its own course.

Dharmadhvaja and Kushadhvaja practised severe austerities and achieved boons from Lakshmi. They married and became kings again.

Kushadhvaja's wife, Malavati, gave birth to a daughter who was born with incredible wisdom. She was named Vedavati as she began to chant the Vedas soon after her birth. She decided to practise tapasya and in spite of dissuasion, she left for Pushkar.

She was immersed in austerities for one Manvantara and had turned into a beautiful youth. One day, she heard a celestial voice announce to her that she would get Sri Hari as her husband in the next birth. She continued with her tapasya in the solitary caves of Gandhamadan mountain.

After a time, Ravana happened to visit the cave. Vedavati offered the uninvited guest water to wash his feet and to drink and fruits to eat.

Seeing a beautiful woman, Ravana became passionate and thought of violating her forcefully. She sensed his intentions and through the power of her tapasya, turned him into a statue, incapable to move or even speak.

Ravana's mind was, however, working. He began to mentally recite praises for Shakti. Vedavati realised it and while releasing him from the spell, cursed him that as he had touched her body out of passion, she would be the cause for ruin for him and his family.

Saying so, she left her body for a transcendental journey. Ravana immersed her body in River Ganga and left.

The same Vedavati was later born as Janak's daughter Sita who was blessed with Vishnu's incarnation Rama as her husband. She also caused the destruction of Ravana and his clan. Sita was jatismara[291].

But before that episode, a brahmin visited Rama while he was in exile with Sita and Lakshmana. This brahmin was Agni Deva. He told Rama that the time was near when Sita would be abducted and, thus, requested that mother Sita be temporarily handed over to him.

In return, Agni placed Chhaya Sita or the Shadow Sita with the promise to return the real Sita at the time of Agni Pariksha, the test by fire. This secret was kept among the three of them and even Lakshmana was unaware of it.

Then Ravana was killed by Rama.'

Janamejaya had an immense appetite for knowledge. He asked, 'What happened to Chhaya Sita?'

Vyasa said, 'After the return of the real Sita, Rama ruled Ayodhya for eleven thousand years and then Rama and Sita left this mortal world.

Chhaya Sita was asked to practise tapasya at Pushkar. After a long period of meditation, she became Svarga Lakshmi and later in Dvapara Yuga, she emerged out of the Agni Kunda as Draupadi. Since she came into existence in Satya, Treta and Dvapara Yugas, she is called Trihayani.'

The king intervened, 'O Muni! Why did Draupadi have five husbands? Is there a background to this too?'

Vyasa replied, 'Devi Chhaya Sita, while meditating in Pushkar, appeased Mahadeva who asked her to seek boons. She asked Shiva to grant her a husband. However, as she had lost the opportunity to be Rama's wife, she, in her anxiety, repeated it five times. And a pleased Shiva granted her five husbands.'

Vyasa continued, 'O King! This completes the anecdote of the lineage of Kushadhvaja. Now hear what Maharishi Narayana told Narada about his brother Dharmadhvaja.

Narayana told Narada that Dharmadhvaja got married to Madhavi who was beautiful, humorous and an excellent amorous companion. They spent years together enjoying each other's company.

Madhavi in due time became pregnant and delivered a daughter on Kartik Purnima, as auspicious and gorgeous as a full moon. This girl was part-incarnation of Lakshmi and was named Tulasi.

Tulasi, despite objections, went to the forest of Badari and performed severe austerities for one lakh years. She appeased Brahma who came on his swan to grant boons to her.

Tulasi told Brahma that she was a gopi in her previous birth and had been caught by Radha in a compromising situation with Sri Krishna. Radha censured Sri Krishna and cursed her to be born as a human on earth. Thereafter, Krishna told her that if she pleased Brahma with her tapasya, then she would get a husband born of Krishna's part. So she asked Brahma to grant her a husband who would be born of a part of Sri Krishna.

Brahma told Tulasi that she was not the only one who was enduring Radha's curse. A gopa name Sudama was cursed too. He had already fallen for Tulasi in Goloka but could not take her as his wife due to the curse. He then had taken birth as a danava called Shankhachuda.

Brahma told Tulasi that both of them, being jatismara, would be married to each other in this birth. In Tulasi's later birth, she would get Sri Krishna as her husband. However, due to an ill-fated curse, she would be transformed into a tree, which would have the properties of purifying the whole world.

As Tulasi would always be a tree in Vrindavan, she would be called Vrindavani too. The leaves from her plant would be a must to complete any worshipping, particularly that of Krishna, and, hence, she would always remain close to him.

Brahma's words brought a radiant smile to Tulasi's face. She thanked Brahma as her desire of consummating and being with Krishna would be fulfilled. She also requested Brahma to find a way to get rid of Radha's fright.

Brahma gave her the sixteen-lettered Radha Mantra, stotram, kavach and method of worshipping through which she could attain siddhi.

On the other side, Shankhachuda received the Krishna Mantra from Maharishi Jaigishavya at Pushkar and proceeded to Badri to meet Tulasi.

The moment their eyes met, they fell in love with each other. It seemed as if both, in their full youth, were meant for each other.

They, on the advice of Brahma, got married in Gandharva form[292] and began to enjoy passionate time in the intimate company of each other. Several years passed by when they got satiated and decided to return to the kingdom of Shankhachuda.

The king expanded the frontiers of his reign with conquests over devas, asuras, gandharvas and kinnaras. The dispossessed devas finally reached the abode of Brahma and narrated to him the tyrannies perpetrated by Shankhachuda.

Brahma accompanied them all to the magnificent Vaikuntha to consult the four-armed Sri Hari. Although the omniscient Sri Hari already knew the cause of their visit, Brahma repeated to him what was reported by the devas.

Sri Hari smiled and told them that Shankhchuda in his previous birth was his chief attendant known by the name of Sudama.

Once, Gopi Virja and Sri Hari had gone to Raas Mandalam. Devi Radha learnt about it from a maidservant and she arrived there to catch them red-handed. While she could not see Sri Hari, she saw Virja turning into a river and leaving the mandalam.

When Sri Hari returned home accompanied by Sudama, an angry Radha rebuked him. Sudama could not accept Radha admonishing Sri Hari. He objected, which made Radha even more furious and she cursed Sudama would be born to a danavi.

Sudama cried in despair. He touched Sri Hari's feet before leaving. By this time, Radha had realised how harsh she had been on Sudama. She took mercy and stopped him from leaving.

At that moment, Sri Hari pacified Radha and told her that half a moment in Goloka was equivalent to a Manvantara on earth. Therefore, Sudama, who would be born Shankhachuda, would return to Goloka soon.

Vishnu then told his visitors that the time had come to relieve Shankhachuda from his danava birth.

Then Vishnu turned to Mahesh and told him to end the life of the danava with the latter's trishul. But before this could be done Vishnu needed to take away from Shankhachuda the blessed kavach that he held in his neck. Vishnu said he would do so under the guise of a brahmin.

Mahesh, thus ordained by Vishnu, camped on the banks of River Pushpabhadra. He sent an emissary Chitraratha, the lord of gandharvas, also called Pushpadanta, to the danava.

Chitraratha arrived in the magnificently constructed city, adorned with gems, crystals and all richness. He carried the message through well-guarded twelve doors, one after the other, to reach the danava king in his sprawling city. He was let in by the guards after he announced himself as Mahesh's envoy.

Finally, he witnessed the king on his golden throne studded with diamonds and jewels and surrounded by an army of danavas all keen to serve their royalty.

He conveyed the message of restoring the devas' kingdom, or else Mahesh would spare no mercy on him. Shankhachuda responded by calling for war preparations.

Shankhachuda broke the news of the imminent war to Tulasi. She was horror-struck. He comforted her by explaining that it was Kaal which was supreme. Kaal brought situations and good as well as bad results according to destiny.

By virtue of being jatismara, both knew the reality and the transient nature of their current existence. Shankhachuda thanked Brahma to have granted Tulasi as his wife. He said he was happy that Tulasi would finally get Sri Krishna as her husband in the next life and he would be able to forsake the body of a danava and go back to Goloka.

They spent the night of a lifetime talking and passionately enjoying the amorous company of each other.

On the other side, Mahesh was joined by all the devas and devis. They began the war preparations.

The next day, Shankhachuda handed over the reign of his kingdom to his son and dressed himself for the war. He was joined by a huge army comprising horses, elephants, chariots, bowmen, swordsmen and trident holders, totalling three hundred thousand Akshauhini.

He, joined by seniors and elders, marched to the camp of Mahesh. They witnessed Mahesh seated in a calm yogic pose wearing tiger skin, with his face radiating like million suns and every pore of his body emanating Brahma Teja.

Shankhachuda bowed down to Mahesh, who was accompanied by Bhadra Kaali and Kartikeya, and received their blessings. The latter exhorted the king, belonging to the lineage of Kashyapa, to return what belonged to the devas. He also reminded him that he was a disciple of Sri Hari.

The danava king reasoned that the dispute between the devas and asuras was eternal. The devas had cheated the asuras at the time of the churning of Kshir Sagar. Not only that, they killed daityas like Hiranyaksha, Hiranyakashipu and Shumbha with the help of gods, namely, Brahma, Vishnu, Shiva and the Devis arising out of Mula Prakriti.

He lamented that by taking sides in favour of the devas, the gods had been unfair as both suras and asuras had their origins in Para Brahma. He smilingly added that as he was battling against god himself, the glory accrued to him in the case of his victory would be far greater than that to Mahesh and conversely, the defeat would be far less ignominious.

Mahesh was amused to hear his argument and told him that there was no shame in fighting against and even getting defeated as the danavas had descended from Brahma too.

What followed was a full-scale war between the two armies. The danava warriors proved to be too good for the deva side, which fled in desperation.

Soon Kartikeya and Kaali joined the forces and in no time turned the tide. Sensing the situation, Shankhachuda began to shower the rain of sharp arrows from his chariot. He did not stop and showered even mountains, snakes, stones and trees.

Kartikeya used his shakti but it was timely negated by Shankhachuda. Kartikeya then used the divine quiver bestowed upon him by Vishnu and nullified the volley of deadly weapons hurled by Shankhachuda. He cut off the chariot and armour of the king and hit his chest with a blazing shakti. The king fell unconscious but only for a few moments.

In response, Shankhachuda hit Kartikeya with an invincible shakti leaving him senseless. Bhadra Kaali immediately carried him to Mahesh who treated him and gave him indomitable strength.

Bhadra Kaali came back to the battlefield to continue the slaughter of danavas. Her fire missile was cut off by a water missile from the other side followed by her Varunastra and Maheshvarastra by Gandharvastra and Vaishnavastra, respectively.

When the Devi hurled Narayanastra, Shankhachuda bowed down to its power, thus saving himself. Her Brahmastra met with a similar one from the king. Finally, she decided to use the Pashupatastra, but she was desisted from doing so by a celestial voice telling her not to waste it until the danava was protected by the Vishnu Kavach.

At this stage, Shiva himself came down to the battlefield. Seeing him in person, Shankhachuda came down from his chariot and prostrated to him. A dreadful war then ensued between them. Innumerable casualties occurred on both sides but devas were rejuvenated by Shankar's divine powers.

As the stalemate continued, the danava camp was visited by Sri Hari disguised as an old brahmin and asked Shankhachuda to give him the alms that he would desire. The magnanimous king asked him to seek what he desired.

No sooner than the brahmin got the kavach from the danava, Mahadeva hurled his trident towards the now vulnerable Shankhachuda.

Knowing fully well that his time was up, Shankhachuda left his arms and sat on the battlefield to meditate upon Sri Krishna. The trident did its job of killing the king by burning him and his chariot into ashes. It simultaneously released Sudama from the danava's body who left for Goloka back to his master Sri Hari and Devi Radha.

The bones of Shankhachuda were, thereafter, used to create conch shells.

The use of conch shells is thus prescribed in the worshipping of devas with water kept in it considered consecrated. The blowing of a conch provides pleasure to Lakshmi. Placing a shankha in homes is propitious as Hari himself resides in it along with Lakshmi. But blowing of a shankha is forbidden for women as it annoys the Devi.

Narayana paused and continued again with a glint in his eyes. He said that the mischievous Vishnu did not stop at taking away that kavach. He disguised himself as Shankhachuda and went to Tulasi.

Narada was surprised. But before he could raise questions, Narayana continued in his flow. Upon reaching there, he projected as if he had returned after winning the war. Tulasi welcomed him and distributed charities on the providential occasion.

Tulasi was overjoyed by the return of her beloved husband. She asked him about the happenings in the war. The disguised Vishnu told her that after the long and lethal war had killed millions on both sides, Brahma intervened to broker peace. He agreed to part with devas' rights and returned.

Later, both slept together.

Tulasi was somehow not convinced and her suspicion deepened when her sexual experience was quite different from what she used to have with her husband. She could not help but ask about the real identity of the masquerading Vishnu.

Afraid of being cursed by Tulasi, Vishnu revealed his true form of handsome and enchanting deep blue colour. Tulasi fell unconscious.

After regaining her senses, Tulasi became furious with Vishnu for having robbed her of chastity. She accursed him that since his heart was like a stone, he would turn into a stone too.

Vishnu mollified her by telling her that Shankhachuda had received the fruits of his tapasya by getting Tulasi as his wife. The time had come for her to get her reward too. He blessed her that she would assume a divine body and marry him.

At the same time, her body on earth would be the virtuous River Gandaki. Her hair would turn into sacred trees by the name of tulasi whose flowers and leaves would be the chief among all others. Tulasi leaves would be used in all venerations.

In order to honour the curse, Vishnu said that he would turn into a mountain on the banks of River Gandaki. The insects would cut and fashion pieces of stone out of that mountain having varying shapes and sizes.

These stones falling into the river would be known as shaligram. Worshipping these stones would be like worshipping Sri Hari and would bring punyas and prosperity provided it was done with tulasi leaves.

The distorted or disfigured or yellowed stones are, therefore, not recommended to be kept in the house.

After Tulasi joined him at Vaikuntha, Sri Hari treated her as he did Lakshmi. Ganga too accepted this. However, Sarasvati could not digest the new status of Tulasi. She quarrelled with her and once she affronted her in front of Vishnu.

Tulasi disappeared from Goloka and turned invisible even to Sri Hari who searched for her everywhere before reaching Vrindavan, the tulasi forest.

There, on Kartik Purnima, the auspicious birth anniversary of Tulasi, he began to meditate upon her with the ten-lettered mantra '*Aum Shrim Hrim Klim Aim Vrindavanyai Svaha*'. He chanted her eight names Vrinda, Vrindavani, Vishvapujita[293], Vishvapavani[294], Pushpsara, Nandini, Krishnajivni and Tulasi.

Tulasi, who needed no invocation but only devotion, was pleased. She decided to come out of hiding. But she was hurt due to the slight. She was respectfully taken back by Hari to Vaikuntha where he worked out an arrangement between her and Sarasvati.'

Savitri and Lakshmi

Janamejaya asked, 'O Vyasa! Did Narada also ask Maharishi Narayana about other principal Devis?'

Vyasa responded, 'Yes, O King! Narada then asked about Savitri.'

'And what did Narayana say?'

Vyasa smiled and continued, 'He explained that Savitri was worshipped first by Brahma, then by the Vedas and the learned sages. King Ashvapati was the first man on earth to worship her.

Narada asked Narayana who Ashvapati was.

Narayana replied that he was the powerful king of Bhadradesha. He was married to Malati who could not bear a child. She, advised by Vashishtha, worshipped Savitri, but to no avail.

Seeing her pitiable condition, Ashvapati joined Malati in Pushkar where both performed tapasya for a hundred years. Eventually, a heavenly voice told Ashvapati to recite the Gayatri Mantra a million times.

Coincidentally, Maharishi Parashar also arrived at Pushkar. Both Ashvapati and Malati took his blessings. He explained to them that recitation or japam of Gayatri Mantra destroyed sins; a hundred thousand times destroy sins of a lifetime, a million of other births and a billion leads to liberation.

He asked the king to recite it million times to purify his births. He also said that the japam ought to be done every morning, mid-day and in the evening. The king meditated duly and, as a result, got boons from Devi Savitri.

Thus, to obtain the best from the Devi, one should observe abstinence on the thirteenth day of Krishna Paksha of Jyeshtha month and break the fast on the fourteenth day with fourteen fruits and fourteen dishes as offerings to the Devi. This vow must be observed for fourteen years consecutively.

Narayana recalled that Sri Hari gave Savitri to Brahma but she did not go to Brahmaloka. Brahma then appeased her with the seed mantra, the eight-lettered '*Aum Hrim Klim Shrim Savitraiye Svaha*' and her stotram, after which she accepted him as her husband.

King Ashvapati chanted the same stotram to appease Savitri. The Devi appeared to him in her gracious white attire and said that while the king desired a son, his wife wanted a daughter. She blessed that both of the wishes be fulfilled.

A daughter was first born to Ashvapati and Malati and they named her Savitri. When she reached her youth, she chose Satyavaan, the son of Dyumat Sena, as her life partner. The king married her off with pomp and show.

After about a year, Satyavaan was ordained by his father to go to the forest to gather fruits and fuel. Savitri followed him.

Satyavaan fell from a tree and died instantly. Yama collected his soul and proceeded. Savitri saw this and followed Yama. When he noticed it, he asked her who she was. Savitri told her about herself. Yama then told Savitri that she could not follow him and urged her to go back.

The chaste Savitri argued that she could not return without her husband. She insisted on knowing about Tattva Gyan, various kinds of karma and their results.

Yama was surprised by such a quest in a young girl. But he knew that she was born with Savitri's boon and, thus, she was a part-incarnate of the Devi. He told her that she was fortunate to get Satyavaan as her husband and that the two were like Lakshmi and Vishnu or Sachi and Indra.

He blessed her that devotion towards Shakti should arise in her mind.

Saying thus, Yama offered Savitri to seek boons. Savitri was sharp to react and asked Yama to bless her that she has one hundred sons with Satyavaan and live this life for a hundred thousand years with him. When both of them depart from this life, they should go to Vaikuntha.

Savitri also wished that her father begot a hundred sons and that her father-in-law should get back his lost eyesight and the lost kingdom.

Yama hesitated as he had come to take Satyavaan away with him. However, bound by his own offer, he granted what Savitri sought.

He then said to Savitri that he would answer her questions.

Yama explained, "Karma is performed only by suras, gandharvas, yakshas, humans and asuras including daityas, danavas and rakshasas. The beasts and animals do not accrue karma, but they bear the fruits of their past karma in previous births. The good karma is finally enjoyed in heaven and the bad lead to hell.

Good karma includes giving away charities, vows, asceticism, performing yagna and worshipping. By doing it, one gets happiness, wealth, long life and power in successive births.

Bhakti is the route to getting rid of all karmas. This bhakti is of two kinds, Saguna that the Vaishnavas do towards Hari or any other manifested form of the devas and Nirguna performed towards the formless Prakriti.

Saguna bhakti is of two kinds too. Sakama is done with desires and Nishkama is the one without desires. With the latter, one leaves the body and reached Goloka, to the highest god, to never return to take birth again.

Sakama, depending upon who they worship, reaches the respective abode of the god, such as Brahmaloka, Shivaloka, Devaloka, Chandraloka and even Vaikuntha. After spending their prescribed time in such heavens, they return to earth to continue in the cycle of life and death.

Of all the bhakti, worshipping the Devi or Mula Prakriti is the highest and the direct cause of mukti[295]." After explaining this to Savitri, Yama asked her to take her husband and go back to their house. He told Savitri to worship Mula Prakriti to live happily.

Savitri paid obeisance to Yama and returned with her husband to enjoy all the boons.'

'Narada's thirst for knowledge was insatiable. He asked Narayana about Devi Lakshmi.

Narayana hoped that Narada remembered how Lakshmi originated from Mula Prakriti and was taken as his wife by four-armed Narayana.

Narada said he did but he wished to know how the goddess of wealth, inhabiting Vaikuntha, came down to earth to become the daughter of the ocean.

Narayana said that once, in the days of yore, Indra became involved with apsara Rambha. They both were enjoying their intimate company when Indra spotted Muni Durvasa en route from Vaikuntha to Kailash, accompanied by a group of his disciples. The muni was holding danda[296] in one hand and a kamandala in the other.

Indra went up to him and bowed down to receive his blessings. Durvasa gave him the invaluable parijaat flower, capable of removing all sorrows and diseases, which was presented to him by Vishnu in Vaikuntha.

A debauched Indra threw the precious flower on the head of his elephant Airavata. The elephant turned into a Vishnu and left his master to enter the forest.

The muni was enraged and cursed Indra for discarding the parijaat that the former had got from Vishnu himself. He told Indra that people got salvation from the use of anything that had touched Vishnu, be it food, water, fruits, flower, etc. Even the dust of his feet and the air that touched him freed a person from all sins. And yet Indra had discarded the parijaat. The muni cursed Indra that Maha Lakshmi would leave him. At the same time, the one on whose head the flower had landed would be worshipped.

The muni's words shook Indra and he came to his senses. He told Durvasa that the curse had helped him to come out of delusion. He requested Durvasa to tell him more so that Indra did not transform into his earlier state.

Durvasa calmed down and agreed to Indra's request. He told Indra that it was wealth, consequent worldly pleasures and manipulation of power that caused all afflictions in life. Their intoxication distanced one from real knowledge, the Sattva Guna. Such a person was either a Rajasika, knowing the Shastras, or Tamasika, with no knowledge of the Shastras.

Two paths were ordained in the Shastras. The first was Nivritti through which sensual desires were denounced. The other was Pravritti, which took one towards pleasures and desires leading to an agonising circle of deaths and births like a bee craving for honey, getting entangled in flowers and hives. One got out of this cycle if and when a saintly person showed him the right path to mukti.

Hearing these profound words, Indra became disenchanted and stayed at the muni's ashram for long. When he returned to Devaloka, he found it under the control of daityas with terror and oppression prevailing there.

Indra went looking for Guru Brihaspati and found him on the banks of River Mandakini meditating upon Para Brahma. He waited for him to complete his session and then explained to Brihaspati what had happened.

Brihaspati told Indra not to grieve or be anxious as everything was transient and under the effect of karma accrued over previous births. There was no way to avoid the karma which followed a being through the cycle of birth like a shadow. Its effects could be diminished or enhanced depending on time, place and the person himself.

In order to dent its effect, charities were recommended. Charities to different persons of different nature in different times and in different places yielded varying results. Those performed on special occasions like Amavasya, Purnima, Sankranti, Chaturmaas, lunar or solar eclipses, Akshaya Tritiya or Navami gave excellent results. Bathing in holy rivers, reciting mantras and other pious acts also added to positive karma along with the charities.

But if Indra wished to end this painful circle, then he should pray to Sri Krishna, who was the creator of the Creator Brahma, preserver of the Preserver Vishnu and destroyer of the Destroyer Shiva.

Following their conversation, Indra took Brihaspati and other devas to Brahma where Brihaspati narrated to Brahma what had transpired.

Brahma told Indra that a man inherited the faults of his father or maternal grandfather or the guru. In his case, Indra was born in Brahma's clan. Daksha was Indra's grandfather and Brihaspati was his guru. So with this pure background, Brahma wondered how Indra had turned out to be so arrogant.

And how could Indra disrespect the parijaat flower, offered to Vishnu's feet, which ought to had been placed on the head by an immortal? Brahma concluded that Indra was obviously under the inevitable spell of fate. The only way out was to seek the graceof Vishnu.

He told Indra to remember that Vishnu was the Atman that resided in the body of each living being. If he left the body, which was meant for the fruition of karma, the being was dead. Consequently, other functions like the mind, signifying Brahma; knowledge, meaning Shankar; and intelligence, sleep and other natural powers which were part of Mula Prakriti would also leave.

Saying thus, Brahma accompanied Indra and the others to Vaikuntha.

The compassionate Vishnu told Indra that Rishi Durvasa was born in part of Shiva and he was Vishnu's devotee. So, no sooner than he cursed Indra, Lakshmi and Vishnu left Indra's place. Devi Lakshmi did not stay in places where there was no aachaar[297] or worshipping of Hari or Shivalinga or conch shells, shaligram and tulasi or sinful acts.

Vishnu then urged Lakshmi to proceed and take birth in the house of Kshir Sagar. He also asked the devas to churn the ocean and told Brahma to give Lakshmi to the devas when she arose during the churning.

As ordained, when the most beautiful Devi emerged out of the ocean, she was worshipped by Brahma and Mahesh.

Thereafter, Indra, having bathed and dressed in cleansed cloth, performed Ghata Sthapana[298] on the seashore of Kshiroda. He prayed to the six deities – Ganesha, Surya, Agni, Vishnu, Shiva and Durga – before invoking Lakshmi as directed by Brahma in his role as the officiating priest.

He offered her parijaat flower smeared with sandal paste and sang praises to her. He then offered sixteen articles – an asana[299], the holy water from Ganga, sweet-scented flower oil, amalaki fruit, a cloth made of silk and cotton, an ornament made of gold and jewels, incense prepared from various herbs and plants, sweet-scented pleasant sandal paste, holy deepa[300], payasam, pakvaan[301], gur[302], svastika made of flour of other grains, a hand fan, betel scented with camphor and sweetmeats prepared with wheat, jaggery and ghee besides a conch shell with flowers, sandal and durva grass; each accompanied by relevant mantras.

He recited a million times the Mula Mantra '*Aum Shrim Hrim Klim Aim Kamalavasinyai Svaha*' given by Brahma. The Devi arrived at the venue in her celestial car. Indra prostrated along with other devas to get her blessings and prayed to her to rid their problems as their possessions were in the hands of enemies.

A glance by Maha Lakshmi on Devaloka freed Indra from the curse and later the devas got back their own kingdom from the daityas.

The Description of the Other Devis

Vyasa proceeded, 'Narada did not want Narayana to stop. He requested the maharishi to explain the significance of Svaha, Svadha and Dakshina.

Narayana relented and said, "At the onset of creation, the devas complained to Brahma that there was no provision for their food. Brahma said he would make arrangements so that the devas could partake in the offerings of ghee in all sacrificial acts.

To accomplish this, Brahma meditated upon Sri Krishna who advised him to worship Mula Prakriti.

Brahma worshipped and chanted her hymns. She was finally appeased and a deep-blue-coloured splendid Devi, called Svaha, appeared. Svaha asked Brahma to seek boons.

Brahma asked her to be the burning power of agni. He requested that oblations accompanied by mantras ending with her name should reach the devas and gods. He emphasised that the mantras would have not any effect if they did not end with her name, Svaha.

Svaha did not refuse Brahma though she desired to be married to Sri Krishna.

Svaha did penance to fulfil her wish. She stood on one leg and practised austerities for one hundred thousand years before the highest Purusha appeared to her. But before Sri Krishna could say anything, she fainted out of weakness and all the excitement.

Comforting her, Sri Krishna said, 'You shall be my wife in the next Varaha Kalpa and called Nagnajiti. But in this birth, you would be Agni Deva's wife.'

Sri Krishna blessed her so that she would be worshipped by all.

Brahma commanded Agni to meditate upon Devi Svaha in accordance with the Saam Veda. She was pleased and they both got married. For a hundred deva years they enjoyed each other's company after which Svaha became pregnant.

She retained her pregnancy for twelve divine years and then delivered three brilliant sons: Dakshinagni, Grahayapatyagni and Ahavaniyagni.

Now listen, O Narada, about Svadha.

Brahma had also created seven pitris before the creation; four had forms while three of them had the nature of teja. Brahma arranged that they would get food through shraadh and tarpan, performed by brahmins. But the pitris could not get the food and so they went to Brahma.

Brahma created a magnificent daughter out of his mind. Her name was Svadha and she was white like a champaka flower and as beautiful as hundred moons. He gave her as wife to the pitris.

Thereafter, all brahmins were advised to chant mantras meant for the pitris with her name, Svadha, at the end. This enabled the offerings to reach them.

Having made arrangements for the sustenance of gods and pitris, Brahma also ensured that a dakshina was offered to the person helping to make oblations or else the sacrifices would not bear fruits.

Now hear how Dakshina came into being.

In the days of yore, Devi Radha had a much loved and respected gopi companion whose name was Sushila. She was pretty and bestowed with a tender and curvaceous build. She was the dearest lady of Sri Krishna as she specialised in Prema Bhakti or love towards god.

Sushila once sat by the left side of Krishna in Radha's presence which made Radha jealous and angry. Sensing her anger, Krishna disappeared.

His absence caused fear among the gopis. Meanwhile, Radha cursed Sushila that if she ever entered Goloka, she would be reduced to ashes.

Radha searched for her lord but could not find him anywhere, including at Raas Mandalam. At last, lamenting, she said, 'A wife derives all pleasures, enjoyment, peace and respect through her husband. He is her friend, presiding deity and the sole haven.

A husband is called by various names: Bhartaa because he supports his wife; Pati as he preserves her; Svami because he is the master of her body; Kaant as he fetches desired things for her; Bandhu because he brings her happiness; Priya because he gives pleasure to her; Isha as he bestows prosperity on her; Praneshvara as he is the lord of her life; and Ramana because he gives enjoyment to her.

As he is regarded higher than the guru and all good deeds, pilgrimages and performing austerities amount to not more than one-sixteenth of serving one's husband faithfully, therefore, O Krishna, do not go away and show yourself.'

Sushila having been ousted from Goloka started practising severe tapasya. Finally, she received blessings and was subsumed into the body of Maha Lakshmi.

On the other hand, the devas went to Brahma as their yagnas did not yield the desired results for them. Brahma became concerned and meditated upon Sri Hari. He created a Martya[303] Lakshmi out of the right shoulder of Maha Lakshmi and named her Dakshina who was Sushila in her earlier appearance.

Brahma brought Dakshina to Yagna Deva who worshipped the chaste and beautiful Devi. He then married her. Later she delivered a son called Karmaphala or the deliverer of the fruits of karma. Since then, everyone is ordained to pay a dakshina, the sacrificial fee, to complete the action or karma of oblations."

Narada requested, "O Narayana! I want to now hear about other Devis too. Kindly describe Shashthi, Mangal Chandika and Manasa."

Narayana agreed and began, "Devi Shashthi is the sixth part of Mula Prakriti and the chaste wife of Kartikeya.

She is the presiding deity of children and is also known by the names of Devasena, Baalda and Vishnumaya.

My father Dharma Deva told me how she bestows sons. Hear what he said.

Svayambhuva Manu had a son whose name was King Priyavrata. He practised austerities and wanted to stay single. But Brahma forced him to marry the virtuous Malini. Despite several years passing by, the couple could not procreate.

Priyavrata undertook a Putreshti Yagna in which Maharishi Kashyapa was the priest. When the yagna concluded, Kashyapa gave the prasadam of charu to Malini who became pregnant.

Malini gave birth to a beautiful golden-coloured son. But the newborn was lifeless. Malini was numbed. None could hold back one's tears in this unfortunate situation.

The king took the corpse of his infant for cremation. He was so depressed that he even contemplated sacrificing his own life. While he was thinking of it, he saw a lavish and lustrous aerial car from which a splendid Devi came out. She introduced herself as Devi Shashthi and explained that, like everything else in the universe, begetting a dead son was also the result of past karma. She then took the dead child on her lap and infused life into him.

The overwhelmed king prostrated and promised to spread the word of worshipping Devi Shashthi in the three worlds. The Devi blessed him with the promise of another son by the name of Suvrata, who would be born with a part of Vishnu.

Keeping his promise, the king performed auspicious ceremonies and gave charities. Since then, Devi Shashthi has been worshipped on every sixth day of Shukla Paksha of each month and particularly on the sixth day after the birth of a child.

She is also worshipped on the twenty-first day of the birth and six months after the birth when the child is given solid food for the first time. Her mulmantra is '*Aum Hrim Shashthi Devyai Svaha'*.

O Narada! Now I will tell you about Mangal Chandika. She is the most auspicious and cherished Devi for all women. She signifies Mangal. She, the Chandika, was worshipped by Mars and also by King Mangal of the Manu family.

A form of Durga, one of the five Mula Prakriti, she became Mahadeva's Shakti in the war against Daitya Tripura. Thus, Mahadeva was the first to worship her with her twenty-one-lettered mulmantra '*Om Hrim Shrim Klim Sarvapujye Devi Mangal Chandike Hum Phat Svaha'*. This mantra acts like the Kalpavriksha and yields all desires.

The third Devi, Manasa is the mind-born daughter of Maharishi Kashyapa, hence, the name. Her name also means that she can play with the mind. Given the nature of the mind, she finds pleasure in herself.

Once upon a time, the human race became petrified of snakes. They went to Maharishi Kashyapa and through his mind power, he crafted a mantra whose presiding deity, Manasa, was also co-created.

The young Manasa went to Mount Kailash and worshipped Shiva for one thousand deva years. Shiva imparted the great knowledge and made her recite the Saam Veda. He also gave her the Krishna Mantra.

She then meditated upon Sri Krishna for three yugas and became a siddha yogini. Due to long austerities, she had become pale and ashen. When Krishna saw her, he named her Jarat Kaaru. Manasa married Muni Jaratkaaru. Chanting her twelve-lettered mantra '*Aum Hrim Shrim Klim Aim Manasa Devyai Svaha*' fulfils one's desire. When one chants her name, one is freed from the fear of snakes.

She has several other names: Jagat Gauri because of her fair colour, Shaivi as she is a disciple of Shiva, Vaishnavi as she is a devotee of Vishnu, Nageshvari and Naga Bhagini for saving the serpents in Parikshit's sacrifice, Vishahari as she can destroy the effects of poison, Maha Gyanyuta because she got great knowledge from Mahadeva, Mritasanjivani as she can infuse life into the dead and Aastika as the mother of Muni Aastik.

Once while observing her duties as a wife, she had woken up Muni Jaratkaaru against his wishes and as a consequence was cast off by him. Jarat Kaaru and her siddha son came back to her father's hermitage. At the Sarpa Yagna by King Janamejaya, she asked her son Muni Aastik to save the serpents from being sacrificed.

Eventually, Surabhi, the heavenly cow, visited Manasa from Goloka. Surabhi bathed her with milk, worshipped her and also revealed to her the Tattva Gyan. Thereafter, Devi Manasa left for heaven."

Narada then asked, "Who was Surabhi?"

"Surabhi, the first cow in creation, appeared in Goloka. She is the presiding deity of cows. One day, Sri Krishna was spending time with Radha in the holy Vrindavan, when he suddenly felt the desire to drink milk. There and then, Hari created Surabhi, with a calf called Manorath[304], from his left side," said Narayana.

He continued, "Radha milked her and served it to Krishna. Some milk was spilled from the earthen jar which turned into the ocean of sweet milk called Kshir Sagar. In no time, millions of Kaamdhenu cows appeared from the pores of Surabhi, thus bringing cows to the creation.

Surabhi is worshipped, in accordance with Yajur Veda, by her six-lettered mantra '*Aum Surabhyai Namah*'. When she is worshipped with devotion on the morning following the Diwali night, it yields excellent fruits."

Narada thanked Narayana for enlightening him by narrating various anecdotes of the Devis arising out of Mula Prakriti. He said on hearing these, one is freed from the endless circle of birth and death. But Narada noted that Narayana had not described Radha and Durga. He requested Narayana to elaborate on their traits and the mantras too.

Narayana accepted Narada's request and said, "O Narada! Radha is the presiding deity of praan and Durga of buddhi. These two are the essential components of creation. From the highest bodily form to the lowest, moving or non-moving, everyone and everything is under the effect of these two. And to achieve mukti, they must be satisfied.

When Radha is worshipped with her six-lettered mantra '*Sri Radhayai Svaha*', one is granted dharma and artha. If it is preceded with '*Hrim*', it bequeaths gems and jewels. Sri Krishna had first received this mantra in Raas from the heavenly voice of Mula Prakriti. Krishna then told this mantra to Vishnu and then Brahma. Brahma had passed it on to my father, Dharma Deva, who taught it to me.

As Radha is the presiding deity of the praan of Sri Krishna, his devotees must worship her first. Radha's name is derived from Radhnoti, which means someone who fulfils all desires; therefore, Radha is the foremost Mula Prakriti.

Now hear about Durga. Irrespective of whether one is a Shaiva or Vaishnava, remembering her name removes all difficulties and dangers. Chanting of her nine-lettered mantra '*Aim Hrim Klim Chamundayai Vichche*' bestows all desires," said Narayana.'

Bhramari Devi

Vyasa paused for a moment so that the king could absorb the intricacies of his narration.

The king asked, 'O Muni! Now that I am enlightened about various forms of Devis arising out of Mula Prakriti, can you also describe the forms that the Devi assumed in various Manvantaras?'

Vyasa smiled because the king's query was the same as that of Narada. He said, 'Narada had the same query to which Narayana had replied as follows.

Narayana said, '"O Narada! You remember that Brahma's mind-born son Svayambhuva Manu had meditated upon Devi Bhagvati to seek her blessings for creating the world without any obstacles.

The Devi had then blessed him and left for Vindhyachal mountain where Varadeshvari, the younger sister of Vishnu in the form of Vindhyavasini, lived. But a problem arose when Vindhya started growing so tall that it disrupted the course of the movement of the sun. The situation could be resolved only after the intervention of Maharishi Agastaya, son of Mitra-Varuna but born of a kumbha[305]."

On enquiring about the details, Narayana smilingly said, "Well Narada, it all began with your visit to Vindhya."

Narada was surprised to hear this. He said, "I do recall my visit to Vindhya once. It was a beautiful and serene locale with forests and fruit trees, plants and shrubs, wild animals and herbivores, and clean and calm rivers where devas, gandharvas, apsaras and kinnaras bathed.

I also remember Vindhya greeting me warmly and I telling him, 'O enemy of Indra! I am coming from Mount Meru where I witnessed the splendid abodes of Indra and the other devas.'

It made me think that while Himalaya as the father of Parvati, Shiva's consort, and Kailash, where Shiva resides, are rightfully worshipped and so do Nishadha, Nila, Gandhamadan and several other mountains for their own reasons, the same, however, does not apply to Mount Meru who arrogantly thinks that he is supreme simply because the sun circumambulated around him.

Saying thus, I had left Vindhya."

Narayana smiled again and spoke, "Now hear what transpired after you had left.

Vindhya began to contemplate how to overthrow Mount Meru. He hatched a plan of growing so tall that he would obstruct Sun in the latter's daily course of circumambulation of Mount Meru. He raised his arms so high that they became mountain peaks that reached up to heaven.

The next day, Sun rose from the east as usual bringing an end to Moon's reign and joy to white water-lilies. People on earth began their day worshipping Surya and tended to their daily vocations.

As Sun moved up through the south, the movement of his chariot was stalled. His charioteer Arun reported that they could not go further since Vindhya had blocked their path and was apparently contending with Mount Meru.

Sun accepted it as an act of destiny and stopped his movement till the crisis was resolved.

Consequently, the day in the eastern parts of earth remained bright. People living in these parts got tired of working with no end to the day. On the other side, people in the west, who were sleeping, had their night prolonged with no daylight on the horizon. The same was the case in Devaloka.

Seeing this grim situation, Indra and his team of devas took Brahma along and sought refuge in Mahadeva. They pleased him with their praises and said, 'O Lord of yoga! Vindhya out of arrogance and envy against Mount Meru has turned himself high enough to hinder Sun's movement, which has upset the system of day and night.'

Shiva advised them to go to Vishnu to resolve it. He also agreed to accompany them."

"In Vaikuntha, the entourage chanted hymns to appease Vishnu. He was pleased and told them, 'You should seek Muni Agastya's help. He is currently residing in the holy city of Benares.'

As advised, the devas reached Benares. They first bathed at Manikarnika Ghaat[306] and proceeded to the muni's ashram. They prostrated before the muni and paid obeisance to him and his wife Lopamudra.

Agastya was surprised to see the entourage of devas. Each one in the group was so powerful in his own right, capable of creating anything in the world, from fire to rain and even death for mortals on earth. He enquired about the motive of their visit.

They explained the crisis caused by Vindhya. Agastya heard them sympathetically and agreed to help them out.

Agastya was not happy to leave the holy city of Kashi as he had planned to settle down in the city, but he took his wife along and began with the rituals to leave the city. They both bathed at Manikarnika Ghaat and worshipped Mahadeva, the lord of Kashi, as well as Kaal Bhairava, known to be the guardian of the city of Kashi. They also visited Sri Sakshi Vinayak.

They left Benares and proceeded south to reach Vindhya at lightning speed by the power of his tapasya. They saw the high mountain from a distance, hindering Sun's path. Vindhya also saw the muni and in respect, he nearly prostrated on earth to greet him, much like a stick fallen on the ground.

When the muni saw Vindhya prostrated, he cast a gracious look to the gigantic mountain and said, 'I am glad you have come down as I could not have ascended your great heights. Now do stay like this till I return.'

Saying so, he crossed the mountain to the other side and went further south. He finally reached Sri Shaila mountain. There, in a place called Malayachala, he founded his hermitage and settled down. He never crossed Vindhya back towards the north lest the mountain rose again. Devi Bhagvati, worshipped by the muni, went to Vindhya where she came to be known as Vindhyavasini."

Narada requested Narayana to describe the other Manus.

Narayana began, "Svayambhuva Manu had two sons, Priyavrata and Uttanapada. The son of Priyavrata was the second Manu, known as Svarochisha Manu. He worshipped Devi Bhagvati at his hermitage on the banks of River Yamuna.

Pleased with his devotion, the Devi appeared irradiating like thousand suns. She granted him the rule of one Manvantara. During his dominion, the Devi acquired the names of Tarini and Jagaddhatri.

Priyavrata's son Uttama was the third Manu who practised austerities on the banks of River Ganga, repeating the bijamantra of Vagbhava, of speech, meditating upon Devi Sarasvati. Priyavarata's other son called Taamas became the fourth Manu. He repeated the Kaam bijamantra on the southern banks of River Narmada to worship the Devi.

The young brother of Taamas, known as Raivata was the fifth Manu. He also chanted the Kaam bijamantra on the banks of River Kalindi.

The sixth Manu was the son of King Anga. His name was Chakshush. Desirous of ruling the world, he went to Brahmarishi Pulaha to seek his counsel. The rishi told him to worship the Devi. He asked the muni how to worship Devi Bhagvati.

The rishi said, 'Anyone who recites the seed mantra of Vagbhava thrice a day gets what he wants and eventually obtains mukti. It is because of this mantra's power that Brahma, Vishnu and Mahesh were able to perform their incomparable tasks.'

Taking the cue from Pulaha, Chakshush meditated upon Devi Sarasvati and performed severe austerities on the banks of River Virja. The Devi appeared and granted him the reign of one Manvantara.

Vaivasvata was the seventh and the present Manu. The son of Surya, Savarni, was the eighth. He had worshipped Devi in his previous birth as King Suratha and received the boon to be the lord of a Manvantara.

Vaivasvata Manu had six sons, Karusha, Prishadhra, Nabhaga, Dishta, Shrayati and Trishanku. They together went for a very difficult tapasya on the banks of River Yamuna to worship Devi Bhramari. She was so pleased that she granted each of them lordship of successive Manvantaras in their next birth.

Karusha became the ninth Manu known as Daksha Savarni, followed by Prishadhra as Meru Savarni, Nabhaga as Surya Savarni, Dishta as Chandra Savarni, Shrayati as Rudra Savarni and Trishanku as the fourteenth Manu by the name of the Vishnu Savarni."

Narada intervened, "Who is Bhramari Devi?"

Narayana spoke, "In the days of yore, a dreadful daitya called Arun lived in the nether regions. In his arrogance to be the victor of the three worlds by conquering the devas, he decided to perform tapasya. He went to the banks of River Ganga and gradually left eating and subsequently stopped drinking water. He survived only on air and meditated for several Ajutas causing jitters among the devas.

The devas took refuge in Brahma and prayed for his help. The four-faced god took his consort Gayatri and appeared before the daitya. He spoke to the daitya and through his deep voice brought Arun out of his trance. Arun opened his eyes and bowed down to Brahma. He said slowly, 'O lord of creation! Bless me that I would not die.'

Brahma smiled at his request as this had been wished by each daitya in the past. He explained, 'O Arun! Anyone who is born will certainly die. Even Vishnu, Mahadeva and I are not immortal, what to say about others. Ask for anything else.'

Arun was immensely intelligent and therefore, more innovative than the past daityas. He said, 'Since you cannot grant me freedom from death, then make sure that my death shall not be caused by any war, nor by any arms or weapons, nor by any man or woman, nor by any being with two legs or four legs or by a combination of any of these. Also, grant me a large army that will enable me to defeat the devas.'

Brahma blessed him and left for his abode.

On receiving the boon, Arun declared a war on the devas.

Knowing well about the boon bestowed on the daitya, Indra marched with his team of devas to Brahma, and, taking him along, went to Vaikuntha. From there, they were joined by Vishnu to go to Kailash. A big congress was held there among the best of brains and braves in the universe.

Meanwhile, Arun took control of Devaloka and all the invaluable assets of the devas. From Sun to Moon to Agni, everyone was helplessly dispossessed and anxious as they knew that Arun could not be killed in a war.

While devas at Kailash brainstormed to find a way out of the unsurmountable problem, they heard a celestial voice, 'Pray to the mother of the universe. She will help you,' adding that, 'if Arun, who is always muttering the Gayatri Mantra, forsakes it, his end would be ensured.'

Brihaspati, at the command of Indra, led the devas in worshipping the Devi. He also acted on the second part of the revelation by disguising himself as a muni and visiting the daitya.

Arun enquired from the muni, 'O Muni! Who are you and why have you come to me? Your visit surprises me as I am not one of you.'

Brihaspati found an opening in Arun's words and said, 'If you are not one of us, then why do you incessantly worship Devi Gayatri who we, the ascetics and the devas, venerate.'

As the daitya was already in maya's trap, he reacted by immediately stopping chanting the Gayatri Mantra, which left his energies enfeebled.

Brihaspati returned with the mission accomplished. Meanwhile, the devas continued to meditate upon the Devi. She appeared in her splendid form with garlands around her neck made of fragrant flowers. The garlands had big black bees that hummed around them and created the sound 'Hrim'.

The appeased Devi asked the devas to seek what they desired. They all cried out together complaining about the excesses committed by Daitya Arun against them.

With one indication of merciful Devi Bhagvati Bhramari, a variety of black bees, hornets, wasps and other insects emanated from her hands. These infinite number of bees engulfed the earth and the sky. They began to sting Arun and his army.

The daityas had no opportunity to use their weapons against the endless stream of tiny enemies and save themselves. They all, including their leader Arun, died there of bee stings.

After accomplishing the task, and that too without a war, the bees came back to Devi Bhramari. And the devas returned to their respective abodes," said Narayana.'

Rudraksham and Bhasma

Vyasa recalled that Narada did not let Narayana stop at the description of the various manifestations of Devi.

Vyasa said, 'Narada further asked Narayana, "What is sadachaar or living in a virtuous manner? Does its observance please the Devi?"

Narayana replied, "Yes, of course, it does. But let us first understand what sadachaar means. We all know that it is the individual himself who has to perform his karma for his deliverance. The mother, father, wife and children do the same for themselves for bettering or worsening their next lives.

The karmas are beyond sharing. Thus, it is incumbent upon each one to live life in accordance with dharma.

Some underestimate sadachaar as a disciplined routine of living and worshipping devas and gods. But it is much more than that. Manu in Shrutis and Manu Smritis have ordained the rules of virtuous living. With virtuous deeds come the knowledge that further improves one's conduct.

The right conduct or dharma of a man is dictated either by Shastras or by prevailing practices. The latter may emanate from one's clan or village or country. But one should not perform malicious acts in the name of dharma such as the killing of other beings."

On hearing this, Narada again interrupted Narayana, "What should one do if there are contradictory approaches in different Shastras?"

The unfettered Narayana continued, "Dharma is as prescribed in Shrutis, Smritis and Puranas only. Among these, Shrutis are the highest, followed by Smritis. In case of any conflict, these have successive authority over the right conduct.

If two varying interpretations exist in Shrutis, then both have to be taken as authoritative. If there are any tantras in Puranas, they shall be matched with the Vedas. In case of disagreement with the Vedas, those cannot be accepted as dharma.

In practice, a person should get up early in the morning, during the fourth prahar of the night, particularly during Brahma Muhurta and recite the Gayatri Mantra thrice. After getting relieved from nature's call, he should take bath and wear clean clothes, apply tilak of ashes on the forehead and put on rudraksha beads.

A total of 251 beads should be worn on the body. These include thirty-two on the neck, forty on the head, six on each ear (twelve in both), twelve on each hand (total of twenty-four on both hands), sixteen on each arm (thirty-two in total), one bead on each eye, one bead on the hair on the crown and one hundred and eight beads on the breast.

One should think about Para Brahma and contemplate performing auspicious acts during the day as well as giving charities. Thereafter, one should sit in the lotus position with the back straight, chin touching the breast and eyes closed. Keeping the tongue with the palate, one should sit quiet, motionless and restrain the senses.

A person is also expected to practise Pranayaam, which is of six kinds. First is the Sadhuma when the breathing is not steady. Then comes Nirdhuma in which breathing is controlled and Sagarbha where breathing is coordinated with mantras. The next is Agarbha when the breathing is without thoughts, even those of mantras. Then comes Salakshya when one is transfixed on the deity and finally the Alakshya when one is beyond the thought of even the deity.

The final stage of Pranayaam is of three kinds: Rechaka, Puraka and Kumbhaka as denoted by the three primary sounds in 'Aum', respectively.

After this, one should focus on the chakras and meditate upon Kula Kundalini, the serpent fire, to carry it to the Brahmarandhra or the crown chakra. The seven principal chakras are Muladhara or root chakra, Linga Mula or sacral, navel or solar plexus, heart or cardiac plexus, throat, forehead or third eye and sahasrara or the crown.

Then one should meditate on one's guru who is equivalent to Brahma, Vishnu, Mahesh and Para Brahma."

When Narayana finished describing sadachaar, Narada asked him why rudraksha was worshipped.

Narayana replied, "O Narada! The explanation is implicit in the name itself as Rudra is another name for Mahadeva. In fact, the same question had also been asked by the six-faced Kartik to his father Mahadeva.

Rudra explained, 'It was long ago when an invincible daitya called Tripura tormented the whole universe. Brahma and Vishnu accompanied the devas to request me to kill the tyrant.

After careful thought, I created a weapon called Aghora in my mind. It was both beautiful and terrible at the same time. It amalgamated the strength of all the devas. In order to energise the Aghora, I kept awake with eyes wide open and thought about it for a thousand years.

Eventually, drops of water fell out of my eyes which gave birth to rudraksham trees on earth for everyone's welfare. This rudraksham seed has thirty-eight varieties; twelve of yellow colour which came out of my right eye, the Surya Netra; sixteen of white colour from my left eye, the Soma Netra; and ten of black colour from my third eye, the Agni Netra.

Rudraksha seeds can be distinguished by the number of faces and are immensely powerful. The faces are created by the lines naturally drawn on them. They can yield either of the opposite results depending upon the desires of its wearer, bhoga or enjoyment as well as moksha or liberation.

Further, the rosaries of rudrakshas consisting of varied numbers depending upon their objective, are used for japam. These rosaries are beyond any comparison vis-à-vis rosaries of any other kind.

The single-faced rudraksha symbolises me, the Mahadeva. Two-faced is like a deva or devi. The three-faced one is like fire and the four-faced one is like Brahma. The five-faced seed is the most common and represents another image of myself.

The six-faced rudraksha is called Kartikeya and seven faced is called Ananga[307]. The eight-faced is Vinayak and nine faced is Bhairava. The ten-faced is like Janardana and the eleven-faced rudraksha epitomises eleven Rudras.

Going further, wearing a twelve-faced rudraksha on ear yields the fruits of performing Gomedha and Ashvamedha sacrifices. The thirteen-faced rudraksha fulfils all desires of its bearer. The holder of fourteen-faced rudraksha on one's head turns a person into my replica.'

Kartikeya asked, 'O Father! I have vaguely heard about an ass carrying rudraksha in the country of Kikata in Bharat Varsha. What happened to him?'

'Somewhere in Vindhya mountain, an ass used to carry the load of rudraksha for a merchant. On one journey, the ass felt tired, fell and died there and then. The soul of the ass was brought to me in the form of myself, Mahesh, by the grace of the rudrakshas he had carried,' explained Shiva."

Narayana further told Narada that this was the extent of blessings the rudraksha seeds bestowed on their bearers who must hold them all the time, whether awake, sleeping or eating. However, while bearing rudraksha on one's body, one must not consume wine, meat, onion, garlic as well as sahinjana[308] and lasoda fruits[309].

Once Narayana finished describing the virtues of rudraksha, Narada enquired about Bhuta Shuddhi.

Narayana described, "Bhuta Shuddhi is done to purify the elements of the body. It begins with thinking of Kula

Kundalini as rising through the Sushumna canal in the spinal cord to Brahmandhra.

A person should unite one's body with Para Brahma by meditating on the mantra 'Hamsa'. The part of the body from the feet to the knees should be thought of as representing earth of golden colour denoting the letter 'Lum', which represents the seed mantra of earth.

Then, the part of the knee up to the navel should be considered as representing water, of white colour, in the shape of a semi-moon adorned by two lotuses at its two ends. The letter 'Vum', the seed mantra of water, denotes this area. From the navel to the heart is considered a triangular form representing the fire of red colour with Svastik mark at its three closed angles. It is denoted by the letter 'Rum' as its root mantra.

From the heart to the centre of the eyebrows, should be considered as the air of smoke colour marked with six dots denoting the seed mantra 'Yum' and of circular appearance. The part from the centre of the eyebrows to the crown of the head is considered akash, clear of any colour and 'Hum' as its bijamantra.

One must be aware that the five elements dissolve in the next level of existence which is their cause; water in fire, its cause; fire in air and air in akash. Going ahead, akash then dissolves in ahamkara which further dissolves in Mahatattva and further into Prakriti and finally into Supreme Self.

Now one comes to Paap Purusha. This sinful man in your body, a tiny man the size of a thumb, is situated in the left abdomen. It represents one or more of the sins, from brahmahatya to stealing gold to drinking to enjoying one's guru's wife.

To get rid of this sin man, one has to inhale air through the left nostril and think of 'Vum' bijamantra of air and turn the body into kumbhaka, like a jar filled with air. The air would then purify the sinful man inside by burning him to ashes with the repetition of 'Rum', the seed mantra of fire.

Thereafter, one has to exhale through the right nostril and expel the ashes of the sinful man in the form of a round ball. This ball can be imagined as turning into a golden egg by chanting 'Lum' followed by a repetition of 'Hum' and thinking of oneself as a cleansed being.

The same process has to be repeated then in the converse order. One has to repeat the mantra 'Soham' and separate the body from the highest being. The Sacral Plexus or the Kundalini has to be brought back to its place. While meditating upon the Devi in her most magnificent form, one has to apply ashes on the body.

Ashes or bhasma on one's forehead is prescribed in accordance with Shirovrata mentioned in the Atharva Veda. Three horizontal curved lines of ash on the forehead, called the Tripundra, are applied. The first line from the bottom represents Brahma, the next one is Vishnu and the top line is Mahadeva."

Narada asked, "Which three fingers should be used to draw the Tripundra?"

"The fore, middle and ring fingers of the right hand shall be used. These indicate the letters 'A', 'U' and 'M', respectively. The application of ash on the forehead is a vital prerequisite for being initiated in the Gayatri Mantra.

The Vedas also prescribe the bhasma bath, besmearing of the body with ash, as among the highest bliss. Yogis consider it holier than a water bath as Shiva himself was the first one to bathe in ashes. It is also termed a Fire Bath as it purifies the external and internal aspects.

O Narada! Let me now explain the effect of bhasma through an anecdote."

Narada was all ears.

"Once Rishi Durvasa, besmeared in ash and adorned with a Tripundra on his forehead and rudraksha over his body, arrived at the lower echelons of existence, where the pitris lived.

He silently chanted the name of Shankar and Devi Jagdambe. The pitris received him with due honours and made him comfortable. While the pitris and Rishi Durvasa were talking to each other, loud, annoying and lamenting voices kept on disturbing them. On enquiring about the cause of the clamour, Durvasa was informed that the racket originated from a close-by city in hell, by the name of Samyamani Puri. The city was ruled by Yamaraj and was inhabited by his tribe. The sinners in that place were being accorded their prescribed punishment.

The pitris also described to him the severe sufferings meted out in various hells, particularly the Kumbhipaka hell, the starkest among the twenty-eight hells. Hearing about the wretched condition of the sinners, the muni decided to immediately visit them.

As soon as he arrived at the Kumbhipaka, the ambience of hell changed. The sinners became happy and laughed. Some even began to sing and dance. The place became replete with the fragrance of flowers rather than the foul smell of flesh and blood.

Yama's attendants were shocked. They ran to inform their king about the wonderous, yet true, metamorphosis of the hell.

A curious Yamaraja mounted his black buffalo to check it out. He also sent a word to Indra in heaven.

The news spread like wildfire and soon Indra from Devaloka, Brahma from Brahmaloka and Vishnu from Vaikuntha arrived to witness the impossible feat of sinners enjoying bliss.

Unable to discern, they all went to Kailash to present their query to Mahadeva. Mahadeva spoke, 'O Devas! This is nothing but the greatness of bhasma. Durvasa had gone to Kumbhipaka besmeared in ash. A speck of bhasma from his forehead flew into hell and caused the transformation of hell.'

Subsequently, the erstwhile dwellers of Kumbhipaka turned it into a pilgrimage by establishing Shivalingam and they all left for Kailash to become Shiva bhaktas. They were named Bhadra.

Yama subsequently rebuilt Kumbhipaka hell in another place and prohibited the entry of Mahadeva devotees."

Narada had another question for Narayana, "O Muni! Some yogis use vertical lines on their foreheads. What does that signify?"

Narayana smiled, "This is called Urdhvapundra and worn by the devotees of Vishnu. Three vertical lines are drawn with space between them.

For this, one should use the earth from the hill crests or the banks of rivers or ocean beaches or anthills or the roots of tulasi plants. Turmeric powder can also be used for Urdhvapundra.

The lines drawn by the thumb give nourishment, the middle finger longevity, the ring finger food and prosperity, and the forefinger bestows liberation. Care should be taken that nails do not touch. Moreover, the colour of the earth is important. While black brings peace, red gives influence over others, yellow bestows prosperity and white enhances dharma," concluded Narayana.'

Sandhya and Gayatri

Vyasa continued, 'At the insistence of Narada, Narayana went on to elaborate the concept of sandhya involving Gayatri worshipping, the presiding deity of the morning, midday and evening.

Narayana said, "O Narada! The sandhya should be performed daily, three times a day. While the morning sandhya should be performed before sunrise when stars are still visible in the sky, the midday sandhya while the sun is in the meridian and the evening when the sun is setting.

The morning and evening sandhyas are also of three kinds. In the morning, when stars are visible, it is best to do the sandhya. After the stars disappear, it yields average results and after the sun has risen above the horizon, it is the least effective. Similarly, the evening sandhya when done while the sun is disappearing, is the best. If performed after the sun has gone down the horizon, it is average and the most inferior if performed after the stars have become visible.

A time period of two ghatika or dandas equivalent to one muhurta at sunrise and sunset is prescribed for performing the sandhya. If one is not able to do so within this period, penance is performed through an added arghya over and above the usual three times in the morning and evening and once in the afternoon sandhya, or chanting of the Gayatri Mantra one hundred and eight times. The chanting of the Gayatri Mantra is the crux of sandhya. Even Brahma and devas meditate upon her daily.

After the aachaman, each body part is touched while chanting one of the twenty-four names of Vishnu, preceded by Aum and ending with Svaha. It is followed by Pranayaam. It involves inhaling through the left nostril, closing both nostrils and exhaling through the right. The same is repeated through the other nostril. The thumb of the right hand is used for holding the right nostril and the ring and small fingers for the left nostril.

The three steps called Purak, Kumbhak and Rechak are accompanied by meditating upon Vishnu, Brahma and Mahadeva, respectively, and by reciting the Gayatri Mantra at each step.

While meditating on Devi Gayatri, it is instructed that one should form twenty-four mudras or gestures by hands and fingers, to appease the Devi and recite only once the hundred-syllabled mantra, which has three components: twenty-four-syllabled Gayatri Mantra; forty-four-syllabled first shloka of Durga Suktam; and thirty-two-syllabled Maha Mrityunjaya mantra.

Towards the end, one should offer water to the sun three times by reciting the Gayatri Mantra an equal number of times. It is said that such water offered in the times of yore became a thunderbolt and helped to kill the rakshasas who tried to impede the path of the sun. It is true for the human body too, if one assumes the sun as representing the mind.

While performing the sandhya, it is recommended that one should sit in Siddhasana. In this posture, the heel should be under the genital and the other below the scrotum, and the back vertically straight.

After the Pranayaam, one should sit in Khhechari[310] Mudra. Here the soul of a person goes to akash, away from the objects of senses. The tongue joins the soul too. Thereafter, the vision is transfixed between the two eyebrows."

Narayana also explained the importance of Gayatri Purashcharan. Here, before a person chants the name or mantra of a deity, the Gayatri Mantra is to be repeated. The repetition is done from a few to even a million times depending on the objective of the mantra to purify it. The mantra has no effect without Purashcharan. But the chanting of the mantra is prohibited in the months of Jyeshtha, Ashadha, Pausha and Mul.

The Purashcharan of Gayatri itself is performed by repeating it two million and four hundred thousand times. This means a hundred thousand times for each syllable, although Maharishi Vishvamitra had placed this number at three million two hundred thousand.

Maharishi Vishvamitra also mentioned the five kinds of yagnas to be performed that would appease the Vaishva Deva, namely, Deva Yagna, Brahma Yagna, Bhuta Yagna, Pitri Yagna and Manushya Yagna. In all these yagnas, curd, ghee, fruits, roots and vegetables and water are needed to perform the sacrifice. If these items are not readily available, then fuel and grass soaked with ghee, curd, payasam or even with water epitomising the recommended items could be used.

He said that oil or salty substances should never be used for oblations. After the offering of food in the yagna, it should be offered to mendicant brahmacharis followed by cows.

Narayana compared the yagna to the human body where the belly is an arani, the mind is the churning rod and the wind is the rope. The fire is ignited thus in the belly and the eyes are considered as the sacrificer.

Oblations to satisfy the five vayus are made through food. It has to be taken by the forefinger, middle finger and thumb for Praan Vayu; by thumb, middle finger and ring finger for Apaan Vayu; by thumb, ring and little finger for Vyaan Vayu; by thumb, forefinger and little finger for Udaan Vayu and by all fingers for Samaan Vayu.

This has to be done with repetition of the respective mantras: "*Aum Pranaya Svaha*", "*Aum Apanaya Svaha*", "*Aum Samanaya Svaha*", "*Aum Udanaya Svaha*" and "*Aum Vyanaya Svaha*".

He also explained the various kinds of vratas[311] a person should observe. These were Krichchhra Vrata, Chandrayana Vrata, Prajapatya Vrata, Saantpan Vrata and Paraak Vrata.'

Janamejaya interjected. He asked, 'O Muni! I am not sure if these kinds of tapasya, yoga, sandhya, vratas and yagnas that you have described are easy to practise for an ordinary person. Kindly, therefore, explain what shall be done by a common man to obtain the Devi's blessings. Moreover, you have described the importance of the Gayatri Mantra as the one that purifies the other mantras. Kindly do tell me more about the construct of Gayatri.'

Vyasa smiled. He was content that his listener had paid attention to his narration which he was about to complete shortly.

He said, 'O King! You are absolutely right in observing that these rituals are not easy to perform. An ordinary man thus needs to repeat the Gayatri Mantra and perform sandhya thrice a day.

The Gayatri Mantra is a powerful and all-pervading mantra. Each of its twenty-four syllables has corresponding rishis, chhandas, sevatas, shaktis, colours, tattvas and mudras.

The twenty-four syllables protect a specific part of the body, beginning with "Tat" protecting the head; "Sa" the forehead; "Vi" the eyes; "Tu" the cheeks; "Va" the nostrils; "Re" the mouth; "Ni" the upper lip; "Yah" the lower lip; "Bha" the face; "Rgo" the cheeks; "De" the throat; "Va" the shoulders; "Sya" the right hand; "Dhi" the left hand; "Ma" the heart; "Hi" the belly; the second "Dhi" protecting the navel; "Yo" the loins; the following "Yo" the anus; "Nah" the thighs; "Pra" the knees; "Cho" the shanks; "Da" the heels; "Ya" the legs; and lastly the "At" protecting all the sides.'

Vyasa added, 'The Gayatri Kavach is a potent mantra. If one recites or holds it on his body, it is capable of destroying all sins. The kavach has its rishis in Brahma, Vishnu and Mahesh; the four Vedas as its chhandas; Para Brahma as its devata; and Bharga[312] as shakti.

Then there is Gayatri Hridyam as mentioned in the Atharva Veda. This mantra should be recited only when a person considers himself as the microcosm of the Devi having all the devas residing on her body. The rishi of Gayatri Hridyam is Maharishi Narayana, the chhanda is Gayatri herself and Devi Parameshvari is the devata. Its recitation yields fruits equivalent to a thousand sacrifices and sixty thousand Gayatri Mantras.

There is yet another Gayatri Stotra that eulogises various forms of the Devi pervading the three worlds. Its recitation brings the results of visiting all the pilgrimages or all the tapasya or all the sacrifices.

In addition, Brahma has composed one thousand and eight names of the Devi Gayatri. He also recited these for the first time. Their recitation, particularly on the Shukla Ashtami of each month, accrues incomparable merits, destroys past sins and unites the devotee with Brahma.'

Janamejaya then asked, 'O Vyasa! Is there a prescribed way to initiate oneself into these mantras?'

Vyasa spoke, 'Yes, the process of such initiation is called diksha after which a devotee is entitled to worship the guru, the fire and the devas. Diksha must be imparted by a guru with due care that both he and the disciple are pure-hearted at the time. It is like a lightning striking the disciple and emancipating his body, mind and soul with divine knowledge.

Certain rituals precede and accompany the diksha ceremony, for both the giver and the receiver. After the ceremony, the devotee is expected to pay dakshina to the guru followed by charities to virgin girls, brahmins as well as poor and the needy ones.'

Janamejaya said, 'O Gurudeva! I am indebted to you for having spoken about all the knowledge contained in the Devi Purana. However, there is one thought that is bothering me after all this wisdom.'

Vyasa replied, 'Go on, O King.'

Janamejaya said, 'If the Devi is all-pervading and her worship is the highest, why is it that people worship other devas?'

Vyasa said, 'I am glad that you asked this question. But to explain it, I will have to take you back to the times of yore. It was after one of the wars between the devas and asuras in which the former won with the grace of the highest shakti, the Devi.'

The devas, out of the intoxication of pride of victory, started feeling as if they were supreme. They became deluded enough to even forget about the merciful Devi.

Knowing and realising the pitiful plight of the devas, the Devi appeared to them in her most splendid form. She was radiating like millions of suns combined. She was glowing so much that the devas could only see a bright light.

Unable to fathom it due to delusion, the devas assembled to discuss this extraordinary light. Indra asked Agni, as he was best placed, to ascertain what this light was.

Agni proceeded towards the light. But before he could say anything, a voice emanating from the light asked Agni to introduce himself.

Agni said, "I am fire. The Vedic yagnas are performed because of me. I can burn anything."

The light threw a straw of grass towards him and asked him to burn the petty object. Agni tried but failed to ignite the fire to burn the straw.

The humiliated Agni returned to inform the devas what had transpired and cautioned them, "Don't be under any false impression that we are the supreme beings."

Indra summoned Vayu, the praan of all, and asked him to figure out what the light was. While he was approaching the mass of light, Vayu was also asked to identify himself.

Vayu answered haughtily, "I am the wind capable of moving anything."

The voice asked him to fly away the straw lying on the ground in front of him.

Vayu attempted his best but could not even move the straw from its place let alone fly it away. Having met the same fate as Agni, he returned equally embarrassed and told his peers that the light was perhaps a yaksha or a ghost.

Finally, all the devas urged Indra, "O Indra! You are our king. You should lead us now."

As Indra was nearing the light, it started fading gradually and eventually disappeared. Indra was flabbergasted. He had no one to address his queries. Instead, he was left with emptiness.

He was ashamed as he could not even speak to the light. He wondered what he would tell the devas. If he told the truth, he would lose his honour and what was life without honour.

Weighing various options, Indra decided to give up his self-conceited esteem. He mentally took refuge in the great light. As soon as he did so, a heavenly voice broke out, "O King of devas! Go and meditate upon the bijamantra of Maya."

Indra quit everything and sat down to recite the seed mantra of Maya. Then came the Shukla Navami of Chaitra and during this time when the sun entered the meridian, the extraordinary light returned. But this time, the Devi appeared from it in an incomparably beautiful form in a lustrous body.

She held a noose and a goad in two hands. The other two hands indicated fearlessness and that they were ready to grant boons. She wore a red saree and was covered with priceless gems and jewellery.

Indra sang hymns in her praise. She explained to him, "O Indra! Maya is nothing but me. It is absorbed in me at the time of Pralaya. When the new creation begins, it is within me, unmanifested, and called Antarmukhi[313]. When it manifests due to the play of gunas, it becomes Bahirmukhi[314].

Brahma, epitomising Sattva Guna, is known as Gross Body, Vishnu, the Rajo Guna, as the Subtle Body and Mahadeva, the Tamo Guna, as the Causal Body. I am beyond the three gunas, known as Turiya where these three are in perfect equilibrium. There is another state of mine which is beyond this and that is formless, the unmanifested or the Nirguna.

O Indra! It is I who mandates the trinity of Brahma, Vishnu and Mahesh to perform their respective tasks. It is again I who manifests in the devas to create sky, earth, wind and fire. Thus, I am the whole universe, the supreme, and every being and thing is under my command."

Devi's words broke Indra out of the delusion of vanity and pride, and she disappeared from his sight.

Since then, O Janamejaya, all the devas continued to worship the highest being, the Supreme Goddess, by performing sandhya three times a day and worshipping her through yagnas.'

Vyasa paused before resuming, 'I must also emphasise that it is only the Gayatri Mantra that is mentioned in the Vedas and must be done regularly and permanently. The same does not apply to the Vishnu or Shiva mantras.'

Vyasa had not finished yet. He continued, 'O King! Let me tell you another anecdote, about Muni Gautama.

Once, there was a long drought on earth owing to the evil karma of humans. It did not rain for fifteen continuous years. People began to feed even on horses, bears, pigs and even the dead bodies of other human beings as there was nothing left to eat.

The brahmins got together to confabulate. They collectively decided to appeal to Gautama to save them from the disaster. They all, along with their families, cows and all possessions went to his hermitage.

Gautama received them affectionately and enquired about the reason for their journey to his ashram. He heard them patiently and told them to stay with him at his ashram till such time that a solution was found.

He then meditated upon Devi Gayatri who was appeased with the worshipping of her ardent devotee, Gautama. She handed him an exceptional vessel that could fulfil all his wishes.

The vessel was a great boon. It churned out food of various kinds as desired, fodder for domestic animals, clothes and ornaments, and all other commodities required for performing sacrifices by the brahmins at the ashram. Gautama also called in other munis and freely distributed the items from the vessel to them.

Gradually, other brahmins and munis started arriving at Gautama's hermitage. It kept expanding with the blessings of the plentiful vessel, feeding and providing for everyone. Even the devas became happy with this new normalcy as they also got their feed from the regular yagnas. Once, even Indra came down to the ashram and thanked Gautama for his kindness.

Twelve years passed by and one day, Narada paid a visit to the hermitage. He was singing praises for Gayatri and playing on his lute. Gautama received him with cordiality and warmth. Narada conveyed to him that he had heard about the muni's praises in Devaloka too.

Somehow Narada's visit and unending praises for Gautama did not go down well with other munis. They decided to move out of the hermitage after the next harvest season, which was not far off.

Soon all the brahmins got together to leave. But before doing so, they, out of sheer envy, decided to teach a lesson to Gautama. They, through their mayic powers, created an old and moribund cow. The cow was pushed into the hall where Gautama was about to begin his routine homa.

Gautama noticed the cow and tried to shoo her away. The cow was so fragile that she fell there and died instantly.

The gathering of brahmins got the opportunity they were looking for. They shouted "Hey! Look! Gautama has killed a cow."

An unfazed Gautama finished his routine of the homa ceremony and sat in the lotus position to meditate on the root cause of the issue at hand. He quickly realised the plotting by his guests. This enraged him no end.

He cursed them, "O wicked brahmins! Since you have played against me, someone who sheltered you in your hour of need, you will be disentitled to mantras and tantras of the Devi as well as Shiva and Vishnu. You will also be debarred from practising sandhya and other sacrificial ceremonies. You will not hesitate in selling your close relatives and being immoral with others' wives. Not only this, the women of your household and all your future generations will also suffer like this."

The disgusted Gautama went to the Devi's temple afterwards seeking peace in her worship. She advised him that this episode in his life was nothing but an unfortunate turn of fate. After receiving the Devi's counsel, he returned to his hermitage.

The cursed brahmins, meanwhile, lost all memories of the Vedas and mantras. They got together and went to Gautama. They fell at his feet in remorse and appealed repeatedly to save them.

The muni had calmed down by this time and felt sorry for them. He said, "The curse is like an arrow. Once shot, it cannot be withdrawn. Therefore, you all will remain in Kumbhipaka hell till Krishna reincartes. After that, you will be born in Kali Yuga and realise my curse."

Brahmins folded their hand and prayed, "What can we do to alleviate the effect of your curse?"

Gautama answered plainly, "Pray to Devi Gayatri."

And that is why, O King, these brahmins in the present day and age of Kali are carrying out Gautama's curse and are devoid of their earlier virtues. Therefore, worshipping of the Devi, the perpetual Shakti, is a must in Kali Yuga.'

Mani Dvipa

Janamejaya asked Vyasa, 'Earlier you had mentioned about the magnificent Mani Dvipa. Kindly describe it to me.'

Vyasa said, 'Devi Bhagvati's permanent abode is more exalting than Goloka, Vaikuntha and Kailash. Called "Sarvaloka" or "Mani Dvipa", it resembles an umbrella that castes away a shadow on the entire universe as if blessing it. It is located above all the regions that I mentioned earlier.

Surrounded by Sudhaa Sagar, Mani Dvipa is filled with fish and marine animals. A huge iron wall stands in the middle of this ocean. It fortifies the dvipa and well-armed guards protect it. It has four entry points.

Inside the dvipa, there is an enclosure made of bronze. Within this, all tree species that exist anywhere in the universe can be found. These trees, separated by water bodies, have the juiciest fruits and provide shelter to birds of innumerable kinds.

Going deeper inside, a brass boundary wall stands that has a forest of Kalpavrikshas. It is inhabited by Vasant with his two wives, Madhu Sri and Madhava Sri, and a host of gandharvas and their wives.

Then comes the next enclosure on the island, surrounded by a wall of lead, and full of santaan trees. This is the abode of Grishm Ritu[315] and his wives, Shukra Sri and Shuchi Sri, along with several siddhas and devas.

After this, there is an enclosure with copper walls inhabited by Varsha Ritu and a garden of hari chandan trees. Varsha has twelve shaktis, namely, Nabhah Sri, Nabhasya Sri, Svarasva, Rasyasmalini, Ambadula, Niratni, Abhramanti, Meghyantika, Varshyanti, Chibunika, Vaaridhara and Sammata.

The sixth enclosure is made of five kinds of iron and has a garden of mandaar trees. Sharad Ritu[316] lives here with his wives Ishulakshmi and Urjalakshmi. The seventh enclosure is made of silver and contains a garden of parijaat trees. Hemant Ritu[317] and his two wives Saha Sri and Sahasya Sri reside here.

Then one reaches the eighth enclosure with walls made of gold. It hosts a garden of kadamba trees. Here resides Shishir Ritu[318] and his two wives Tapah Sri and Tapasya Sri.

Thereafter, one comes to the ninth enclosure built with pushparaga[319] gems. Everything in this enclosure is made of gems and jewels, including the flooring, water canals, etc.

On the eastern side of this enclosure is Amravati, the city of Indra and on the south-eastern part is the abode of Agni. He lives here with his two wives Svaha and Svadha. On the south and south-west are the cities of Yama and Rakshasa Nirriti. On the west side is the city of Varuna, the northwest is Vayu Deva, the north has the yakshas and the north-eastern corner is of Rudra.

These devas are the aggregates of all of their respective kinds in various Brahmandas.

Next, the tenth enclosure is built with red padmaraga[320] gems. Here sixty-four kalaas of the Devi live. These are Pinglakshi, Vishalakshi, Samriddhi, Vriddhi, Shraddha, Svaha, Svadha, Maya, Sangya, Vasundhara, Trilokadhatri, Savitri, Gayatri, Tridasheshvari, Surupa, Bahurupa, Skandamata, Achyutpriya, Vimla, Amala, Aruni, Aaruni, Prakriti, Vikriti, Srishti, Sthiti, Samrhiti, Sandhya, Mata, Sati, Hamsi, Mardika, Vajrika, Para, Devamata, Bhagavati, Devaki, Kamalaasana, Trimukhi, Saptamukhi, Surasur-Vimardini, Lamboshthi, Urdhakeshi, Bahushirsha, Vrikodari, Ratharekhahvaya, Shashireka, Gaganvega, Pavanvega, Bhuvanapala, Madanaatura, Ananga, Anangmathana, Anangmekhala, Anangkusuma, Vishvarupa, Suradika, Kshayamkari, Akshyobhya, Satyavadini, Bahurupa, Shuchivrata, Udara and Vagishi.

The eleventh enclosure is made of gomedamani[321] where thirty-two Maha Shaktis or Devis reside. These are Vidya, Hri, Pushti, Pragya, Sinivali, Kuhu, Rudra, Virya, Prabha, Nanda, Poshini, Riddhida, Shubha, Kaalratri, Maharatri, Bhadra-Kaali, Kapardini, Vikriti, Dandi, Mundini, Sendukhanda, Shikhandini, Nishumbha-Shumbha-Mathani, Mahishasura-Mardini, Indrani, Rudrani, Shankarardha-Sharirini, Naari-Narayani, Trishulini, Palini, Ambika and Hladini.

The twelfth enclosure is made of diamonds. Here reside Devi Bhuveshvari with her attendants. Each of her attendants is eager to serve the Devi as they have specialised skills bestowed on them. The Devi has eight main attendants or sakhis, namely, Anangrupa, Anangmadana, Madanaatura, Bhuvanvega, Bhuvanpalika, Sarvashishira, Anangvedana, Anangmekhala.

After this comes the thirteenth enclosure made of vaidurya mani[322]. This octagonal enclosure is inhabited by eight matrikas[323], which are also the aggregates of individual matrikas in every universe. These are Brahmani, Maheshvari, Kaumari, Vaishnavi, Varahi, Indrani, Chamunda and Maha Lakshmi.

The fourteenth enclosure is built of indraneel mani[324]. This has a sixteen-petal lotus; each petal hosts one of the sixteen dark blue coloured shaktis of Devi Bhagvati. These are presiding deities of respective shaktis in each Brahmanda. These are named Karali, Vikrali, Uma, Sarasvati, Sri, Durga, Usha, Lakshmi, Shruti, Smriti, Dhriti, Shraddha, Medha, Mati, Kaanti and Arya.

The fifteenth enclosure has an eight-petal lotus. Everything here is made of pearls. The petals are the abode of eight shaktis, the principal advisors to the Devi. They inform the Devi about the happenings in various Brahmandas. They are Anangkusuma, Anangkusumatura, Anangmadana, Anangmadanatura, Bhuvanpala, Gaganvega, Shashirekha and Gaganrekha.

Next, the sixteenth enclosure is hexagonal and made of emeralds. The east part is inhabited by Brahma and Devi Gayatri, the south-west corner by Maha Vishnu and Savitri, the north by Maha Rudra and Sarasvati, the south-east by Kubera and Maha Lakshmi, the west by Madan and Rati and the north-east by Ganesh with Pushti Devi.

The seventeenth enclosure is made of pravaal[325] where lives the goddesses of five elements, namely, Hrillekha, Gagana, Rakta, Karalika and Mahochchhushma.

Then, there is an eighteenth enclosure built with navaratnas[326]. This is inhabited by the presiding deity of Aamnaaya[327], the ten Maha Vidyas and all the manifestations of the Devi who came into being to kill various daityas at various times in history.

The final nucleus of the dvipa is the abode of the Devi, built of chintamani[328] gems. Her palace has thousands of pillars, built of suryakanta mani[329], chandrakanta mani[330] and vidyutkanta mani[331].

Here in the central part of the dvipa, the Devi rules and directs all the universes. Her own palace is known as Sri Chintamani Griha.'

Vyasa continued, 'O King! I have now described what all Narayana told Narada who in turn spoke to me. This is what comprises Srimad Devi Bhagavatam. Anyone who hears this, achieves all success in his lifetime and moksha thereafter. Therefore, you must perform your yagna in the name of the Devi to save your father from any evil that might befall him.'

Epilogue

Janamejaya prostrated in front of Veda Vyasa and began the Devi Yagna. He also ordered the Bhagavatam to be read by the assembled brahmins. He observed the Navratri fast, fed many brahmins and young girls, and gave away alms to the poor, orphans and brahmins.

The moment the yagna was completed, Narada visited the king. After he had relaxed and settled, Janamejaya enquired Narada about the objective of his unannounced visit.

Narada replied, 'O King! I am here to share the good news with you. I came from Devaloka where I saw your father in a divine form enjoying his stay. I was told that soon he will go to Mani Dvipa.

Your Devi Yagna, observance of Navratri rituals and recitation of Devi Bhagavatam have borne fruit and delivered your father, King Parikshit, from hell. You are truly blessed.'

Janamejaya was overjoyed. He had fully comprehended the virtues of reading Srimad Devi Bhagavatam.

Notes

1 The Lunar race
2 Somnath, about 230 km from Dwarka, in Gujarat, India
3 Kali Yuga is the last of the four aeons, preceded by Satya Yuga, Treta Yuga and Dvapara Yuga
4 Meditation
5 Water is taken in hand as a witness to the act (because fire as a witness cannot be taken in hand) as well as to channelise the energies for its fructification and then thrown on the ground
6 The Supreme Goddess
7 Gems
8 Spiritual chanting
9 Medicinal herbs
10 Sage
11 Celestial nymphs
12 Celestial musicians in the service of devas
13 Aachaman signifies purification through pouring water in one's hand and sipping it thrice followed by taking water in hand for the fourth time and throwing it on the ground which means symbolic washing of the hand
14 Chanting of mantras
15 Meditation or penance depending upon the context
16 Hermitage
17 Offering of food or fruits made to gods and later distributed to the devotees
18 Philosophy and law
19 Economics and sciences
20 The city of Benares
21 The fire rites
22 A sacrificial ceremony
23 It is I who is the entire creation; there is nothing eternal in this creation other than I
24 Righteousness

25 Prosperity
26 Fulfilment of desires
27 Liberation
28 Stage of gradual withdrawal from worldly affairs
29 Stage of complete renunciation
30 The manes
31 Double tongued
32 Seven elements – skin, blood, flesh, bones, sinews, marrows and semen
33 Vishnu's serpent bed and the lord of snakes
34 Night jasmine
35 Attendants
36 Blue-coloured linseed or flax
37 Hibiscus
38 Saraca asoca
39 Mimusops elengi
40 Umbrella tree or screw pine
41 Magnolia champaca
42 Red amaranth
43 Six-angled
44 Manifestations of powers
45 Newton's first law of motion, in modern science, says that 'an object continues in the state of rest or in motion at a constant velocity unless it is acted upon by a net external force', which means that the entire world would be inertial unless it is acted upon by a shakti, the external force
46 The cosmic ego
47 Karma which is ripe for fructification in a particular incarnation
48 The subtlest of the three bodies – physical, astral and causal – experienced in deep sleep or pure awareness
49 In mathematical terms, each gross element is 50 per cent of its subtle element combined with 12.5 per cent of each of the four other subtle elements
50 Having none of the three traits or gunas
51 Ascetics who have achieved ultimate enlightenment
52 Present-day Ayodhya in Uttar Pradesh, India
53 A prenatal ceremony performed soon after a woman conceives, with the objective of begetting a son

54 Involves parting of the hair above the forehead of the mother-to-be, observed in the fourth, sixth or eighth month of pregnancy aimed at protecting the child in the womb
55 Fourth of the sixteen ceremonies, held soon after the birth to remove impurities of the child who has been in the womb for nine months; a mixture of ghee (clarified butter) and honey is tasted by the baby
56 Naming of the baby
57 The ceremony of tonsure or shaving off of the head
58 The ceremony, initiating a boy's life as a student, in which he receives a sacred thread to be worn across his chest from the left shoulder to the waist
59 The daityas or devils
60 A ceremony performed to consecrate a king
61 The Solar race
62 Lord of love and desire
63 One Akshauhini comprises 21,870 chariots, 21,870 elephants, 65,610 cavalry and 1,09,350 infantry; the ratio is 1 chariot:1 elephant:3 cavalry:5 infantry soldiers
64 A ceremony where a woman chooses her husband out of several suitors present
65 Nine days/nights of celebrations
66 The waxing moon
67 Made of boiled rice and ghee
68 Washing of the feet
69 Offering of water
70 Offering of a mixture of honey
71 A vow or resolve
72 Sandal paste
73 A fragrant wood, the aloe wood
74 Incense
75 Another name for Sita
76 Vasavi is another name for Vyasa's mother and, thus, Vasaveya means Vyasa
77 The living beings
78 Vasudeva was popularly known as Aanakadundubhi as aanakas (a divine musical instrument) and dundubhis (drums) resounded celestially when he was born
79 A part

80 The 14 Manvantaras together form a day of Brahma; these 14 Manvantaras are Svayambhuva, Svarochisha, Uttama, Tamasa, Raivata, Caksusu, Vaivasvata, Savarni, Daksha Savarni, Meru Savarni, Surya Savarni, Chandra Savarni, Rudra Savarni and Vishnu Savarni
81 Foot
82 Badrinath, one of the four dhaams
83 Persuasion or appeasement
84 Corrupt or buyout someone by exploiting their greed
85 Punish, usually through war
86 The god of the spring season
87 Seeing, hearing, smell, taste and touch
88 Nether region, commonly known as hell
89 Also called Rewa
90 The thousand-spoke disc
91 Householder or married man with a family
92 The divine play
93 Pied cuckoo bird, known for heralding the onset of monsoon
94 Also known as Sumeru
95 Pieces of wood for kindling the fire by attrition
96 A kind of parrot or green parakeet
97 Lotus pose
98 A kind of white ant
99 The sacrificial pit
100 Fate
101 Buddha is the lord of Buddhi (intelligence and wisdom)
102 Great sinner
103 Manifested form, with the gunas
104 Celestial beings considered expert musicians
105 Secondary Puranas
106 The stanza
107 Modern laws of physics also say that 'energy can neither be created nor destroyed'
108 Chapters
109 Sweet, sour, salty, pungent, bitter and astringent
110 The prayers
111 There are eight praharas in a day
112 Penultimate muhurat before sunrise, begins typically 96 minutes before sunrise

113 Intrinsic tendencies or virtues
114 Ultimate powers that can be attained by seers
115 The Supreme God
116 The cycle of four yugas
117 Horse sacrifice usually performed to expand the frontiers of a kingdom
118 Yagna performed to maintain harmony in the kingdom
119 Eight elemental gods, representing aspects of nature
120 Ganga's son
121 Breathing regulation exercises
122 The king of fishes
123 Smell of a fish
124 Earth
125 A layer of Patala
126 Four-armed
127 Fearlessness
128 Posture
129 One of the twenty-eight types of narakas or hell where the sinner is roasted in Kumbhī fire, i.e., big vessels full of boiling oil
130 Beings with human bodies and snake heads
131 Unclean, impure or unrighteous people
132 One of the eight forms of marriage; the other seven are Brahma, Daiva, Arsha, Prajapatya, Asura, Gandharva and Pischacha
133 Sacred fig tree
134 Unrighteousness or unjust
135 There is natural enmity between buffaloes and horses
136 Juice extracted from the soma creeper
137 A barbed missile
138 Clubs
139 Pickaxes
140 Maces
141 Tridents
142 Discus
143 Half moon
144 Thunderbolt
145 A kind of mace
146 Reliever of problems

147 The ocean of milk, which was churned by the suras andasuras together
148 A kind of energised weapon for trapping someone and rendering him ineffective
149 Fire weapon used by the god of fire, Agni Deva
150 A pot, could be of any material, usually used for water
151 Create discord among the enemy
152 Celestial beings known for their knowledge and wisdom
153 Attendants of Kubera, having a human body and the head of a horse; they play musical instruments and sing with the gandharvas
154 Victory, Victory!
155 A part-lion, part-bird beast, considered more powerful than an elephant
156 A treatise on the art of love
157 A kind of missile
158 Literally means flavour, signifying sentiment or emotion here
159 Love
160 Peace
161 Shiva's messenger; dut means messenger
162 Flower from screw pine or umbrella tree
163 Equal and opposite reaction in intangible form
164 Literally means Five Fires (it amounts to penances in the heat of four live fires in the four directions and the sun on top with the objective of taming the five internal weaknesses – desire, anger, greed, ego and attachment)
165 Pigeon
166 Sparrow or goraiya bird
167 Partridge
168 To kill a brahmin
169 The ceremony accompanied by chanting of Vedic mantras for good fortune; in this case, to secure victory and avert calamity in war
170 Invocation of mantras for malevolent purposes
171 The ceremony in honour of a departed one
172 The physical configuration of an army in the formation of flying vultures during war
173 Mantras from the Atharva Veda used to cause magic spells

174 Ten thousand human years
175 Rishis of Devaloka
176 An oath
177 The tree that yields all desires
178 Future
179 Present
180 Purification of materials used in worshipping
181 Clarity and channelisation of action
182 Purification of one's heart and mind
183 Faith or devotion
184 Human sacrifice
185 Usually an inauspicious period of a certain number of days observed by the family after a child's birth or a death
186 The ceremony after a boy finishes his study and returns home from hermitage
187 Old name of oedema
188 Crane
189 Also called adi bird, the king of goose
190 Literally means essence; in this case, the essence of a man, that is, semen
191 Implies the atomic form
192 Descendants of Maharishi Bhrigu
193 Born from the thigh
194 Another name for lotus flower
195 Attachment
196 Date and time
197 The ceremony of offering water and black sesame seeds to the deceased or manes
198 Pure consciousness
199 True knowledge
200 Serpents
201 A fire ceremony like yagna but undertaken at an individual level, usually at home or hermitage
202 In praise of Agni Deva
203 A female deity born to annihilate enemies
204 Another name for Balarama
205 Relatable to the concept of theory of relativity of time based on the velocity of an object that modern science has also established

206 Unsullied meat straight from the hunt or sacrifice
207 An outcast by virtue of dealing with the disposal of corpses at a cremation ground
208 Malevolent demons with hideous appearance
209 Conical spikes
210 Invocation of the deity
211 Homage
212 Twice-born
213 Charity, usually given to the poor
214 Gifts to brahmins or priests
215 One hundred million
216 Coins
217 Ten million
218 Cremation ground
219 One of the twenty-eight types of hell
220 Endurance of difficulties in life
221 Pure maya or Shuddha Sattva joined with Supreme Self
222 The five-faced (Ishaan, Tatpurusha, Aghora, Vamadeva and Sadyojata) form of Shiva, which exists in the causal plane
223 Akash and ether have been interchangeably used in the Puranas and basically mean vacuum or space
224 Juice of flowers
225 Seat of deity; in this case, of Shakti
226 Known by the name of Vishalakshi in Kashi where Gauri's face fell; Linga Dharini in Naimisaranya; Lalita Devi in Prayag; Kamuki in Gandhamadan; Kumuda in southern Manasa; Vishvakama, bestower of all desires, in northern Manasa; Gomati in Gomanta; Kamacharini in Mandar Mountain; Madotkata in Chaitraratha; Jayanti in Hastinapur; Gauri in Kanyakubja; Rambha in Malaya Mountain; Kirtimati in Ekamrapitha; Vishveshvari in Vishve; Puruhuta in Puskara; Sanmarga Dayini in Kedara Pitha; Manda atop Himalayas; Bhadrakarnika in Gokarna; Bhavani in Sthaneshvara; Vilvapatrika in Vilvake; Madhavi in Shrishaila; Bhadra in Bhadreshvara; Jaya in Varaha Shaila; Kamala in Kamalalaya; Rudrani in Rudra Koti; Kaali in Kalanjara; Maha Devi in Shalagrama; Jalapriya in Shivalingam; Kapila in Mahalingam; Mukuteshvari in Makota; Kumari in Mayapuri; Lalitambika in Santana;

Mangala in Gaya Kshetra; Vimala in Purushottama; Utpalakshi in Sahasraksha; Mahotpala in Hiranyaksha; Amoghakshi in Vishakha; Padala in Pundra Vardhana; Narayani in Suparshva; Rudra Sundari in Trikuta; Vipula Devi in Vipula; Kalyani in Malayâchala; Ekavira in Sahyadri; Chandrika in Harishchandra; Ramana in Rama Tirtha; Mrigavati in Yamuna; Kotivi in Kotatirtha; Sugandha in Madhavavana; Trisandhya in Godavari; Ratipriya in Gangadvara; Shubhananda in Shiva Kundam; Nandini in Devikatata; Rukmini in Dvaravati; Radha in Brindavana; Devaki in Mathura; Parameshvari in Patala; Sita in Chitrakuta; Vindhyavasini in the Vindhya range; Mahalaksmi in Karavira; Uma Devi in Vinayak; Arogya in Vaidyanatha; Maheshvari in Mahakaal; Abhaya in Ushna Tirtha; Nitamba in the Vindhya mountain; Mandavi in Mandavya; Svaha in Maheshvaripura; Prachanda in Chhagalanda; Chandika in Amarakantaka; Vararoha in Someshvara; Pushkaravati in Prabhas; Devamata in Sarasvati; Paravara in Samudratata; Mahabhaga in Mahalaya; Pingaleshvari in Payosni; Simhika in Kritashaucha; Atishankari in Kartika; Lola in Utpalavartaka; Subhadra in Shona Sangam; Devi Lakshmi in Siddhavana; Ananga in Bharatashrama; Vishvamukhi in Jalandhara; Tara in the Kishkindhya mountain; Pushti in Devadaru Vana; Medha in Kashmiramandalam; Bhima in Himadri; Tushti in Vishveshvara Kshetra; Shuddhi in Kapalamochana; Mata in Kayavarohana; Dhara in Shankhoddhara; Dhriti in Pindaraka; Kala in Chandrabhaga river; Shivadharini in Achchoda; Amrita in Vena; Urvashi in Vadari; Aushaddhi in northern Kuru; Kushodaka in Kushadvipa; Manmatha in Hemakuta; Satyavadini in Kumuda; Vandaniya in Ashvattha; Nidhi in Vaishravanalaya; Gayatri at the mouth ofVedas; Parvati near Shiva; Indrani in Devalokas; Sarasvati in Brahmaloka; Prabha in the Solar disc; Vaishnavi in Matrikas; Arundhati amongst the Satis and Tilottama among the Rama Apsaras

227 Repeated recitation of a mantra to achieve the desired objective, usually accompanied by burnt offerings

228 Fasting observed on the third day of Shukla Paksha of

Magh month commemorating the wedding anniversary of Shiva and Uma (or Gauri)

229 Hymns from the Rig Veda praising the Devi
230 Inner sacrifices
231 Offering of oblations to the fire of life
232 Dissolution or end of the world
233 Unborn, existing eternally
234 Gigantic
235 Abode of Brahma
236 Space between the earth and the sun
237 Topmost region of heavens, the abode of most enlightened souls
238 Abode of the sons of Brahma
239 Abode of Tapas
240 Region between the sun and the polar star
241 Subtle channels in the body through which energies flow
242 The Supreme God or the highest Self
243 Sahasrara or crown chakra
244 Highest Shakti
245 Root Chakra
246 All fifty letters of the Sanskrit alphabet are placed on the body through hand gestures accompanied by Om as the prefix and Namah as the suffix
247 The five Pretas are Brahma, Vishnu, Rudra, SadaShiva and Ishvara, located under the feet of the Devi
248 Consecration of the idol, meaning infusing life into it
249 Here, it means a country
250 An asterism in the moon's path or lunar mansion
251 Alley
252 Path
253 Zodiac constellations
254 Fast; when the planet traverses perihelion, the part of curvature nearest to the centre of its orbit
255 Slow; when the planet moves through aphelion, the part of curvature farthest from the centre of its orbit
256 Uniform
257 Season
258 One muhurta is 48 minutes and, thus, a day has 30 muhurtas
259 Seven sages, namely, Vashishtha, Marichi, Pulastya, Pulaha,

Atri, Angiras and Kratu; also known as Great Bear
260 Polar star
261 The attendants or messengers
262 With sharp edges like swords
263 Brahmins, kshatriyas or vaishyas
264 Clan; traditionally no nuptial relations are permitted in the same gotra
265 Celestial she-dog
266 Pointed objects such as horns, swords, spears
267 Pits
268 Brahmin, kshatriya, vaishya and shudra are the four varnas
269 The radiant spirit of Brahma
270 Literally means life; here, it means the flow of energy within the body in the form of vayu (wind)
271 Danavas, born of mother Danu and father Kashyapa, are also demons like daityas who are sons of mother Diti and father Kashyapa
272 Traits or attributes
273 Krishna's habitat
274 The left part of the body and signifies the wife
275 Universe
276 A protection; could be an armour or an amulet
277 Verse
278 The span between the extended thumb and little finger, nearly 8 inches
279 Four days, 10th to 13th of Krishna Paksha of the month of Ashadha
280 Also called Pitri Paksha, the Krishna Paksha of the month of Bhadrapada
281 Another name for Durga
282 A sacred stone found in River Gandaki and iconically represents Vishnu
283 One of the twelve houses in the zodiac
284 The four-month period from Shukla Ekadashi of Ashadha till Shukla Ekadashi of the Kartik month
285 The anniversary of the first day of a yuga
286 Circular dance performed by Sri Krishna with gopis in Goloka
287 In Tantra, the deity and corresponding energy are the

same, e.g., Shiva and Shakti; in scientific terms, it makes no distinction between potential and kinetic energies

288 Forgiveness

289 Fearlessness

290 Measure of time equal to one-sixtieth of a day, that is, 24 minutes

291 Someone who has a recollection of past lives

292 One of the eight forms of marriage, based purely on love and passion

293 Worshipped by all

294 Purifying the universe

295 Liberation

296 Stick, usually of bamboo

297 Proper conduct

298 Consecrating an earthen jar

299 A sitting mat

300 Lighted lamp

301 Food delicacies

302 Jaggery

303 Earth

304 Desire or wish

305 A jar of water

306 A descending path or stairway to a river or a body of water

307 Another name for Kaamdeva

308 Moringaceae

309 Indian cherry or glue berry

310 Tongue is rolled back and drawn deep up to the nasal cavity

311 Vow or fasting

312 Another name of Shiva

313 Internal

314 External

315 Summer

316 Autumn

317 Pre-winter

318 Winter

319 Yellow sapphire

320 Ruby

321 Quartz

322 Cat's eye stone
323 Literal translation is mother, signifies mother-like goddesses
324 Blue sapphire
325 Coral
326 Nine jewels (Mukta, Manikya, Vaidurya, Gomeda, Vajra, Vidruma, Padmaraga, Marakata and Indraneel)
327 Sacred texts learnt by heart and passed on in the spoken form, such as the Vedas
328 A gem capable of fulfilling all desires
329 Sunstone
330 Moonstone
331 Shining like lightning

About the Author

Dinesh Bhatia is a career diplomat with over 30 years of experience. He is currently India's Ambassador to Argentina with concurrent accreditation to Uruguay. He has earlier served as the Ambassador of India to Cote d'Ivoire, Guinea, Liberia and Paraguay as well as the Consul General in Toronto.

He holds a B.E. in Electronics and Communication from Delhi College of Engineering.

His wife, Seema, and he have a daughter and a son.